anything can happen

Also by Susan Hampton

Poetry
Costumes
White Dog Sonnets
A Latin Primer
The Kindly Ones
News of the Insect World

Essays
Blood in *Family Pictures*, ed. Beth Yahp
Scale by Scale in *The Best Australian Essays, 2007*, ed Drusilla Modjeska

Edited
The Penguin Book of Australian Women Poets
(with Kate Llewellyn)

Non-Fiction
About Literature, with Sue Woolfe
Don't Take Your Love to Town, ghost-written with/for Ruby Langford Ginibi

Fiction
Surly Girls

anything can happen

Susan Hampton

Puncher & Wattmann

© Susan Hampton 2024

This book is copyright. Apart from any fair dealing for the purposes of study and research, criticism, review or as otherwise permitted under the Copyright Act, no part may be reproduced by any process without written permission. Inquiries should be made to the publisher.

First published in 2024
Published by Puncher and Wattmann
PO Box 279
Waratah NSW 2298

http://www.puncherandwattmann.com
puncherandwattmann@bigpond.com

A catalogue entry for this book is available from the National Library of Australia.

ISBN 9781923099012

Cover photograph by Susan Hampton

Cover design by David Musgrave

Printed by Lightning Source International

Could there be a speck of my original self anywhere?—that I have left behind. God, and if I have forgotten about it, can it save me?

Diane Williams

strict nonchalance. the myth you discarded

joanne burns

It is the absence of a sense of what one is living at the moment one lives it that multiplies the possibilities of writing. To explore the gulf between the frightening reality of what happens, at the moment it happens, and the strange unreality, years later, of what happened.

Annie Ernaux

Who are we when we are together with no one but ourselves.

Hannah Arendt

1 Night

The puzzle of childhood is never complete, and the missing pieces—down behind the lounge, under the house, in the bin of memory—reappear at intervals at the behest of the gods or fate or dreams. In old age there is a strong sense of the appearance of any piece being placed into a gap giving the picture shape and colour, a willow tree climbed then forgotten then suddenly there, its leaves draping and surging into the river of childhood. A schoolfriend, unseen for fifty years, may search you out and find you, handing you pieces. A white horse called Ricky appears in your driveway and three of your cousins are hoisted onto his back.

*

In memoir, I think, omissions are not accidents. Surprises are welcome.

Whereas in autobiography 'everything' is told, often in chronological order, the memoir is partial, with the capacity for time loops—you are sitting in your car when the movement of your arm to turn on the radio brings to mind your mother's arm reaching to do the same thing when you were a child and had to endure those long or long-seeming Sunday drives in the 50s and 60s. The scenes of your childhood, the river, the back lane, the silo, rise up to replace your mother's arm. That dissolves and you find you're hearing or in fact making up a conversation. Yes, you're making it up. What did they say? That person you can't see yet.

But I have turned the radio on in the car and they're playing Patti Smith, *Radio Ethiopia*. Groaning out one of her monologues. It's a track I haven't heard for a long time and I lean back in the seat to listen. My friend Bird and I played this album a lot when she was sharing the house in Annandale with my son and me. It was a hot summer in the late eighties. The insistent bass and Patti's gravelly voice and her androgyny.

I listen to the end of the song and reverse out of the garage, grinding slightly against one of the many cardboard boxes. I step out of the car, move the box to a corner and on impulse open it—on top, a scrap of paper from the summer of 1970. It was about going to Stockton to stay with Violet, my mother's mother.

I got to Violet's by nightfall and she welcomed me in. I had rung her from a petrol station on the highway from Sydney. I didn't have much stuff and brought it in from my bike panniers in two goes. Violet dogged my steps, not saying much.

Does he know where you've gone?

No, I left him a note. But no address.

Later—

Did he hit you?

No.

It was obvious she thought it was marvellous luck if you had not been hit. I could see she was not able to understand why I would leave my husband. When he turned up, she gave him a subtle look, meaning he was welcome.

Joe had rented out his house in Blacktown to some other Slovenians, driven to Newcastle, got Uncle Norm to take him to the main gate of the BHP and sign him up to the union and then gone in and got a job as a fitter's mate, starting Monday—afternoon shift. Violet again gave him a kind look. He had also visited my parents (across the river) and told them his side of the story while at times weeping. He was beautiful to look at. They thought he was "doing the right thing".

I put this sheet of paper back in the box, almost scrunching it up. And now rather afraid of the box I walked away from it. Fifty years had not been sufficient to erase the guilt and at the same time, the sense that I had been in the hands of society and not myself. Or, worse, that my self was as yet so undeveloped that I had colluded with other people's perceived wishes. Yes, I ought to take some responsibility.

Also, the page didn't seem like a normal diary. Instead of talking to the self, the voice is already telling a story—why explain that my parents lived "across the river"?

The tide was turning. I put the car away and spent the day on the back deck. On the lawn four plovers were pecking at the grass, then moving on a few steps, pecking again. While they walked, they seemed to be getting intelligence through their feet. Slightly digging their claws in when they were stopped. As if listening through their feet. Walk and stop, wriggle your claws into the grass—is a worm moving under there? Slugs? Nothing, walk on.

Across the grass and sedges of the swampy reserve, I watched the estuary, a wide saltwater lake. I could hear Charlotte in the garden cropping the broad-beans. We have fetched up in a shorebird sanctuary, in effect.

It took us a while, when we first came to the Central Coast, to realise the screaming we heard at night from the peninsula was birds.

At about three a.m. I'm woken by the rising calls of the stone curlew, uncanny, feral, endangered. They live across the estuary on a peninsula that was once a nunnery, now the Mary MacKillop retreat centre.

Sal was visiting from Melbourne and woken by the curlews and called them the Screaming Marys. It is almost a scream, it's operatic, and slightly curdles your blood. Sometimes oyster-catchers call at night too, a thin high pip-pip-pip, a sound you can put in the background. Domestic. But I wait for the curlews. They don't call every night.

Sometimes I hear voices off the water, and it gives me a strong feeling of solitude. We're eight weeks into a lockdown, it's even quieter than before. Wind amplifies the voices and carries them to our veranda. Not that you hear the exact words or get the meaning, as an unintended recipient.

On the water surface there was a moving area of glitter, and when I looked again it had travelled out on a slow tide and was hidden behind the mangroves where the water rounded a bend and headed for the coast.

All our childhoods, for the Christmas holidays, the family had gone from our inland town of Inverell to the coast, down the New England highway through the Hunter valley to Violet's. Her house was on Stockton peninsula across the river from Newcastle.

Over the road from Violet's was the beach. At that time it was accessible by a series of tracks through sandhills, hollows and saltbush and pigface, good places for kids to hide. The sea itself was a long way away, which now it is not.

On the other side of Stockton, four streets away, was the river.

Violet's husband, who we called Pappy, worked shifts at the BHP. One night he had laid his rifle across the table when he thought the boys were too noisy. When he was an old man, and my sisters and I were there on holidays, he chased us up the beach with this gun. I think we had been too noisy.

Pappy rowed himself across the river to work. We didn't see much of him, but Violet was always there, coming out through the screen door to the back veranda to greet us, a pinafore over her house dress, always reticent. She did not quite know how to deal with Mum. Their hugs were awkward. When Mum was about two, Violet had to give her away to people who could afford to feed her. She managed to hang onto the three boys. For a while they lived in a tent in the bush near where Pappy was working on building a silo.

There was no way I would be able to read all the material in the boxes, I would have to employ a method of making raids on them, taking out a page or two, or a notebook, reading a few pages, then putting it back. Try a different box next time if I was not ready for that one. Unreadiness would usually be obvious by the state of my health or my inability to concentrate. Every sound was something that needed to be interpreted.

In the boxes there would be corroborating detail, or in some cases, conflicting detail. Or accounts of things I had no idea had happened to me. In 1979 apparently at the Verona in Paddington I saw *Now Voyager* and *Dark Victory* with Bette Davis. Or the fact that I had gone along with certain things. A kind of unintentional collusion. At those times it could take a day or days to absorb what had gone on, and how absent I was from my feelings, and the events of my life.

At other times I might skim read a whole year's diary in an hour. One year was so inarticulate and abstract I put it in the recycle. In one part, pages of my attempts to understand quasars and quantum theory, along with diagrams.

Today's box has a diary I kept in Glebe, where I had rented a small terrace near Sydney Uni. On my second attempt I had been able to leave Blacktown.

I bought bread at the Demeter Bakery and walked the streets. I was going to poetry gigs in the city at a pub called The Royal Standard. Changing my enrolment from Macquarie Uni to Sydney went smoothly and I started my honours year. In order to live, I was casual teaching. Certain days at uni I was studying sixteenth century poetry, where the rituals of courtly love were so far from my experience of life, it was relaxing.

Diary 1979

A hot morning, even at eight a.m. I made myself wake up, and "taught" at Balmain High School. In one lesson I was explaining the intellectual history behind *The Bishop Orders his Tomb* to a Year 12 boy whose essay had 'could of' in part of a sentence.

I then had Year 8 and was supposed to take them through a few scenes in *A Midsummer Night's Dream*. It was impossible. They couldn't see why they were being subjected to something in four-hundred-year-old English about fairies. I went to the Deputy's office and said, 'That Year 8 will be needing you. Don't call me, and I won't call you.'

For many years I'd been telling friends about that day and it went more like this: I went to the Year 8 room and tried to quell the noise. Finally I got them all to sit and some of them listened, but there was a big boy more or less in the centre who was eating lollies out of a bag and running a book on the Melbourne Cup, which was on that afternoon. I would read out about Bottom and Quince and there would be wild giggling about Bottom's name and paper planes being thrown and the boy running the book would be calling out Blue Dream, anyone? and some kids would pass money across. Then the few kids who had been listening to me lost interest and turned their attention to the bookmaker. All this I could stand but then two boys from the back of the room climbed out a window and ran across the oval and jumped into the harbour just near a sign with a shark in a circle and a diagonal line through it. I found I had lifted up a chair and brought it down hard on an empty desk. The legs broke and bits flew everywhere. There was silence. I was so appalled at the fact that I'd lost my temper I just stood there, and the bookmaker said,

Miss. Those bits could've hit someone.

In the eye, Miss, another boy said.

You were just lucky, Miss, a girl said.

This whole scene, the boys swimming gleefully in the harbour, the boy munching lollies and running the book, the smashing of the chair, does not appear in the diary. But then in my telling over the years it gets inserted into the story between the fairies and the going to the Deputy's office where I have quoted myself correctly. 'That Year 8 will be needing you. Don't call me, and I won't call you.'

Yet in reality it seems I may have simply walked out of the room.

To save myself from further confrontations with my perfidy I did not go near the boxes now but sat and stared at the water.

Today on the surface there were three areas of glitter, proceeding east in three thin strips, in a tide that was speeding up. The tide had now made up its mind and all the water was going the same way.

There were times during the change of the tide when one current of water was coming in, and beside it another current going out. There must exist between these currents a film or membrane of water that is dancing in a kind of stasis to accommodate the two streams.

On quiet days at still water I wait for any puff of wind to jiggle the broken reflections of trees on the peninsula, something I must have done as a kid, at the river. The amnesic haunts of childhood. History, muffled and disordered by repression and time. What we weren't allowed to say, and weren't allowed to know.

There are many ways that unreliability may come about. A person may be born with a nature inclined to deception and fudging and lies. Or they may find their childhood reality banal or lacking in stimulation, and cover it over with wild invention. They may enjoy telling stories, and for want of material, make it up. Or they may find it hard to understand the self and what it is and where it fits, long after others seem to know who they are.

A thunderclap bangs through the upper air and shakes the brick house. *Crump*, another one, jolting everything. Birds of every local species arc and fly about in crazy patterns yelling at each other. In an animist culture this event would be the very God, and Milton's armies make sense. My thoughts are sparking off at all angles, trouping through religions and historical geographies and loved landscapes and emails from friends. All the air is zinging and now the thunder is rolling towards Avoca and the rain settles to a mild dimpling on the surface of the water.

In the night the Screaming Marys woke me up, first one calling, then the other, plaiting its call through the first one, wild and loud.

The weather calms for a few days and I turn to sit with my back to the estuary, to get the sun. I can tell from the door glass what the tide is doing. All the important things are happening in the reflections. I could be in Plato's cave, where other realities juggle themselves wanting my attention. Why am I writing here? I could be out in the kayak, where it's perfect.

I watch the night come in. Into the silence, the ring of the phone—it's Matthew, one of the best men when Charlotte and I were married a few years back. He lives in the nearby suburb of Saratoga, and is the person who found us this house. I slide the green button on the screen.

Anything happening? he says.

Eleven spoonbills are standing near the jetty, I said. Completely still. I think some of them are sleeping. They spend a lot of time being still, unlike other birds.

We don't have them here. We have cormorants and seagulls.

We have godwits who are just now leaving for some remote part of Russia.

No need to up the ante. How's your health?

Er—

I did wonder.

You're lucky your body is staying so young, I said.

I feel that! It's still strong and healthy. I thought turning sixty would be my *death*! Anyway, what if my body wants to outlive the rest of me—maybe someone else would like it—I imagine a world where these bodies are seeking inhabitants—it would make a great short story.

It's not the sort of thing I write.

Ah well. But think of it, the person narrating the story in a seemingly neutral voice might turn out to be *selling the bodies*. And you realise this as you read on.

Yes, that's good. In literary criticism it's called 'the unreliable narrator'.

Oh, it's a thing?

Yeah, it's a thing.

2 Annandale and Blacktown

The eels

Back when my son was in high school and we lived in Annandale, he and most of his friends did not live with their fathers, but saw them at weekends, or in some cases hardly at all. It seems a wind swept through our community then, I'm speaking of the 80s, and the women left their marriages and became single parents. My son and his two best friends had even more in common—they were the only child, a male, of a mother who was now at university or was becoming a writer.

My mother came to visit and said, 'I know it seems the thing to do, but I can't say it's good for these boys not to grow up with the father.' My son said, 'But my kung fu master is a man in my life, I'm learning good moves from him, would that count? Not forgetting I see Dad every weekend and we go to the Eels games.' He paused. 'And even though they're a crap team at the moment, and need a better coach, we always go, would that count?'

Wax

For a while there was the top half of a man in my bedroom, a Chesty Bond from a skip on Johnston Street. I'd found him poking up between the plaster and boards, hardly damaged, and took him home and sat him on a kitchen chair.

Introduce me, said my son.

Oh, would you like him?

Yeah!

The following morning the man had on a pink Rip Curl T-shirt and a pair of dark glasses. A beach towel was draped around his neck. My son was painting the man's hair yellow. He'd decided to call him Wax, short for waxhead. In the weeks that followed I was hoping Wax would say something.

Doesn't Wax speak?

No, he's a statue, right? He can't talk.

Why don't we change his identity? Maybe he'd talk if he wasn't a surfie.

Wax was transformed into one of the Blues Brothers, a medieval knight, and a detective in the Vice Squad. In no case did he speak. Whether he had on a hat and tie, a T-shirt and towel, a sword and visor, he was silent. His name was always Wax.

Home Movie

Bored, affronted and annoyed, my son had to write a composition. He was fourteen then. He sat at the kitchen table while I cooked. Then I went to him and stood behind him and put my hand on his shoulder and looked at his page: 'It was a dark and stormy night and I was sitting at my desk when there was a knock, and a dirty blonde walked in.'

After that time, he began to make short films. He borrowed a video camera from my friend Heather. I came home from work to find him at the door, ruler in hand as a microphone.

Mrs Hampton, where were you on Thursday afternoon last at 4.15pm?

Er, ahh.

Ma'am, you may have seen something, after all you're a neighbour of the crime scene.

He put down the mike and began filming my response. 'What has happened, Officer?', and so on. He was tight-lipped, I would need to improvise.

I know the neighbours quite well—as far as I know they are law-abiding.

Did you ever hear them argue?

I didn't.

He would need me to get my old clothes on and lie on the lounge room floor so he could pour tomato sauce on me and film me as the victim. Later he sat at the table and propped the camera on a cake tin and spoke on TV as Head of the Homicide Squad. He would be as vague as possible about the murder, saying they were following every lead.

I watched as he changed his clothes and became the deranged husband who may or may not have killed his wife Stavroulou. A change of tie and he was the detective again, falling into brevity and low intonations, speaking from the corner of his mouth, shrugging, wanting any information he could get, guessing and second-guessing what people knew. This time he was interviewing the husband, who said in a European accent, 'Stavroulou she was the love of my life. I never will kill her, never.'

'Sir, somebody killed your wife.'

Harry Dovellini

By this time, he was old enough to go into town by himself or with a friend. They played the machines at Timezone and investigated George Street. One day he came home with a plywood box on legs and wheels that was full of vintage magic tricks and had been owned by Harry Dovellini. The man at the magic shop in town had also sold him some books on how to perform the tricks. Rather than the murder victim, I was now the beautiful assistant who had her head cut off and 'magically, she still speaks'. He practised the tricks for hours, sometimes in the kitchen while I was cooking dinner, where he stood in front of the mirror on the dresser.

At the weekend he painted the box and next day painted his new name on it: Beni Bizarre. I made him a cloak, and he bought a wand. Now the practising took on extra elements: his entry and the swirling of the cloak, the lifting of the wand.

The following weekend I drove him to a park in Rose Bay where he was performing at a fourth birthday party. Two of the invited children were twin dwarfs, girls, dressed in shorts and T-shirts, fair-haired and with muscled little arms and they didn't take their eyes off him. For the whole of his show, they stood near him, under the tree, next to his magic box and his new name. The other kids sat back where they were supposed to be. The dwarf sisters were a gift, and once my son realised this, he included them in the show, looking at them and raising his eyebrows to see if they could tell how a trick was done, from their better position. They gave nothing away and were perfect.

Kung-fu

While Ben was in the city, he discovered the kung-fu academy and began to go to classes every week, working with Sifu Bennett, learning the positions and the moves. Posters of Bruce Lee appeared on his walls and he talked to me about Bruce's films.

In the mirror he practised his kung-fu moves, particularly the opening gestures of the bowing. But also, some sudden aggressive poses. But then back to stillness and the whispering. 'Respect yourself. Respect for all sentient beings.'

Later he also practised with his nunchakus, flicking his hands around. He showed me some metal stars you could throw at people. I cautioned him against taking these out of the house. I asked him how things were going at school but he never wanted to talk about school.

Then for a while, with Bird and me as audience, he practised his magician's patter and gesturing to misdirect the audience. He stuffed a single red silk hanky into his clenched fist while asking us to watch closely. Then saying abracadabra he pulled a string of brightly-coloured hankies from the bottom of the fist, raising them in the air. His cheeks glowed.

Heather

Heather was coming over to show Ben how to edit his films. My good friend, she was a high school maths teacher whose front room was gear—video cameras, scuba gear, a bow and arrows. She came early and we sat on the back step in the sun. She said she was reading *Emma*, 'enviously'.

Austen's so cool, my God she's cool. I'm reading it for the second time to find out what she gets away with, and how.

Are you writing a novel? I said.

Isn't everybody? she laughed.

I have no idea, I said. What is it about?

It's a murder mystery set in the Grampians in Victoria.

I was silent. I'd been wrestling with a novel about a winged life-sized statue who came alive, and called herself Nike after the runners she found abandoned in a skip. I was getting lost in some rather literal problems such as: how is it that she can read? How do you write about someone who has not had a childhood but was born an adult? The statue had stood just outside the front doors of a Garden Art store in Haberfield, a real store, which did sell life-size 'classical' statues. I mean, I had seen her. And even though I thought the reader would suspend their disbelief long enough for me to get the statue aloft, flying over the city, and landing in the park at the harbour end of Glebe, I couldn't see how I could get away with the fact of her being able to *read the word on her shoe*. How did she know anything? I was stuck in epistemological, even ontological, problems, when I ought to just believe in her reality and forge ahead, the way EB White had done when he wrote Stuart Little. The people in that story had a child who was a mouse, but they just dealt with it, made him a small bed, sewed him small clothes etc, and away the story went, carrying the reader with it. It was a matter of confidence in the sleight-of-hand you were performing. But my story kept jamming and was going nowhere, so I didn't mention it to Heather. Nike had become a non-topic.

Heather had made friends with Bird, and they often went out together at night to Ruby Reds or Hellfire or the Freezer, places I rarely went, and they spoke about their adventures or swapped notes on the women they were interested in.

Library

I was interested in getting my kid through high school but he wouldn't take any tuition from me or talk to me at all about school. I knew he wasn't really doing any work. One day he did mention he'd got into trouble at the library, for lying.

What did they think you had lied about? I said.

I went in the library and on the front desk was a copy of your textbook, that you wrote with Woolfie.

About Literature, I said.

That one. So I said, oh, here's my name, Hampton, that's my mother, she wrote this book, and the librarian got me in trouble for lying because *no one like me* would have a mother who wrote a book, so it was *evident* I was making it up just because of the coincidence of the name.

What happened?

Sent to the deputy.

Sorry, son. I will ring the librarian.

Won't make any difference.

What are you doing this week-end. Any magic shows?

No. Going to Dad's for the Eels game.

Most weekends he walked up to Booth Street for the 470 bus to Central and got the train to Parramatta. I wondered if his father had a current girlfriend and how he was. If I asked Ben, he always said Fine, and never carried tales between parents.

I wondered if Joe was lonely, and waited for Ben to be there.

Cleveland

Joe had come from Slovenia. His parents and six of the eight siblings had gone to America, to Cleveland where his father had got work after escaping during World War II. His father was dead by then, but his mother was alive, a finer-featured version of Joe, the same eyes. Only one sister was here, Slava, Australian name Gloria, married to a truckie who cashed in his life insurance to pay for Joe's ticket to Australia. Joe's father had mandated it that Joe come here rather than go to America with the rest of the siblings, so that Slava would *have someone* here. They didn't get on.

Joe's brothers Srecko and Branko, and the rest, were in Cleveland. Joe felt he'd been pushed out, away from the family, and lost all his younger siblings. In those days people didn't phone each other all the time, or at all. I'm speaking of the late 60s, now.

Granville

My life at that time had reduced itself to a room in a boarding house in Granville, a Yamaha 50cc motor-bike and the western suburbs primary school where I taught. It was my first year out. It was becoming clear that we had been royally conned. Two years of lessons at Teachers College had given us lots of lesson *content*, but no hint about crowd control: or that we would have to find a way, at age nineteen, to deal with forty or so kids, some of whose parents were in jail, or junkies. Some kids were wards of the state. One girl lived in a caravan with her grandma, parents whereabouts unknown at that time. The girl was nine.

Some kids were OK of course but the atmosphere in the room was ruled by the damaged or upset or abused ones, creating areas of signal quiet, and areas of irruption. It was all very well to teach spelling, and the rule of I before E ... if you could get them to look your way. I had been given no tools at all on this part of the job.

Those children we couldn't control were to be sent to the Deputy who had an office near the staffroom. He would verbally reprimand the girls and give them lunch-time detention; he caned the boys. So it is that I have on my conscience a boy called Martin, who was nine, coming back into the room with a reddened palm and a hardening brave look in his eye. Not that he tormented me but he never shut up and I couldn't get any teaching done. If I tended to his trouble, the others rioted to the extent of getting out windows and wandering away to far ends of the playground and sitting in small groups. I will probably never get over having Martin caned. I would like to know where he is now, and if he's all right.

At night I ate at a café in the main street, wiener schnitzel, and a coffee. I didn't know how to cook. I always sat alone. Some of the nights I must have bodged up something to eat in the kitchen of the boarding house. The other inhabitants, refugees, cooked there. I didn't know any of their languages and they had not much English. I would have two boiled eggs and a gin and tonic.

Into this solitary café scene walked a tanned Slav with a hurt look in his eyes, and a quiet manner. He wanted to sit with me, and pay for my dinner. We ate schnitzels which he had already paid for.

That night in my upstairs room I heard a noise at the window and saw through the dark it was Joe who had got an extension ladder maybe from the back shed and was opening my window and whispering to me, could he come in? The moon was shining on his face. I moved over in the single bed.

He invited me to a Yugal soccer game the next Saturday and then we were going out. Then he looked through the boarding house and thought I should move in with him—he had a house in Blacktown, it would be better. After a few weeks I packed my things.

Blacktown

Joe was shocked I only knew how to boil an egg and make porridge. He taught me to cook and I wrote down the recipes.

At weekends he took me to meet his Slovenian friends who like him were in their early thirties. They called Joe 'Joze', pronounced 'Yozheh'.

Rudi and Maria lived in a shed at the back of their block in Blacktown. At the front of their land, Rudi was building their new house. They had a daughter and young twins. I had five younger sisters and was so used to babies I sat and nursed them. Maria had made a cake with a hole in the middle.

Afternoon tea over, we played rummy for a few hours, keeping scores, smoking, and after a while Rudi started to sing, just a few notes, getting in key. Singing was as natural to them as speaking, even when they were not singing actual songs but just trying out notes, going hee hee hee hee, while they were thinking what to do, or making harmonies and now and then doing quarter tones, a kind of keening note up against another note that someone was holding.

Joe and Maria joined in, old Slovenian songs they knew. Some songs were very fast, dancing type songs. *Terezinka-zinka-zinka.* At times they sang in parts. When Rudi had a losing streak he angrily sang out the priest's part of the mass, satirically, and the others responded. They laughed and Maria got the slivovic down from the shelf.

Another couple sometimes joined us, Ivan and Malchka, for card nights. They brought filana paprika, stuffed capsicums. Ivan worked at the locomotive workshop at Chullora and one night was describing partly in Slovenian, partly in English, what sounded like an industrial accident. The others were clicking their tongues while they laid down their cards. At the end of the story Ivan sniggered, the story stopped, the game went on. When we got home, I said to Joe, why did Ivan snigger like that at the end of the story?

What is snigger?

That strange little laugh.

Oh. Must be he frighten.

I gave Joe credit for psychological understanding, I gave him credit for wanting to learn more English. The first I think was true.

He was the oldest boy. He had a big family, eight siblings. Here are some of his family.

There were a lot of Yugoslav migrants in Blacktown and Toongabbie at the time, Slovenians, Bosnians, Croats, people from Adriatic islands like Korchula, places with long traditions, thousands of years of settlement and resettlement, unlike Blacktown, which had not yet 200 years of white settlement, and before that, as I explained to Joe, who had no idea, an almost completely hidden and mysterious continuous settlement by black people, for probably thousands of years.

Someone said Blacktown was named that because blacks on the coast were pushed west by colonialists and settled there. Or had a base there.

Flying

The Slovenian Club was in Wetherill Park and we went on a Saturday evening. Joe helped organise the club, doing thankless things that kept the community together. That night there was a small band and about sixty people were eating and drinking at tables, relishing their food, cevapcici, raznici, filana paprika.

Joe's strong hand went into the small of my back and took me onto the edge of the dancefloor where a fast polka was in progress.

The dancers were in a circle, in pairs, and moving around swiftly. Part of the expertise of the male partner is to choose the moment of entering the stream. The more difficult, in a way, is the female learning the art of submission, which done well can be taken in a sort of spiritual sense, rather than a gender-political sense, where you let go your desire to alter the course of events, and respond to the promptings of the other.

The dance got wilder and wilder, it was early in the night but some of the people had been pre-drinking because it was cheaper to drink at home. They were hooting, the women as well, the women in particular, as they swept around past the others at their tables watching.

Before he had stepped me in, Joe and I watched for a while. He wasn't the type to say, Watch how it's done—he expected me to keep up, pay attention. I was a good student. Once we were on the floor it was very soon that I was also able to let go of my will, or it left me, and I entered a floating sensation that hovered above me even during the stomping which had now become lighter, more athletic.

Something had changed in the dance, the men were beginning to catch each other's eye. On the other side of the circle a man called Alagich picked up his partner and literally threw her to another man who had just let go of his partner. The man who caught her let her bend her knees into the landing then fluently took her up into the dance right on the beat, and on it went. Watching the women fly across the circle was so thrilling I waited for it to happen to me. I hoped I would not be thrown to Alagich, he looked a bit rough. Or rather he looked smooth but handled the women a bit rough. I kept bending my knees waiting for lift-off when Joe caught some man's eye and up I went, thrust by one hand in my side-waist, and one in my back. I flew to a man I hadn't noticed before, who received me well but wasn't as natural a dancer as Joe.

In the progress of the bodies I was soon back with Joe, and we went on in the dance with me still breathing heavily and my hair on end.

I kept a Slovenian dictionary

I was 19, Joe was 32. We were married in Newcastle in a little church my mother found near where my family lived. What marriage would be like was a blur in my mind, though I hoped at some time we would go to Slovenia.

It would be forty years before I got to see Slovenia and by then we were both with other people.

The reception was at home, consisting of my parents and five younger sisters, Violet, some aunts and uncles, Joe's sister and her family, my Hungarian friend Marti from college, and Joe's best man, Korchula Joe.

Just before going to the church, in the bathroom checking my make-up, I realised that the big roller-curlers the hairdresser had used gave me unsightly tunnels in my hair which had then been sprayed into place. It was disgusting and stupid. I washed my hair in the handbasin and quickly dried it. I realised now it wasn't the right length, I found the scissors and cut it shorter, then roughed it up, like the style was meant to be a bit everywhere. I repaired my makeup to minimal, then took the bobby-pins and put my veil on. It was time to get in the car.

On the way, watching the suburbs glide by, I said in my mind a goodbye to my friend Tommy, a woman who lived near Violet, and who had taken up all my attention since I was fourteen, when I first fell in love with her. And even through meeting up with Joe I remained somehow attached to Tommy. She was thirty, married with two kids, kept different hours from her husband who was a fisherman and went to work at three or four am.

I still had a cache of Tommy's letters. I stared at the reflection of a bride in the car window, realised I'd have to burn the letters.

Back in Blacktown, we sat up many nights till late or set the alarm and got up to watch the European soccer. On Saturday nights Maria and Malchka and their families came over and we played rummy. At times Joe cooked pancakes and fed us while we played. I played two hands, one for him, and now and then he came to me and looked over my shoulder 'Put that five on Rudi's'.

In the back of my recipe book I kept a Slovenian dictionary. 'Me gremo na mesno': 'I'm going to town'. But I am no good at learning languages, just as I'm no good at remembering poems or the words of songs, or major areas of my childhood and even most of my adulthood. At some point I stopped being able to remember things. I remember being with my sisters and cousins in the hometown down at the river making a raft, but maybe only because there's a photo of it. At any rate I kept up the Slovenian words for what seemed a long time.

One day when Joe was at the factory, I went to my shelves and reached behind the books for the letters from Tommy. At the incinerator in the back yard, I started a fire and watched as my history puckered and curled. I thought for this marriage to work, I had to burn Tommy out of me.

Since I didn't know myself, I didn't know Blacktown would be a mistake. I lasted eleven months and began to talk to Joe about it, that I would need to leave, and it was hard to say why. I did still love him. But it wasn't the life I could live. In one of my memories of this moment, he kept shaking his head and crying. But I know that isn't true. In fact he was angry and hostile. In the end I just had to go.

I rang the Department of Education and said my husband had got a job in Newcastle and I would have to move to a school up there. They said Wickham which was on the wharves and suited me. I packed my few things and rode my motor-bike to Stockton—a 50cc, it took five hours on the highway. Violet came to the back door and stood waiting for me.

It wasn't hard for Joe to make a call to my parents and find out where I was, but, as with everything else, I hadn't thought that through. My ability to think about the future, or imagine it, or create it in some intentional way, was absent. I have tried to improve on that but with little success. Joe arrived on Stockton having lined up the job at the steelworks, and our life continued on. My ability to trust people was very high. To the extent that I was able to think about it, I thought he had made a big change for me and I ought to give it a go. Probably he meant well and maybe he was prepared to get over his anger at me leaving. Soon enough I was pregnant, and I just got on with my life. I went across the dunes and swam at the beach, I rode my motor-bike to work, I cooked with Violet, I lived in the back bedroom with Joe.

When I was three weeks overdue to give birth and I got a back pain, I rang my mother. Is this it? She thought very likely, and asked where I had booked in, which hospital.

I didn't know I had to book in.

Susan, for Christ's sake.

No one said. You or Violet could have told me. Or the doctor.

Ben is born

My mother found me a place and my son was born, sweet and well, looking just like his father. I had trusted it would be a boy, after the six daughters of my family. I held him tight against me. I was so used to holding a baby, especially after Trisha and then Barbie were handed to me while Mum was busy. I'm sure Linda felt the same when her kids were born. We had no qualms about babies.

Soon it was time to register Ben's birth, and I wondered when Joe wrote his own name, Jozef Pisorn, whether he minded changing the spelling for Ben's name, Benjamin Joseph. Whether Jozef was losing yet another part of his history and his culture. When I asked, he shrugged.

Back on Stockton, presents began to arrive. Tommy handed me a shoe-box, and when I opened it, nestled in tissue paper, there were ten pairs of home-knitted bootees, in three colours. I thanked her and put them in the bassinet which was on the floor beside the bed.

I was enjoying being a mother and I could see why Mum thought a new baby was a kind of magic. His hair smelled warm and good. His fontanelle pulsed. We had created a life.

It seemed Joe had forgiven me for leaving, but not so. Ben was three weeks old when Joe said that as soon as Ben was big enough to walk, he would take him to Slovenia and not come back. This frightened me so much I lost my milk.

I couldn't imagine why he would do this when we had been, I thought, repairing our marriage. I realised I would never understand him. Nonetheless we had a new baby and had to go on together.

My response to having a baby was a great need to study. I rang the scholarship Board to find out if I could still take up the Commonwealth Scholarship. They said I could. I enrolled at Newcastle Uni, and Joe and I bought a house at West Wallsend. Ben was about one and we managed because I went to uni at night and Joe worked day shifts—he was by then at the floating dock as a fitter-and-turner's mate. His workmates were called Big Pig, Little Pig, and Auntie.

Korchula Joe's prediction

We had a visit from Korchula Joe, and while I was making tea I heard him saying quietly to Joe that Susan wanting to be a writer could be *a problem.*

What problem, my husband said.

You think she will have babies, the other Joe said.

Look, her mother had six, of course she will be like that.

Er, I said—

The best man read my hesitation and cut in, She will go to university like she say, Joze, then she will leave you.

During the first term I discovered the existence of the Shorter Oxford Dictionary in two volumes, which I then bought. Two large hardback books, each about two inches thick.

When one of the lecturers said, Oh, that's Cod Latin, I looked it up in the Oxford to find that cod 'reliably thought of as a fish was also in Old English, Norse and Danish a bag, or a husk; in Swedish a cushion, pillow… in Germanic *kud, keud,* whence Old English *ceod,* pouch… At the same time, as a verb it was slang or dialect for hoax…'

Hoax Latin, someone just making up the likely sounding words.

The lecturer could do that with Gerard Manly Hopkins in the poetry tutorial, and though it was wasted on some of the students I thought it was pretty funny. He had memorised so much Hopkins he could pluck words from any of the well-known poems and put them together at will.

Speck for Branko and Srecko

'But that klobassy, he doesn't have any. What do they call him here? salami, Sir, hello, do you have salami, no, no, he only has this sausage, so pale, nothing spice, bits of some rubbish from the floor, he push it in some bit of plastic, we can't eat this.

Sir, do you have speck? He doesn't know, smiling to me like a nice idiot, very happy, doesn't know anything.

Speck is from the pig, I wave my hands, ah, I point to a picture on the wall here, see? Now I lift my shirt and show him my ribs, I pat myself, my ribs, he is laugh at me. Mother Maria. No, no, he has got me, he show me some bones here, bacon bones, he say.

Ah, but the speck it has more, what is this? I pinch my arm, Mary give me the word, flesh, skin, more flesh, I say. But he has not, speck is a no-thing here. No speck, no proper sausage, how can I eat this expensive steaks and this mincey-wincey—ah! I see the bacon. Sir, half a kilo please, of this and now I wait, I rest, while he smiling wraps me a bacon, at last some bit of the pig. But not the part I want for Branko and Srecko.'

Shaving the Pig

In Joe's childhood there was always a pig in the family, which they fed on scraps and corn and turnips and milk all year, watching it fatten up, till the day when with great ceremony the pig would be killed. He talked about this a lot.

In Newcastle at one point Joe was working at a spinning factory in Raymond Terrace. It was in the north, and he drove through farmland to get there. Looking at the country, wondering what the soil was like. At times when we have been driving, I have seen him get out and pick up a handful of soil and sniff it.

One afternoon he came up the driveway and popped open the front of the VW where there was a big fat pig. In all its recently dead glory, pink, with a large snout, and on its hide stiff white bristles.

I stared at its pale eyelashes and waited.

He had seen the pig when driving home, and gone in and asked the farmer if he could buy it. The farmer agreed, and helped him slit its throat and bleed it. Then they cleaned it up a bit and hefted it into the boot.

Joe explained that I was going to help him manhandle the pig into the laundry tubs where we would pour boiling water over it to loosen the bristles and then we were going to shave it. The whole pig. Then he would take it outside and slit it open and take out the guts. We would be able to eat the liver and kidneys and heart. It would be beautiful and the meat would last for months, we would have to put some loin chops or trotters in my parents' fridge and also ask my sisters.

I went to get my razor. The rest is a blur of glistening organs and a sense of a deepening understanding of the insides of a pig, the arse, the ribs, the cut oesophagus. The smell, in Joe's childhood nose, of so many meals to come, after nearly a year of eggs and flour and milk and turnips and spuds. Meat! The satisfaction of digging your molars into a loin and chewing hard at the gristle on the bone. Every bit of the pig was important. He asked me to boil some water for the eyes and trotters so we could make brawn. The gelatinous brawn, so good on a sandwich later with pickled baby cucumbers. He couldn't wait, his eyes were gleaming.

It has taken me fifty years to get over ingesting so much pork in one year. Only now at the age of seventy am I able to consider and enjoy a barbequed pork loin chop, and only last night did I sink my teeth into the gristle on the bone and really work at it. It was good.

A chess game

I finished first year Arts at Newcastle and the following year we went back to Blacktown to live. Fiction and Poetry were subjects that could be part of your BA at Macquarie Uni, so I enrolled there.

One night we were invited to visit some friends of Joe's I hadn't met. The men were going to play chess. I had played Joe a few times but he had studied the game and been some sort of chess champion in Slovenia. At least that's what he said. At any rate in our first game he defeated me in five moves; it was a known gambit, he said. I tried a few more times, avoiding that trap but encountering others, then stopped playing. Went back to my books.

It was the first time I had seen him play with a friend and although I think I was expected to sit and talk recipes with the wife, I sat and watched the men to see how to stand up to Joe's game. The other man was pretty good too and I saw a look of silent determination come across Joe's face. From that moment he slowed his own responses to such long times that the game went on again after dinner and until late as Joe would sit apparently considering his next move, for up to fifteen minutes at a time. The other man began to get bored and lost his concentration which I suppose was Joe's method, in this case. I turned my attention to the wife who was kind and good but had nothing interesting to say. She had made a great cake.

Glebe

At the second attempt, one September, I left my husband after seven years, and went to live in Glebe.

It was a Thursday night and I'd just come out of an evening

tutorial. I realised I couldn't put it off, so I drove home and told Joe I was going, that it would be madness to pick up Ben out of his sleep and take him now, Sorry but I need to go, I'll find somewhere to live tomorrow, and come back for Ben on Saturday.

He must have been in shock but didn't show it, said it would be fine, just go. We'd talked before about me leaving one day and how we would amicably arrange to share Ben.

A few days later at my front door in Glebe a sheriff arrived with a document saying Joe had been awarded custody. He had apparently gone straight to a courthouse on the Friday morning and found that since I had not taken Ben with me *at the time of leaving*, it would be assumed I didn't want him, so custody went to Joe. I found this out when I went to the courthouse in Glebe and showed them the document. I was allowed to have Ben at weekends and for half the school holidays.

Joe was again saying he would take Ben, who was three and-a-half, to Slovenia and not come back. He was telling Ben that the police would come and take Mummy's boyfriend away and put him in jail.

Why did Mummy leave?

Because she doesn't love you.

These things were relayed by the child at weekends. I would get him to draw and the drawings would be men with guns, everything black.

I tried speaking to Joe about it.

Can't you think of it from his point-of-view? I said. It's messing up his head, he's a little kid.

Who is messing up his head?

Well, you're not helping.

I am supposed to help you? Mother Maria.

If you are mean about me, it won't help him.

He should know the truth, Joe said. And later he said, I'm very disappointed in you, Susan, as if he were a headmaster. Dogs seemed to follow me on the street. Or they were really there and I couldn't shake them off.

I changed my enrolment from Macquarie Uni to Sydney Uni, had a boyfriend and later several girlfriends, and fought for three years with perhaps six different lawyers over custody of our son.

I bailed from Sydney Uni on the last day it was possible to discontinue without failing subjects, and stopped trying to read 'The Fairie Queen', a long text by Edmund Spenser written in the sixteenth century. The passage for required reading concerned a well-born woman chained up in a dungeon, and the approaching men.

I was glad to read the newspaper instead, or sit at an outside table at a Badde Manors on Glebe Point Road and watch people passing. I would sit very still. It was while I was sitting one day that I remembered not the event but the sensation of the teacher in kindergarten handing me a pencil and saying That's yours, it's just for you. I suppose I'd always had to share my pencils before. Then the sensation of holding the pencil and being so ready to learn to write. I copied the letters from the board and my hand seemed to know what to do. Once I had learned to write 'house' I could not help revelling in the fact that from a few marks on paper, the reader went straight to their imagination and invented my 'house'. It also thrilled me that you can change one letter and get 'horse', or add one letter, and go from the word to the world.

The teacher came by and touched the hair at the back of my head and said, You're a good writer. It may have been the first time someone paid me a compliment. Or touched the back of my head affectionately. For whatever reason, the sentence 'You're a good writer' stayed in my mind, something I spent my life practising to be.

And later in Primary School there was a subject called Composition. Each week I waited for the new topic. I was so ready to do Composition.

These memories of my early competence rubbed uneasily against my inability to know how to manage my adult life. I got up and walked away from the café, berating myself along the street. Crossing the road into the uni I went to ask if I could re-enrol next year and do Honours again—yes—I started swimming laps in the pool at Victoria Park, and at other times walked around the suburb—the cafes, the Primary School, Gleebooks, the Housing Commission terraces, women with three kids from three different fathers, up to the PO, down past the library to the bigger houses and the harbour and dredges going by with mobile cranes.

Finally the year Ben was ready to go into third class, I was awarded custody, and the arrangement was swapped: weekdays he was with me, weekends and half of school holidays, with Joe. Joe's vengeance had died down and we could speak easily now about any alterations and what Ben wanted. It was far from ideal and I had grinding sensations in my heart about how it was for the child.

A prize

About this time I submitted a poem about Violet and Stockton and the steelworks and the life there, to a competition being run by the ACTU for poetry. The prize was $750 and I had no expectation of winning. But perhaps there were few writers in Australia who wrote about working class people and I was in luck. To celebrate my win I took Ben to Violet's for the school holidays and told her my news. She looked sceptical and was amazed by the amount.

And you say it's about me? she said.

Yes, want me to read it to you?

I suppose so.

I read it out and waited.

Well that's as may be, she said, but without me you wouldn't have had a poem.

That's right, Violet.

Well by rights shouldn't you be sharing the prize with me? What's half of $750?

Here I was, uncomfortable, young, and stupid, and I'm pretty sure I refused to share the prize. She put on her big hat and we went across the road to the beach where she kept walking into the surf, in higher waves than normal. I always held her hand in the water as she had never learnt to swim. I was worried she'd get swept off her feet but I think that is what she wanted to happen. She ended on her knees, laughing and calling Ben to come and help me pull her up. She got her dress and her apron and her bloomers wet and had to change everything when we got back to the house. All day she seemed elated and in the late part of the afternoon we played cards and she won every game.

By the end of the year I had published a set of poems in an anthology, and was reading at the Harold Park Hotel where the performance poetry scene was centred. The hotel was opposite the trotting track and often in those times in the early morning in Glebe you would see people leading horses down to the bowl of the track. As well as pacers there were greyhounds racing there. I thought the greyhounds' names were good. Like horses' names. Arctic Princess.

Adelaide

I reeled out of the tent mid-some-writer's speech or discussion, needing tobacco and fresh air. I stood on a mound and lit up. Judith Rodriguez, a poet from Melbourne who I didn't really know, was standing nearby. I waved. I squatted on the mound and thought of Winnie in *Happy Days*, buried to 'just below the breastline'. Judith came across and sat near me.

How goes it? she said.

Couldn't take any more.

Yeah. She smiled at me and said suddenly, You know, I think we may be the only two women in the poetry world here who married immigrants.

What was your name before Rodriguez?

Green.

Not quite the same Latin twist, is there?

She looked at me. We sat on the mound. Is Hampton your real name?

No. I was married to a Slovenian man who had a name no one could pronounce.

Oh?

I was a school teacher at the time, and our name was Pisorn but the 's' was pronounced 'sh', so, 'Pishorn', so you can imagine what fourth class made of that. I was mocked for my name for months.

So we were looking for a new name. Joe worked at the floating dock, we were in Newcastle then. They were always on strike, an electrician would walk under the ladder of a painter and docker, everybody out. So there was no money. And one day Joe came home and said, 'Bloody that horse, he took my money, I'm taking his name.'

I asked him what he meant. He said his workmate, a man they called Aunty, a fitter-and-turner, had given him a hot tip on a horse in the fifth race in Adelaide. Joze had gone to the bank and from our 'either or both to sign' account had taken out all we had, six hundred dollars, and put it on 'Hampton's Pride' which came second last. He had to have something, he was *taking its name*. I thought of Hampton Court, and The Hamptons off New York, and agreed. So I got my name from a horse.

A horse.

She was quiet for a while. Then she said, I thought, neither of us has ever written a word about the experience—of marrying a migrant, I mean.

No, I said, would you excuse me? And saying this I went away behind a garden on the riverbank and on the back of a paper bag, I wrote

Yugoslav Story

Joze was born in the village of Loski Potok,
in a high-cheek-boned family. I noticed
he had no freckles, he liked playing cards,
and his women friends were called Maria, Malcka, Mimi;
And because he was a handsome stranger
I took him for a ride on my Yamaha
along the Great Western Highway
and we ate apples; I'd never met anyone
who ate apples by the case, whose father
had been shot at by partisans in World War II,
who'd eaten frogs and turnips in the night,
and knew how to make pastry so thin
it covered the table like a soft cloth.
He knew how to kill and cut up a pig
and how to quickstep and polka. He lifted me up in the air.
He taught me to say, '*Jaz te ljubim, uganzi luc*'
(I love you, turn off the light)
and how to cook *filana paprika, palacinka,*
and *prazena jetra.* One night in winter
Joze and two of his friends ate 53 *palacinke*
(pancakes) and went straight to the factory
from the last rummy game. Then he was my husband,
he called me *moja jena,* and sang a dirty song
about *Terezinka*, a girl who sat on the chimney
waiting for her lover, and got a black bum.
He had four brothers and four sisters,

I had five sisters.
His father was a policeman under King Peter,
My father was a builder in bush towns.
Joze grew vegetables and smoked Marlboros
and he loved me. This was in 1968.

The following weekend I caught the night train to Melbourne for the first Poets' Union conference. People came from every state, and it was bizarre and wonderful to be surrounded by poets, to be talking poetry all day, to go to a gig where someone from Darwin read followed by someone from Hobart.

Joe visits

After another time I was away, I came home to a note on the table with the names of people who had called. Ben was now in Year 9 at Glebe High. My girlfriend at that time, who lived in North Sydney, had rung three times. Joe had rung—not for Ben, but for me.

Do you know what that's about? I said to him.

What's that? He was practising magic in the mirror.

Daddy ringing me.

No.

Isn't it time I told him I'm a lesbian? Then he'll let it go.

No, Mum, you mustn't! He would have no idea. I mean, his idea of lesbians would be pornography. He will get weird images in his head of what you do and he'll be really upset and come over and be angry and just want you to be normal. It will just cause a fight.

Once again I was confronted with the fact that my child had a better understanding of people and situations than I did, that he lived in the real world, which I tended to avoid, that he accepted and understood it. Its time-honoured practices. The likelihood of what a person might think.

But because it wasn't a good idea to tell my husband I was a lesbian, and because I was at this time not living with a lover but as an independent person in her own house with her son, I had an aura of availability around me apparently—Joe didn't wait for me to return the call but arrived the next Saturday with a bottle of Riesling.

His affable side was on display, his body language expansive, his big gardener's hands, which I had always liked, sat like plates on the table. It was weird to have him sitting in the kitchen visiting, trying to think of things to chat about.

It's good to see you, I said. But you mustn't get any ideas that we might get back together. In a way I do still love you, but we're not suited, it's very sad.

What's mean not suited? We're very suited! We have a child! We need more children.

But you don't know anything about me, who I am.

I know everything.

How many books I've written, for example.

Books? No.

Well, that's important to me. But it means nothing to you.

You don't want more children?

Sorry, no. I want to write more books.

Anyway, he said, have a drink. He opened the wine and waited for me to bring glasses.

I will just have a sip, I said—knowing it would be sweet and horrible—I don't really drink in the daytime and I don't drink Riesling.

What? You used to drink Riesling!

Yes, but I was nineteen. I didn't know what I wanted from life then. I didn't know how to talk to people.

He took a swallow of the wine. But, he said, you always talk to people very well. All my friends think you are good talker.

That's different.

With you, everything is different.

Yes. I hope you will try and understand.

I understand nothing. I make big effort, I forgive you, I come here with wine, I'm dress nice, I offer you a life.

It's not the life I can live. Joe, I'm sorry. I got married and then I grew up. It should have been the other way around. I was so young, a child.

Your Mum she marry at nineteen and she have six children!

Christmas holidays

That year Ben and I were in Stockton for our annual holiday with Violet. Mum visited Violet on Sundays, then went to see Tommy. I went with her and we talked about nothing, as usual. They never spoke of anything personal. Something that had changed, in my generation. Tommy was making it clear by her body language and her expressions that I was using the word 'lesbian' far too freely.

Back to Violet's and a few days of peace and the sea at the front door. I didn't feel like going to the Wreck and fishing with Tommy, so I walked into the sea with a hand-line. The spritzy and marine smells played in a light wind. I didn't catch anything, but it was fine.

A few days later, Ben and I drove down to the punt and crossed the river to see my parents. When he went into the next room to watch TV, I sat in the kitchen with Mum and Dad.

I told them Joe had visited, and he was unable to understand why we couldn't get back together. Mum and Dad shook their heads, and rightly had nothing to say on the topic.

I then told them about the National Conference of the Poets Union and said I'd met a woman there who came from Adelaide, and who wanted me to co-edit an anthology of Australian women poets.

The Poets' Union? Dad said, really? What happens when you go on strike?

No one notices, Mum said.

We called Ben in for morning tea and Mum asked him if he remembered, a few years back, asking her if she knew anything about our ancestors.

Yes, he said, leaning forward, what did you find out?

Mum gestured to two ring-binder folders on the dresser and said, Well, quite a lot. I've been collecting birth and death and marriage certificates and putting them in order in the folders. They tell you some things but not—she hesitated—

Ben understood, and said, You want their stories.

Yes, it would be good.

He went to look at the top folder, flicking through it. OK, he said, farmers, farmers, a tinsmith, a butcher, a boiler-maker. So that's who I come from.

Dad said to him in a quiet voice, I wouldn't recommend farming.

I asked Ben what he knew about Joe's side.

Farming, he said. That's why Daddy has such big hands. Hard physical work.

I don't know if I realised that, I said.

Stories

Violet as a child had lived with her family up the valley at Lochinvar, in the cottage set aside for people whose job it was (the wife's job) to close the railway gates when a train was approaching. One day when her mother was closing the gates, Violet looked under her parents' bed and found a trunk, and when she pulled it out and opened it, under some spare linen she found a long plait made of dark hair like her own. When she asked her mother about it, or the woman she thought was her mother, it was revealed that the plait belonged to her real mother. The real mother had run out one day to close the gates when she saw her toddler son on the railway line. She rushed to the line and threw him free but she did not get away in time. Violet's father had cut off his wife's plait and hidden it in the trunk, and some time later remarried. This second wife was really Violet's stepmother, and her actual mother was the plait.

My mother also did not grow up with her real mother. We knew some of how this had come about, but questioned Violet for detail.

It was during the depression, she said. She sighed heavily and stared down at her hands which were on the tablecloth.

Among all the things I forget, I recall this moment so well that I can remember the tablecloth, and when Violet died I asked for it, and I still have it.

When Violet married Norman McLean, who we called Pappy, and had my mother June, Pappy was building silos in the bush. They were living in a tent. Mum was a toddler, and during this time two more kids, boys, were born quickly … although this isn't clear, they might have been born in Maitland or Stockton, then come back to Binigai.

One morning Violet got a lift into the nearest town, Inverell, and arranged to rent the front two rooms of a house owned by two sisters in Urabatta Street. The shared kitchen and laundry were in the back yard.

Twenty years apart in age, the sisters lived together in a quiet Methodist way. Aunty Mi (they pronounced it My) and Aunty Pearl were sixty and forty.

Pappy was still living in the bush and when he came to town he drank most of the money and gave what was left to Violet. It wasn't enough. The ladies helped Violet with food and low rent, and they minded my mother. They got attached to her.

When Violet was pregnant again, and desperate, she wrote to her sister Daisy who came up on the train. They went with the kids to Maitland to their parents, who said to Violet some version of You've made your bed so you can lie in it.

Pappy followed Violet to Maitland, and they lived in a shed and tried to make ends meet, but it wasn't possible. The two oldest kids, June and young Norman, were about to be 'put on the state'. It was at this point that Violet started to cry, telling the story. Aunty Pearl appeared: she had come to Maitland to visit some relatives. She said she and Aunty Mi would to take Mum 'till there was more work or money about'.

During the telling of this story, Mum asked how old she (Mum) was, when this happened—but Violet was so overcome at this point we never found out. Mum thinks she was two or three.

Aunty Pearl took Mum back on the train, and Violet managed to hang onto young Norman.

Somehow though, Mum lived with the aunties all her childhood and then for the four years she worked in a solicitor's office till she married at 19. She stayed in Inverell and had six daughters and kept us fed. Dad was a builder and Mum ran the business.

Pappy had eventually become a boiler-maker at the BHP, and he and Violet bought a house on the beach at Stockton, paying it off at a pound a week. Every Christmas holidays we drove down—it was then about a ten hour drive—and stayed a few weeks. My sisters and I ran wild in the sandhills, hiding from each other, building barricades with driftwood. Sometimes alliances were formed, and the driftwood was moved.

Violet never said much. She rarely roused on us. Pappy retired a few years before I finished high school, and died soon after.

When I finished school, we all went to Newcastle to live. My family lived on the Newcastle side of the river, and I lived on Stockton with Violet, waiting for news of a scholarship.

Later when Violet and I were alone—we all called her Nana—she told me she had always been called Mrs Mac or Sis or Vi or Mum or Nana, but no one had ever called her by her full name, not even Pappy.

From that day, when we were alone together, I never called her Nana again, always Violet. I don't know if she appreciated it—she never showed her feelings much except now and then when she was overcome by silent crying or very occasionally at a game of euchre, a hoot of laughter.

At that time Mum began to try to get to know her mother and to bring Violet out past her grief and shame and to love Mum, even to be able to hug her. But this never happened.

We didn't tell all this to Ben, but talked about the BHP, and the men's jobs (three generations of our men worked there), and how good the fishing was.

The women's line was a more-or-less silent line in the story. And in fact Mum hadn't started researching her side of the family, but only Dad's side, which went back to the First Fleet. When I mentioned this one day, and said, Mum, what about your side? she said, Oh. Yes. I'll start looking into the McLeans and the Murphys.

I took Ben fishing with Tommy and we stood looking across the river at the BHP. It covered a big site, and all the sheds were a dark red-brown.

So that's where Daddy worked for a while? Ben said.

Yes, and my cousin Steve and your great-uncle Norm and your great-grandfather, also called Norm.

You mean Pappy?

Yes.

His line plunged, and carefully, as taught by Tommy, he wound in.

We caught a good feed of flathead. Violet would be glad.

Rockdale markets

When school was almost over, Ben decided it was time to sell his toys. We would have a few more months in the house while I had it cleaned and painted, then my plan was to rent it out, and go and live in Daylesford in country Victoria and look for a farm. A ten-hour drive, but I knew people there. In particular, a woman I'd met at a Mardi Gras event, who I had been in love with for the past year and whose farm I'd been visiting.

Eventually, Ben was going to live in Parramatta with his father. It would have been much better for him if I'd stayed in the city till he was ready to leave home. But in my family, my generation were the first to finish high school and most of us left home straight after that, for work or university and part-time work. I simply followed the plan, and it suited me because I was attached to the farmer. It's impossible not to feel regrets in hindsight.

I will need help, Ben said, looking at me, meaning, to do such a thing as sell my toys. We drove to the supermarket for boxes and methodically sorted and packed almost everything.

At the Rockdale market, as soon as we put the toys out he began joking around with people nearby, especially men with stalls. One man called him over. 'You new here young fella?'

My son slipped between his personae of canny businessman, martial artist, magician, Blues Brother, sullen schoolboy, joker in the pack.

After lunch the stall-holders began to pack up. We had not sold a lot, but some of the big things went. 'Mind the stall,' my son said, and raced off, haring through the last of the crowd, checking out other stalls still selling toys and asking their prices, offering them an amount for a job lot. These toys which he got so cheap at the end of the market he would sell for normal prices at the beginning of next week. I was surprised and thrilled that a person like me so uninterested in money could produce a child like this. I watched him operate and so did everyone else, and there was a sense of amusement in the air. From another stall I bought some books I thought he might like to read, one by Groucho Marx.

My son disliked literature except for Charles Bukowski and disliked maths and everything else about school. He only went to school to see his friends.

When high school ended he was set free into the world. He got his licence, and a car appeared, I could only suppose he had saved the magician money. His car-horn played a tune, so I often knew where he was in the suburb, or when he was arriving home. He treated it as if it was an ironic joke. He bought a suit and got his first job, all within a few weeks of getting the car.

Meanwhile I was still teaching two days a week at a university, on the basis that I had now written a couple of books, and I taught Bukowski and no one ever disliked him. The drunkenness, the humour, the racetrack, the dead-end jobs, his conviction that no one was a whore.

Tina

Wax, though basically a surfer, was one Saturday morning sitting on a kitchen chair dressed as a businessman. My friend Tina came over and sat and talked to him about her super fund, should she get one? How did a person go about it? How should she think about her future, given that she was a sculptor and made little money. Wax was silent as if he were thinking. Eventually we got to work on the clay goddess we were making.

For a while, years before I found the Annandale house, I'd lived with Tina who had a small stone house in Lilyfield. Her son was the same age as Ben. She was making things in boxes to exhibit, had been to the desert and collected red sand, twigs, claws, and was putting them inside the segments of the boxes. We liked the same music.

The goddess was set up on my kitchen table. We'd got the idea from a hardback art book, and had the page open at her torso and head: she was from some early culture, with huge eyes and no mouth. Tina had provided a big block of clay and we were cutting into it with her tools. After each session of work, we covered her in wet cloths so she wouldn't dry out and crack. When we had the outer shape we turned her on her side and dug out her innards so she would be a certain thickness only and good for firing. Tina took care of that.

She asked how Nike was going and I said it was hard trying to create the consciousness of someone who had *no childhood.* A statue who had only come alive as an adult. Tina wondered whether thinking about amnesia might help me.

Packing up

My son was taking down his Elvis poster from the wall, then Groucho, Dirty Harry, Bruce Lee. He had given away the fish and was deconstructing his aquarium. The tasselled red lantern came down from the light and his clothes were folded in boxes. In the centre of the room stood the wheeled wooden box containing his magic tricks, with its painted sign, Beni Bizarre. Folded into this box was his velvet robe with its satin lining. He was 18, and was going to live with his father. He did not want to move out. But his mother had decided to go to live on a farm near Daylesford in Victoria. We were sad and sorry around each other, not saying much.

Mum, what do you want to do there?

Sit and stare at trees for two years.

Annandale has trees.

Uninterrupted trees.

He shook his head and began to fold his kung-fu clothes. I went to my study and began to pack up my notes and my books.

Joe rang to see whether Ben was doing a magic show that weekend, or coming to Parramatta. I said he was doing a kids' birthday party in a big park in the eastern suburbs.

He snorted. Is what rich people do for kids' birthday, hire magician.

I guess so, I said. Did Ben tell you I've decided to buy some land?

There was a silence.

I was very conscious Joe had grown up on a farm, then had always had vegetable beds when we were married. A jolt of guilt went through me that when we lived in Blacktown I had been so concentrated on university and studying to be a writer that I had bought tomatoes one Saturday and when I came home, he patiently took me out to the garden and showed me his tomatoes on their stakes, a big bright-red crop. I had not noticed his tomatoes. I remember groaning. I groaned again now.

Joe's deprecating laugh came down the phone line.

I'll get Ben, I said.

Photos

While they talked, I went to my study and took down some photo albums to put in one of the boxes I was packing. Here were the two albums of my childhood, and again I wondered who that kid in the pictures really was.

It was hard to relate to my childhood self, since she was so covered with accretions of later selves accumulated to deal with the world. I've discussed this with my sisters in recent times and both Kathleen and Barbie have talked about how shy they were as little kids, and how they've had to make themselves fit to the social world, to put on a persona that made them credibly confident in the professional worlds they inhabit now, where they have teams of people working with them and looking to them for advice, and where they fit in the realms of government and university. They're both successful in their work, and seeing them operate you would never know their background as reserved children.

There was a whole year of Kathleen's early life where she became mute. Barbie found it such a shock when the family moved to Newcastle, going into an Infants class of people she didn't know, that she cried so much the head teacher asked Kathleen to take her home. This happened more than once. Yet these girls as women—

as with Linda, Gwennie and Trisha, are great at their jobs and can be called on to operate in any emergency. They are all good parents with loving children. They have been hospitable to me and tried to understand my life, though some aspects of it may have made little sense to them. And though there have been sisterly disagreements, I feel loved by them all, in some sense cushioned by their presence. Our parents may have had little idea how to raise children beyond the practical details, and we were radically unsupervised in the way of that time. The river was our haunt.

Recently in the *Weekend Australian* newspaper Kate Miller Heidke, a singer, song writer and musician, was interviewed for a page called Confessional.

'The older I get,' she says, 'the more I'm convinced there is no such thing as "authenticity". Everybody inhabits a persona, and not just when they make music, even when they go about day-to-day life. What does it mean to be an "authentic" person; an "authentic" artist? I think everything is a construction.'

I had been watching Ben try on various selves to deal with his world, and noticed how adept he was and with what good humour he did it. His childhood was so different from mine.

His first suit

Appearing in the doorway of my study, Ben looked at where I was now packing the albums in boxes. He'd bought himself a suit off the rack in a George Street mens' store and was so practised at a magic trick that the manager had given him a job, on two weeks trial.

Did he interview you? What did he ask?

Held up his pen and said could I make that disappear.

I laughed.

It's not that hard.

Is the trial period paid? I asked.

Yeah. Not the full amount, but something. Do you want me to pay rent?

No, but thanks. Let me see you in the suit. Did you remember to get a tie?

I have ties.

He reappeared in the lounge room as a businessman—though the suit referenced the Blues Brothers—and turned in a slow circle in front of the wood stove.

Good? he said.

Yes.

I've been watching the men.

Unbeknownst to myself, I began inventing the story of my son's first suit, in which he had been playing the machines at Timezone in town and had come out onto George Street and walked along behind a man in a well-cut suit. He had excused himself and stopped the man and asked where he got the suit.

A conversation ensues, the man is a barrister, he's Jewish and has a Jewish tailor whose rooms are near there. My son looks at the suit again and the man asks him about himself. He says he just finished school and is applying for jobs and needs a suit, and his mother is a single parent on the pension and he has saved some money from working.

The man considers him and then says he will take my son to the tailor and introduce him, and will have my son choose the cloth and he the barrister will pay for the cloth. My son can then pay for the tailoring. They agree and shake hands and my son thanks him and they go upstairs to the tailor.

In my story the suit was made and my son got a job but I couldn't remember what the job was. For years, I had been telling this story.

When I began to doubt my confection, I told my son the story of the suit and going upstairs to the tailor. By this time my son was married and about forty-five. We were at his house. As I told the story he smiled and nodded his head.

What really happened? I said to him.

My son's wife, Louise, came and sat at the table too.

My son leaned back in his chair and said, Mum. It's really simple. I went into Mick Simmons and bought a suit off the rack, went to the interview, also at Mick Simmons, got a job selling suits and worked there. End of story.'

Into the silence, Louise said, I prefer Susan's version.

By now I knew I was a pathological liar. It took a while for this to sink in. I was sure there was more to this.

Then I remembered something. OK, I said, is this bit real? The job interview. You go into the manager's office for the interview and he sits you down and takes out a gold pen and says, 'Can you sell things? Sell me this pen.' And during the process of selling it, you make it disappear. And he hires you.

Yes, that happened.

That's something.

We sat up after the granddaughters were asleep in their beds, his wife going to bed was bidding us goodnight.

We were quiet for a while. I recalled a dinner with Ben, in some degree the last dinner of his childhood. I asked if he remembered that dinner.

Yes. We ate garlic prawns our favourite food and talked about the holiday we'd had in Bali … do you remember the name of the place? he said.

Mrs Alit's Cottages, I said. Local boys used to come on motor-scooters to the boom gate and beep their horn, and they took you on adventures. Did you feel safe?

Yes, very safe.

You never said much about where you went.

One day we rode up into the mountains where their grandparents lived and their mother pig was giving birth and we watched the other piglets being born. She licked them all clean.

I wish you'd told me at the time.

I was probably worried you might think I shouldn't go with them as far as the mountains. We were gone all day.

I tried not to worry about you. I knew you were having adventures.

We sat silent, then I said I remembered him doing his paper run, when he was at Annandale Primary, standing on the corner of Johnston Street and Parramatta Road, breathing in the fumes and getting filthy legs. On hot days retreating to the Empire Hotel where some old geezer would buy him a lemon squash. He remembered that he had bought the wheeled box for his magic tricks from 'Harry Dovellini, chief illusion maker' and that he got it from Alf in the shop in George Street.

This loved section of George Street contained the magic shop, the Menswear Store and Timezone, the electronic barn of games where you learn to hunt and kill, and how to avoid being killed.

3 Bird

Annandale, in the eighties: it wasn't hard to make a living, but it was hard to make it happen all in one place.

I had a day's work each at universities in Newcastle, Sydney and Wollongong. I was on and off trains, marking up assignments from the Narrative Fiction Workshop, watching the landscape, and dreaming up exercises in point-of-view or repetition. Reading them the first page of *Bleak House*.

One semester I was invited to do a three-week residency in Darwin. I had never been there and said yes. My main memories of Darwin are of alcohol and lesbians.

People were drinking as I got off the plane, from stubbies and hipflasks, openly, amongst getting on with their day, no one making comment. I thought of Charles Bukowski. He would've liked Darwin. Someone collected me from the airport and delivered me to campus and the office of the Head of School. He smiled and turned to a bookshelf which he pushed, and revealed a bar. 'Beer? Too early in the day? One thing you'll learn about the territory, it's never too early. Wine? Glenfiddich? What'll you have?'

Doll

At the end of the first workshop a few stayed back to talk, the last remaining one a woman about ten years younger than me, Janice, who the others referred to as J-Bird. Part of her hair was dyed red, part black. Side-on she looked like Nefertiti. She wore vintage clothes from op shops, and highly polished Cuban-heel boots. She wasn't saying much. Then she said, 'You should come back to my place, you'll fit in there.' I agreed. In class she had put on some lens-less black horn-rim glasses and performed as her alter-ego Doll Drone.

'She came out of the closet
very well-dressed
She came out of the closet
on American Express'

Her house, shared with an unstated number of others, had many louvres and sliding doors, and geckoes on the walls, that is, live geckoes. I scanned the titles of the books that were everywhere, on shelves, in piles, on tables, under a cat. We sat in the kitchen over cups of strong tea.

Bird had come to Australia from a small coastal town in New Zealand years before and prided herself on never having had a job. Her mother already had three kids and had not meant to have her, called her 'the mistake'—and though her father tried to compensate by being extra kind, it was not ideal. After Bird the mother had another child to be a companion for her, but these two never got on.

At about fifteen Bird left town with a gang of women who were passing through, women she liked the look of. They had teased hair and lots of makeup and fancy underwear, and stopped in each town to conduct business they did not discuss with her. She copied their look, however. They had money and splashed it around, they drank and laughed a lot and she had a great time with them. Eventually she got a plane to Sydney where one of her older sisters lived, and altered her look to suit the ghetto, though she kept the teased area of her hair and the lipstick. She stayed with the sister till she got on the dole, then set off on her travels. Her excuse for moving around was that she was always 'looking for work'. She had lived in Sydney, Byron, Darwin and Perth. Since she had no skills other than living the good life on a frugal income, and being Doll when required, she never got work.

She was writing a book called 'Dykes' Travels in the National Ghetto.'

She asked after my family and I told her about my father's mother Lucy Swinfield. Lucy was in my mind because on the plane to Darwin I'd been trying to read a tiny leather-bound book called 'Work' that was given to me from the few things in Lucy's house when she died.

Poor, I said, subsistence farmers. Lucy was in the Temperance Union—her father had been an alcoholic.

So, Bird said, not all writers are middle-class and come from money.

Not quite all, I said.

We talked about the difference between our ancestors, who endured real poverty and fear of starvation, and our poverty, which was chosen, mild, and mitigated by the welfare state.

She threw me a sarong and put one on herself.

Let's take a bath.

We went outside where amongst the ferns and lilies she had put a clawfoot tub on brick footings. She filled it from a hose that came out the laundry window, threw in some lemon balm, and lit candles. We were drinking Stella.

Great bathroom, I said, why don't you go first. I'll go after you.

OK. She took off the sarong and got in. She seemed to be tanned all over.

I could read to you, I said.

She went under and came up again, shining, her wet hair now back against her head.

You could! What would you read me?

What about 'The Faerie Queene'.

Yes! That sounds ideal.

Do you know anything about 'The Faerie Queene'?

No. And please don't tell me. Let's just have the work.

I went inside. It was all there, Anglo-Saxon Poetry, Langland, Chaucer, Bunyan, Spenser, Wyatt. Someone had done a good degree. I took down the Spenser and flipped through it, looking for a likely segment.

At the end of the workshops Bird asked for my address and said she'd come and stay with me in Sydney. I wrote my address on the back of a matchbox and beside it she wrote 'Ham'.

When months later she arrived in Annandale with a suitcase and a backpack, it seemed the spare room was meant for her. Due to exceptional foraging skills she had within a week acquired a double bed, a large tin trunk that had belonged to a soldier in World War II, an oval full-height mirror, bricks and boards and rope to make bookshelves and a wardrobe. In the kitchen, her poetry persona, Doll Drone, had conversations with Wax. Wax never replied or added anything to her thoughts, just sat immobile in his manliness. I thought sometimes Ben might do the ventriloquy for Wax but he ignored Bird's attempts to befriend him.

She had been living with us for a month and my son didn't like her walking his dog to the shops because friends would recognise his dog and he didn't want Tigger to be seen walking with a witch.

It was understood from the start with Bird that this was a friendship and we would not be lovers—I had no interest in her that way. A lot of other people did, and were surprised I didn't. I loved her though. She had an understated style and knew how to be quiet about the house, so you could get on with your own life.

She took up the third of our four bedrooms and made a wardrobe from a broom handle and ropes. She located the best local op shops and bought some summer frocks for performing in, and clothes for clubbing. Clothes were her thing, though she could leave them all behind in one town and start again in another. Within weeks she had a pile of costume jewellery on her dresser. It was hard for her to believe I was such a plain dresser and never wore make-up; she was constantly cutting my hair to a more interesting shape and offering me ear-rings and pendants. She bought me frocks and a pair of Cuban-heeled boots. It was strange having a style queen living in the house but I liked it. I can't remember whether I charged her rent.

Heather came over and I introduced her to Bird. Heather was wearing her aunt's cast-off jodhpurs and a cotton shirt with a thin gold chain around her neck. They got on a wavelength straight away, single women, no kids, keen on the stylish look, plenty of nightclub experience, many adventures to be recounted. I felt so normal and somehow confined, not having given myself time between childhood and parenthood to be simply an adult and have my adventures. Several of Bird's adventures I was glad I had not had.

These women were accomplished performers and it was always good when the three of us were together.

Because of Bird, my Sydney friends began to call me Ham as well.

Bird's writing was all in capital letters. Had she left school before getting the hang of running writing? Or just preferred to print?

She arranged to have fifteen of her poems printed on A5 size card and was putting sets of them in envelopes to sell or swap. Performing at pubs, she didn't need them, spoke from memory, a true auto-didact. She did a gig at the Harold Park Hotel, her black-gloved Doll finger now and then touching her glasses frames, her leather jacket, her hat. A few women approached her and she sold them her poems and let them buy her vodka tonics or Stella.

While I was at work, teaching a Fiction class at UTS, Heather and Bird had been to the Mardi Gras workshop in Darlinghurst and consulted with the artists and sculptors about a lesbian float. They were keen. They wanted to make a flying Wonderwoman.

We sat at the table discussing ideas, Ben standing near us practising kung-fu moves Sifu was teaching him in the studio on Broadway. He would pause and say quietly again into the sideboard mirror, 'Respect. Respect yourself. Respect for all sentient beings.'

Wonderwoman

The Mardi Gras workshop was a warehouse full of benches and tools, stored artefacts, costumes, bags of cloth, giant gowns hanging from the metal struts that supported the high roof. All around, an atmosphere of making. Bird and Heather went from bench to bench feeling bits of cloth.

The previous year Heather and I and a gang of her friends had made a larger-than-life-size Martina Navratilova who in her tennis frock and swinging her racquet glided along in the parade on the top of a flat-bed truck, and we in our tennis clothes and brandishing racquets danced around her to some Chrissie Amphlett songs. It was the 90s, a high era in women's rock music.

Today a beautiful poofter was walking in among a thicket of giant painted papier-mâché high heels mounted on broomsticks. The vibrant reds and blues shone onto his pale skin. His name was David McDiarmid. He was starting to look other-worldly because of AIDS. He introduced his friend Fabian. Heather introduced Bird.

I remembered Imelda's shoes from a previous parade, held aloft by a band of buff dancing poofters so they seemed to *float in the air* above the noise and the music.

But now we came to the head of a man, papier-mâché, ten times its normal size, on a platter. I recognised Fred Nile, an anti-gay Christian minister. The head, which now that I looked closer seemed to resemble a turkey, was surrounded by plastic fruit—grapes, bananas, rockmelon.

I said he'd been in the news that year for having his congregation pray for rain on parade night. And threatening to turn up at the parade and make *citizens' arrests.*

It didn't rain, David said.

And no arrests, Fabian added.

At that time Fabian was Mother Inferior of an order of gay male nuns, The Sisters of Perpetual Indulgence. They had carried the head of Fred Nile in the parade, while other nuns from their order, all in full habits, danced around him, while Fabian, as usual, danced and swung the censer, creating an aura of holiness.

Are you a sister? Bird said.

I am the head of the order, Fabian said. Fred Nile could only exist within a swarm of us.

And only beheaded, David said. Though he wasn't exactly John the Baptist.

But we were Salome! Fabian said, and they laughed as if this were exactly true—and to them it was true. They had played a Biblical role, only it was, 'Bring me the head of Fred Nile.'

And Fabian, David said, have you heard there's a move to take the head to the next Sleaze Ball and blow it up?

David now turned to me, and asked if I had a car.

I do.

I wonder could you drive me to the flitter shop? I need to get 20 kilos.

Sure. What is flitter?

Like glitter but more fabulous.

Just then Bird and I noticed a dusty twelve-foot-long Barbie Doll lying on a bench. Parts of her papier-mâché body had come away from the wire armature. Even so, she was impressive. I looked sideways at Heather who was surely thinking the same thing.

Heather leaned forward. Do you boys need this Barbie?

No, no, Fabian said, do you want to do something with her?

Can we have her? I think we have an idea for her.

Wonderwoman? I said.

Heather and Bird smirked at each other.

We discussed the transformation of Barbie, then Heather went out to do research. Bird and I were worried about Heather—she didn't look well. As usual she had high energy but it had begun to seem febrile and her colour was bad. If she was sick and had been seeing doctors, she probably wouldn't admit to it.

David gestured to us to come outside where the air was gritty and more real. I felt like I'd seen again the backside of Mardi Gras.

In the car we cruised along to the radio. After all it was a sunny day.

You direct me, I said.

Next left.

He wanted to know what we did for a living and I said we were writers. From the back seat Bird performed a few of Doll's pieces and he told her she was groovy. And you? he said to me.

I'm finishing a book of stories and short pieces about …

Dirty low-down lezos, Bird intercepted.

That's right, I said, looking at David, but I don't have a title yet.

Oh. Turn right here. Quick!

Is this the way to the flitter?

No, but I want to show you something. Now, look up, on that building.

High up a graffiti said SURLY GIRLS.

There's your title, David said.

Can I steal it?

Looks like public property to me, he said.

At the flitter shop the other two seemed to be in heaven whereas I was bored and went back to the car to wait. I thought the title was good, and took an old bill from the glove box and wrote a piece to incorporate the words. Now I would be able to finish the manuscript.

For a while I sat in the car in the sun and thought about how even autobiographical pieces such as these by the time they hit the page, were partially confected, altered, made more symbolic, exaggerated, even invented. After all you wanted the reader to be swept along in the story, to turn the page. It further occurred to me that some factually true thing which had been in the manuscript, I had taken out because it didn't fit, or was irrelevant, or ruined the energy or rhythm in the paragraph, or changed the mood too much, —there are so many times when strict truth was really not useful.

It's not on these grounds I absolve myself of being an unreliable narrator, or even on the grounds of some prior unremembered trauma inflecting the ability to tell or know the truth, but simply that it's a sunny day in Darlinghurst, people are getting flitter for the parade, and Barbie is waiting patiently on her bench to become Wonderwoman.

Back home Heather arrived with vintage comics. Wonderwoman it turned out was an Amazon, Princess Diana of Themyscira. 'She wields the lasso of truth—also known as the magic lasso or the lasso of Hestia. The lariat forces anyone it captures into submission, compelling its captives to obey Wonderwoman and tell the truth.'

At the workshop we took a closer look at Barbie and dusted her down and wiped her with damp cloths. Could she tell the truth? Her arms were by her sides. To make her into Wonderwoman we would have to remove her arms and *reset* them so one arm could be soaring out in front of her as she flew, and the other could be holding out the lasso. David and Fabian helped us cut out her arms and showed us how to reconfigure them.

While we were remaking her body ready for flight, David asked about her backstory.

She was an Amazon, Bird said.

Aren't they just a legend? he said.

It said they were nomadic steppe horsewomen, I said, from north and west of the Black Sea. Way back.

Err, I don't think the archaeology professors at Sydney Uni would agree with you, he said. Where is your information from?

The comic!

Oh. Yes.

When the repairs were done and dried, days later, we began to paint her. Bird did the face and under instructions I painted her costume blue and red, with stars. Heather mixed up a skin tone and painted her legs. She had brought a real whip, which had belonged to her aunt. We were in a mood of happy concentration. The armature held, and the papier-mâché.

We hired a truck and planned how we would position her to look like she was flying. The boys helped us.

On Mardi Gras night we wore silver and black, and danced along Oxford Street beside the flying statue—danced all the way to the showground. I noticed Heather's energy was at about half-speed but she had fallen in love with the woman who was running the Mardi Gras office, Q.T., young, dark-haired, private-schooled, and Heather was making a determined effort to keep up. She was pale under her scattering of freckles and Q.T. looked at her in a concerned way sometimes. I decided to quiz Q.T. later.

I wanted to be alone for a while and drift through the whole parade. The drugs were good and I started along the road, walking through Dykes on Bikes, who in their nakedness and engine noise set the tone. One or two women sat on each bike and often one in the side-car, many of them bare-breasted, tattooed, with ear- and lip- and nipple-rings, revving themselves up.

Then I came further into the parade and encountered a feral gang from Victoria who in a general atmosphere of flirting, surrounded me (you were not supposed to walk through the parade but go straight to your float and keep with it, rules I never obeyed). Instead of being hassled by the marshals I was entranced by these women who looked like they spent their lives gardening or herding sheep and driving around in old utes (this later turned out to be true). In some sense, I *recognised* them—people who had grown up in small towns, gone to the city, then made a return to the paddocks and sunrises and outdoor work, bringing their drug habits with them. I stayed with them for quite a while, quizzing them about where they were from, what they did with their lives, meanwhile we danced around each other to house music from speakers on the next truck, waiting for the parade to move off. It was a humid night and the crowds were pressing in, wanting to see the trannies and the dreaded lezos in their ripped clothes and the buff gay guys and really anything different from themselves.

By the time I had segued through to Wonderwoman rising above the truck on her frame and holding out one arm with the lasso of truth in the air, I had formulated a plan. Once Ben was finished school, I wanted to find maybe twenty acres with a mud-brick cottage, sheds, fruit trees if possible, off the grid, solar panels, tank water, a big dam. I wanted to be down the end of a white road in country no one cared about, and look after it. For a few years at least.

Q.T. admitted when I rang her that Heather had been in hospital twice for cancer treatment and was on heavy drugs to keep her going, but that she would not last long, it was thought. Months perhaps.

What? I can't believe this, I said. What sort of cancer?

Melanoma. She's having an operation on her hip next week but they don't expect it to be more than a holding operation. Q.T. started to cry quietly and I took a deep breath.

Where is she now?

She's here, at my place.

Give me the address, I'm coming over.

It's really bad. We've only just fallen in love and had our

honeymoon. Q.T. was now sobbing quietly into the phone.

It was the beginning of many visits to RPA to be with Heather before and after the surgeons did what they could. Her friends were on a roster and we were allowed in at any time of day or night as they didn't expect her to last long. Bird often came with me, my right-hand woman. We would wait till peak-hour traffic was over then drive to the hospital.

One morning when Heather woke from a drug-induced stupor, she pointed at Bird's arm and said to me, You know I saved her life?

I didn't, no.

I noticed sun damage and made her go to the doctor. It had to be cut out. She paused for breath then said, Right, Bird?

Thank you.

Pleasure. Whereas in my case I think I may have traced the melanoma—pause—on my hip to a lazy afternoon—in my early twenties when I was—uh—sunbaking under a tanning lamp, trying to cover up my freckles, which I didn't realise were actually attractive to some people, uh, and sipping on a few gin and tonics, when I went to sleep. I may have irradiated myself.

Or it could simply have been from the sun, I said. Think how our parents always told us to go outside and play. And out we went.

Don't give yourself a hard time, Bird said.

Did you read that book about the Bardo for me Bird? What am I to expect?

Later Heather recited her Coral Sea poem written on the honeymoon for Q.T., then sang to us, or rather moaned and hummed, while she garnered her energy to launch into one of her Bette Davis routines, then lapsed into what seemed like a coma. She had been awake for ten minutes and would now sleep for hours. A nurse came in to find Bird and me sitting on either side of the bed, each holding some part of Heather's body, looking at each other and crying, we both cried with no sound, just the tears running and the shaking of the head, what the fuck did we know about the Bardo.

Within weeks Heather was moved to a hospice called Ravenwood and in the afternoon a string quartet arrived, a surprise arranged by Q.T. Tall-stemmed champagne glasses, pastries, an audience. We asked Heather if we could move her to the big sitting room but she was already beginning to withdraw into herself. I'll listen through the window, she said.

Half my time I spent crying and taking notes, and half trying to be bright for Ben, cooking, being there for him in our last weeks together. He wore his new suit to work at Mick Simmons in the city. There was no way he would ever want to go to uni but I had no doubt he'd make good. He was street-smart and could read the room and spin a story and he knew when to be quiet. It was strange and sad hugging him goodbye, the end of an era, our heyday, his magic years. In private I cried.

Those weeks of tears were perhaps the last time that I cried with such a sense of inner collapse. And I have rarely cried since, and not at all for many years now.

4 The Gardener and the Radiographer

During the month of social events that had led up to the Mardi Gras, I went with Heather to an event called 'Return to Lesbos', held on a party boat where we were to have a lobster feast, and dance to a small band who were tuning up as we came down the gangplank. On the wharf Heather had introduced me to a friend of hers from the country north-west of Daylesford, a farmer—though later I realised she was more a gardener than a farmer. Tanned and blue-eyed and good-looking, she gave me a firm handshake and looked me in the eye for slightly longer than was necessary. Onboard, we sat at one of the tables set around the small dancefloor, and when the band struck up *That Ole Black Magic*, the gardener stood and held out her hand to me, as if she had decided I was the one. By this I mean I had noticed her looking around the women in the boat, in a choosing sort of way.

She came home with me and sometime during that long night I felt the years strip from me and that this was what I wanted: in a sense I was a done deal. It was a hot summer. In the morning as we sank against the sheets she positioned herself by my side so that she could kiss the skin beside my eye. We went to sleep like that and when I woke an hour later her mouth was still in the hollow beside my eye, and her arms wrapped round me. I watched the curtain shadows wafting on the wall, how short our lives are, and across my books, waiting for her to wake.

Later we talked. She had left school early and always done physical work. At one point she had a restaurant—coincidentally in Annandale, an illegal restaurant, in a house—she waved her hand towards the high side of the street. At that time she was in love with a girl called Coralie who was studying French at uni. When they made love, Coralie would touch her arm, her stomach, her eyes, and say the French words. Coralie had wanted kids and moved on to a man.

As the gardener spoke in her almost too quiet voice, it seemed to me that Coralie was the gardener's equivalent of Tommy—someone you never really get over, because you are so young, all your senses wide open, and you are so unprotected by defences later constructed during grief. At this time of life—I was almost forty—my defences were an armoury—or so I thought—I note in passing the word amour in armoury. From this distance in time though, I see the chinks were caused by what had not happened with Tommy.

At the time I only noticed the main *difference* from Tommy—that the gardener felt very happy to be making love with me. There was not that constraint.

As far as I know Tommy never read books. Whereas the gardener said that in winter she often lay on her bed and read a novel, books people recommended for her, or had given her. People like Coralie and Heather, who had been to uni.

Her mix tape was mostly Chrissie Hynde, The Pretenders, *Don't Get Me Wrong, Stop Your Sobbin', Brass in Pocket, Hymn to Her.* I was playing Miles, Coltrane, Billie.

Bird came home from somewhere and I introduced them. They liked each other immediately and we sat around the table while Bird performed a few of Doll Drone's best, the gardener chuckling and enjoying herself and rolling joints. I noticed that neither Bird nor the gardener had any interest in talking about New Zealand, in fact, once they established they were both from there, and named their home towns, that was it—no further mention—I guess they simply had to leave all that behind them. If I asked questions, they shrugged.

Do you want to talk about Inverell? Bird said.

Not a lot happened.

Well then.

Ben came home from school and set up his trolley of tricks "Beni Bizarre" in the lounge room and invited us to sit on the lounge and watch his show. He went out to the garden and brought in his rabbit, Alfie, a black rabbit—he hadn't been able to get a white one—and Alfie after coming out of the hat, roamed around the lounge-room while the tricks were being performed. The gardener was entranced.

At one point Ben said, And now I will need my beautiful assistant, gesturing to me, and I stood near him while he put a square hinged wooden board around my neck and produced a plastic sword and said he intended to put it through my neck. I stood still, as I knew how the trick worked. He inserted the sword into a slot in the board and it seemed to go right through my neck and came out the other side. I made no move but allowed myself an expression of pain and endurance.

And now! Ben said, shazam! and quickly he withdrew the sword, pressing a cloth to it as if to clean it, but really to put some red paint on the blade, and held it aloft, whereon I cried out, seeing my blood, and Ben said, Miraculously, she still speaks!

When he finished his show, the gardener asked if she could use my phone and went straight into my study and rang her farming partner and I could hear the delight in her voice. She asked if she might stay in Sydney a bit longer than planned, and I got the impression this was granted rather unwillingly.

Bird came and went, often having meals with us, and Ben went to his father's for the weekend.

The gardener and I went to Chinaman's Beach for the day and I took some photos of us using the timer on the camera. When the pictures came back we looked so elated, even with our eyes closed.

The water was just spritzy enough to be getting in and we lapped along parallel to the shore.

Over the week she spent in Sydney, the gardener spoke rarely of her upbringing. For long hours she would be quiet. Then little bits seeped out.

One story concerned a man with a beautiful garden who lived up the road. All the kids loved to visit because he'd set out the garden with gnomes, grottoes and a stream, lily pads that attracted dragon-flies, a cubby with toys under a weeping willow. Then one day he made a move on her, and she realised what he was doing with the kids.

How old were you then?

About six, seven.

Later she overcame her fear and the silence, and dobbed him in—and he was convicted and taken to gaol. She did not say how far he had got, with her. Also, I didn't want to know.

From this time on, at school, she was teased and hassled for getting the *nice old man* in gaol, as if the whole thing were her fault. Perhaps it was part of the reason she left school early, though also, she couldn't spell, and still couldn't spell, she said. She was sitting on the hearth of my wood stove as she told or almost whispered this story. She had a strong profile and quite strong views, but always spoke quietly. I think the quiet speaking was to keep everything liminal, for erotic purposes.

Before she had the restaurant in Annandale, she worked at a brothel, for a woman called Madame Hildegard. I must have looked taken aback. She said she was saving to buy land, that she wanted to live on a sheep farm and spend her life gardening. And this had really happened—in Melbourne she had met and fallen in love with a woman who had been to Israel and worked in a kibbutz with sheep and also wanted to buy land. This woman was a radiographer and was also saving up. They began to plant veges in big polystyrene boxes ready for planting out, and drove to the country every weekend looking at farms.

They found a place, twenty-five acres, and the radiographer bought some coloured sheep and started breeding them, giving them Jewish names, the first lot all beginning with A; their lambs had names starting with B and so on. The gardener could not have been more happy, but after some years she fell in love with a local woman called Glenda, also a good cook, and they secretly planned to run away together and start a restaurant. Somehow though this didn't happen, the radiographer won out, Glenda withdrew from the scene. Glenda had however given her a poodle-cross puppy, who the radiographer immediately named Grimshaw. When Grimshaw grew up they bred from her and one of these pups, also now grown, was kept for the radiographer, who named her Nicey Hapgood.

Why Grimshaw? I said.

Because if I moved out and lived with Glenda, things would *sure be grim*.

I looked at her face: she showed no embarrassment or anxiety, only, if anything, amusement.

It was at this point in her narrative that the gardener said she felt she ought to tell me she wasn't monogamous. Also that Grimshaw would be sleeping on the other side of her in the bed when I came to visit. She had beautiful brown curly fur and did not shed.

The gardener had tried to be monogamous with the radiographer, she said, but it didn't suit her so they no longer had a sexual relationship but had agreed to go on being farming partners no matter what. They had an *arrangement*—that the gardener could go away at times or even bring lovers to the farm and the radiographer would stay in her own part of the house, out of the way.

This was said with a smile that didn't quite reach her eyes.

I'm not sure how it would work, I said.

They each had their own end of the house, she said, with their own kitchen, lounge and bedrooms, separated by a library area and the bathroom. The radiographer had no friends and didn't go any further than the nearby small town where she worked three days a week at the hospital. This was so they could afford to have the farm. They ate their own veges and meat and milk and fruit but needed money for irrigation and pumps and repairs and the vet and the car and so on. The gardener was on the dole, that helped a bit.

They had been there for nearly ten years now and both loved the place and worked hard to keep it looking good—it was the life they both wanted, up early to do chores, and animals everywhere—the sixty coloured sheep, chooks, rabbits, three dogs, eight cats, and a tame magpie called Malvina. There was an orchard and big vege beds, a barn, and extra paddocks they rented so they could move the sheep around.

All this came out only slowly over the week and only because I asked questions. No photos were shown. She was reluctant to talk about herself. In the years I knew her, this did not change. Another thing. She never said anything negative about herself. And that is the main difference I have noticed between men and women. In that sense she was a man.

No was quite an important word. It seemed that areas of her were not coloured in, or perhaps hidden, and, as I came to realise, hidden for strategic purposes.

I asked the gardener to talk to me about non-monogamy. She spoke about a share-house she'd lived in with some gay men, years before, and said the way they lived suited her. She thought monogamy was a bit of a trap and wanted to experience more of life, not less, to be open to what might happen. I couldn't see how it would work but I didn't want to give her up. She invited me to visit the farm in about a month. I drove her to Central and the bus station for the Firefly to Melbourne, from where she would then get a train to Ballarat, then the radiographer would pick her up from there.

In the meantime I went as usual at that time of year to stay with Violet and go fishing off the Wreck with Tommy. One night I was watching 'Who Wants to be a Millionaire' with Violet, when the phone rang and it was the gardener. I asked her to wait—the phone was in the loungeroom but had an extension cord—I wrangled it into the breakfast room and shut the door. Because of the cord only reaching so far I was sitting on the floor against the wall, leaning in to the mouthpiece. We had built up a week of longing until our letters started to arrive.

She said something had happened—she had fallen *in love* with me. I stared at Violet's lino and had a micro-second glimpse of meeting Tommy in that room. Tommy as she was when I fell in love with her at age fourteen. She had been squatting on the floor. Then it was gone, and I tried to speak. Nothing came out.

I wasn't sure whether 'in love' meant the gardener would not be taking other lovers—for now—or for how long? But it didn't seem cool to ask and perhaps she didn't know the answer. Did being in love cancel non-monogamy? Or not always? Was she my girlfriend now?

Are you there? she said.

In a month I packed to go and visit her farm. I cooked some meals for Ben, put them in the freezer, gave him some money for his week's expenses and went over with him the ground rules for what he could do while I was gone. Was he sure he would be all right? Would he not rather go to his father's in Parramatta and get the train to school? He was sure. I caught the bus to Melbourne, then a train to Ballarat, where my girlfriend and her ex came to collect me. Since my girlfriend didn't drive, she relied on her ex to ship the lovers in and out, unless they drove there. This was seemingly done with laughter and good will and a few punning statements that hid, I was guessing, a tight anger. The ex was smart, plump, with curly brown hair, pink cheeks and blue eyes. It was clear she was the one with executive function and the one who managed the relationship. She didn't seem to have a sex life. Or any friends, apart from the gardener. Between them, it was looking like a folie a deux, though I didn't let myself think that then. The letters had been so joyful.

Once at the farm I saw by the gate it was called *Radclyffe*. We were greeted by three standard poodles and an array of cats. They'd had rain and the paddocks were green under the flock of grazing sheep, not your ordinary sheep but dark brown or beige with black faces and noble Arabic noses. They had been bred for carpet wool, though there was no money in it—the women loved the look of the sheep and ate or sold the rams except for the breeders.

The large two-part house sat on a sweeping lawn surrounded by flower beds in full bloom. Beyond the house-yard gate, where I was not encouraged to go, were the vege beds, the dams, and a large barn where they stored hay and birthed the lambs.

They watched *Rage* on TV early Sunday mornings, Tina Turner, *What's Love Got to Do with It?* Whereas I learned about relationships from novels, they took their cues from pop songs and rock'n'roll. Roosters woke us in the morning, and in the night peacocks screamed from the barn roof.

Every morning I went with the gardener to collect the eggs.

Large white hens with an array of black feathers at the neck, Wyandottes, I think, also Isa browns, the best layers, she said, and bantams. Their sheds were large, and the eggs were swapped with other farmers for their produce.

Next to the chooks were the rabbit pens—not your ordinary rabbit but plump flop-eared black, white, a soft grey, and cream creatures living and mating in an area large enough for them to have burrows. (Deep under the burrows was wire mesh.) A white one with black spots appeared. Dalmatia.

Did they eat the rabbits? Not often, no, the rabbits were there so they didn't have to buy dog and cat food. The ones being bred to feed the other animals were not named, only the breeders like Dalmatia were named. But the rabbits were really the radiographer's area, perhaps I shouldn't hang around there too much. I noticed the radiographer did more of the chores, and didn't smoke or drink. She consumed a 1.5 litre bottle of Coke every day and was about two stone heavier than me and twice as energetic.

By the arrangement, the radiographer was asked not to come into my friend's house when I was there, but this rule was constantly being violated on the grounds of loneliness, or the need to discuss pressing farm matters, or because she'd had an annoying phone-call, or one of the cats who slept with her had had a litter in her underwear drawer. A weird effect during these interruptions was the radiographer's rather forced laughter presented as good cheer.

The gardener and I visited back and forth for a year, and in the winter when the radiographer's interruptions became unbearable, the gardener pulled me down on the hearth beside her and said, We'll be together one day, I promise. She was looking into my eyes.

It was during one of these visits that I had the sudden feeling Heather had died.

I had known when I left Sydney I shouldn't go, even for a week, but when I told Heather in one of her waking moments, she had said, Go, take a break—she knew I'd been practically living at the hospice, sleeping on a camping mattress in her room, checking on her during the night. Stupidly, I went.

Now I was sitting on the hearth by the gardener's fire, shivering though it was hot. I reached for the phone and dialled Ravenwood.

Where are you? the nurse said.

Victoria.

I'm sorry to have to tell you on the phone, but Heather died ten minutes ago, at a quarter to nine.

I felt a low sharp noise come out of my throat, and held the phone away for a minute. The gardener slumped on the hearth next to me. In the night we held each other like dumb children. We went to Sydney together for the cremation and stood with her other friends watching her smoke come out of the tall chimneys.

Once I had decided to leave Sydney, I was invited to live at Radclyffe for a month while I looked for land. I put the house on the market and drove south for ten hours, the windows down to receive the fresh dry country air. In the back of the car I had the clay goddess, who was perhaps blind though she had large eyes, and was mute since she had no mouth. She was wrapped in towels and coats.

We joked that I was a love slave. 'Hurts so Good' was a popular song at the time. *Come on baby, make it hurt so good.* I was given the second bedroom in the front part of the house and a desk where I could finish 'Surly Girls'. I handed over the goddess and a place was found for her in the garden that abutted my friend's bedroom.

One afternoon after some private time with the gardener in her part of the house, I went round the back where the shared toilet was, to be met by the radiographer who was brandishing a bloody knife—having just killed a rabbit to feed the dogs and cats—and who whispered as if conspiratorially, Having a *nice* time? Her pink cheeks and blue eyes gleamed. Her surface sweetness hid a wish to do me harm. Stunned, I returned to the front house and spent the afternoon helping the gardener plant a camomile lawn in the square of space outside the French doors of her bedroom. I considered telling her about the knife but something stopped me.

Between the two houses and joining them together was a shared area consisting of a library, also shelves for storing bottled fruit and vegetables, bright with their colours, and on the other side of the passageway to the 'back house', the bathroom. The next day after a bath as I browsed in the library area I noticed most of their books were by or about lesbians. Only books by women, it seemed. I took down 'The Well of Loneliness' and scanned a paragraph and responded as I always had to that book, I was bored and appalled at the self-hatred and the weird psychiatry. An invert, for God's sake. I shut it just as the radiographer came into the library and hissed at me, *You don't exist, You don't exist.*

Telling this part of my life I feel it as if through gauze—that is, I entered a kind of oblivion and it continued in various forms for five years. Then I went on with my life in other towns.

When I begin to write about it, thirty years later, the gauze disappears and I become unwell or suddenly lose energy. Food goes straight through me. I have to stop and recover.

After the hissing I left the library area and went to 'my' room to work. It was against this background I finished 'Surly Girls' and sent it to the publisher. Once it was posted I stopped writing and was becoming numb. Or I should say, a combination of numb and frightened.

Only once I tried to explain to the gardener how the radiographer treated me behind her back, but this was not believed. After that I gave up.

It is unfortunate that any passing rational thought had zero effect on the state of still being in love, and it would take the five years I lived at my farm, on and off, for the emotions to catch up with the truth of the situation: I was not debauched enough, or free enough, to step onto the carousel of the non-monogamous, the poly-amorous; and not astute enough to deal with the weaponry exhibited by the radiographer.

After three weeks of the planned month at Radclyffe, I began to pack my gear. The gardener came into the room bearing two cups of tea and looked shocked.

What, leaving? Are you going back to Sydney?

Still intent on finding my own land, I said I would find a place in Daylesford.

Wait a moment, she said, and went to the phone and made a short call, then came back and asked for a piece of paper. She then drew a map: the road into Daylesford from the west, the town, another road out of town, a by-road off this, a turnoff, a picture of three small houses on the left then an arrow going into a property on the edge of the forest and one word: Mase.

If you go here, a good friend of mine will be expecting you. She's happy for you to stay till you find somewhere in town. I'm sorry you're going.

Your friend has reduced herself to hissing at me in the library.

Oh, come on, Ham.

When I drove off, apparently I was laughing. I don't remember doing this, but it became a bone of contention later—How could you have been laughing? It was sad!

In a while the gardener got her licence and drove over to visit me. Finally we had privacy but the damage had been done, and it was becoming clear she would not be living up to a statement made by her hearth the previous winter, 'We'll be together one day, I promise.' A woman called Zoe from Taradale was becoming a frequent visitor.

Hepburn Springs

The almost magical country around Daylesford and the many mineral springs seemed welcoming and I pulled the Toyota into the main street and got out to look around and buy groceries. An old-fashioned town with good views and friendly people. It was such a relief to be gone from Radclyffe.

When I turned into the driveway of the house labelled Mase, a man was mowing the front lawn. I got out to ask where Mase might be when he turned the mower off and came towards me saying, You must be the person from Radclyffe. Ham? I'm Mase, short for Mason, Lesley Mason but I never use the Lesley. Come in.

I looked more closely at my host while she made tea. The beard was short, and only on the chin, there was no cheek stubble. There was a strong jawline as you might see on a man but there were breasts, I now saw, not noticeable at first, but there. She had hips but not so you'd notice, and was wearing the usual lumberjack clothes of the local lesbian, or the local male, indistinguishably.

The face was symmetrical and handsome rather than beautiful but so good-looking, the voice was deeper than a woman but higher than a man. The books on the mantlepiece were all by women.

The house was one big room, with a bathroom at one end. There was a kitchen along the back wall with a gas stove. Near the fireplace in the lounge area, her mattress was on a wooden base. Sheepskins and rugs were strewn across it. Under the base rested her chainsaw.

Thanks for saying you'd have me here sight unseen.

You come highly recommended.

I'll find a flat soon I imagine.

She stepped back from the fireplace where she'd been squatting to make tea from a blackened kettle, and handed me a mug.

Stay as long as you like. She pointed to a ladder that went up to near the roof where a loft platform contained a mattress and a wooden fruitbox for a bedside table.

You can sleep up there. I live alone but I don't mind company sometimes.

I can't tell you the relief I feel.

No, but I can imagine, she said. Need anything to eat?

Not yet.

We talked all morning and she somehow picked up from my voice that I came from northern NSW near the Queensland border.

I didn't realise I had an accent, I said.

You mentioned bringing in your port, but most people say suitcase, she said. I get picked up for it. I come from Inverell.

Oh, I said, same here.

We shook hands on it, and sat and stared at the fire for a while. Nothing much to say about Inverell. I wished I had known her at school but she was just younger enough than me to have started each stage of school just as I was leaving. We never met. We talked about people we knew, but didn't know anyone in common.

She was so open and easy in my company I took a risk and asked when her beard had grown, and she said at puberty, when her breasts also began to grow. Her parents took her to the doctor who examined her and said she had an atrophied womb and would probably never have children, that she had an enlarged clitoris, and that she was a hermaphrodite.

A what? her mother had said. And what is a clitoris?

Her father had sunk down into a chair and couldn't even speak.

The doctor asked Mase if she felt she was a girl, since she had been regarded as a girl so far, and wore a tunic to school and used the girls' toilets etc.

Not only, Mase said.

The doctor thought it best if Mase shaved her beginning beard and continued as a girl, but Mase liked her beard and her deepening voice, didn't like school anyway and wanted to get out of Inverell. She hitched out of town and made it as far as Melbourne.

How old were you then?

Fourteen.

Everything seems to happen at fourteen.

Yeah, well, I got out. There were other reasons I had to get out.

She now had a logging coupe in the forest where she was allowed to cut trees to sell as firewood.

Is that how you make a living?

That and the dole, she grinned. Want some music?

While I brought the groceries in and then my port, she hooked open the bonnet of her ute which was parked facing the front window, and clipped two leads onto the car battery from her 12-volt music system. No electricity then. I looked around the room and saw several lamps of the sort you can pump up to go brighter if you're reading. Put my head out the back door and saw a tank up on a tank stand. Fridge and stove both worked off bottle gas.

No town water? I said.

No town nothing. Don't want it. Don't want the bills.

Keep warm enough in winter?

Cut my own firewood.

Everything in her house was neat and in its place. Patti Smith surged into the room and Mase went out to finish the mowing.

Every night we had good talks and she liked to cook. I read one of her books about women on the Left Bank in Paris in the early part of the century, Gertrude and Alice, Sylvia Beach, Bryher. So many lesbians with good educations and family money. Natalie Barney, her life built on the same principles as the gardener. So many lovers. HD and her pain and her analysis with Freud. Urban lesbians with inherited wealth. I was encountering the opposite. Rural lesbians on the dole.

Did you read this book? I said to Mase.

I surely did. Did you read the part where Gertrude is dying and she says to Alice, What is the answer? And when Alice doesn't reply, Gertrude says, In that case, what is the question?

I walked 20 minutes into the forest and stopped to listen. Small birds, now I saw they were wagtails, played near dew in spiderwebs, lizards crept in rotting logs. Further away, a roo with a bulge in her pouch. Stacks of wood that probably belonged to Mase were seasoning for the following year, their sap drying. I got well lost and took an hour to find my way back just on twilight. It was cold and I missed Heather. I missed Bird. I missed Ben and my family. I didn't miss Sydney itself. I was ready to be in the bush again, the strong eucalypt smell and the still trees. Mase had cooked a roast for dinner.

Daylesford

After three weeks in the forest in Hepburn I rented a flat in a big house near the lake in Daylesford. Linton House had once been a lying-in hospital for women giving birth, and my flat was on a corner of the veranda which went four sides round the building. Down in the garden, springs gushed from the lawn and trickled into the garden beds where lilies and foxgloves and lupins were standing tall in semi-shade.

It was a short walk to the main street. I was meeting people just from the look of them on the street, or because Mase introduced me. Most of them had come up from Melbourne. Any woman who had a place in the district, and there were plenty, had no trouble populating a weekend party with interesting guests. Phoenix was small and muscley and shy and worked for Forestry. She spent her days in a work gang pruning trees on backroads in Victoria.

Sal was looking for somewhere to live, so came back to Linton House with me and I took her to the landlord's flat. She moved in that afternoon with her few things and her dog Lupa. Sal was tall, thin, dark-haired, and was learning Italian from the parallel text of the *Inferno*. Every day she would come to my veranda and read me some, in Italian, to help take my mind off the disintegrating love situation. Every time I tried to think about the gardener, my thoughts started to congeal.

Despite a glutinous brain I was ready to find out what it would be like to live alone. 'Surly Girls' was away being printed. I began to unpack. Here at last was the cubby. From Bird I had learned how little you need to live. My Sydney things, including most of the books and clothes and all the furniture, were under my sister Barbie's house in Marrickville. It took me half an hour to unpack and make up the single mattress on the floor. I went up the road to Centrelink.

I wasn't sure what Sal did for a living. One day we walked to the mineral springs and the beautiful lake where she explained to me in English the layers of hell. It was ingenious, just like love.

In town on Friday Sal saw a girl she liked the look of, and said, Let's kidnap her and steal all her clothes. Sal had spiked hair and at that time she drove a big iridescent green car and was on the road a lot. It was something she'd wanted for a long time in high school, she said, to buy a car and get away.

Sal's father was a solicitor she said, and her mother volunteered as a guide at the art gallery. Sal just wanted to mooch around, take a job here, a job there. Didn't want to do anything with her private school education. Or not yet.

Drug-free, Sal was unusual in that community. She cleaned houses and later went to Melbourne and painted trompe l'oeil scenes including once a garden of Eden on the sides of rich peoples' houses. Then she was living in North Fitzroy and enrolled at uni and did a semester on Dante. Like everyone, she preferred hell to heaven.

It was on my veranda some months later that I had a launch party for *Surly Girls*, which billed itself as performance pieces. I invited all the local women I had met, Sal, Mase, Di Jest and Chrissie from Deep Spring House, KD from Mollongghip, Phoenix, Megaera, various others who had changed their names, and Andrea Lemon, her real name, from outside a town I can't now recall.

I put on a mix tape and when a certain track came on, nine of the women who unbeknownst to me had been learning tap-dancing, got up and did a tap to that song. It was a high moment of my life. It seemed, and maybe was, spontaneous. I can remember the intent expression on Di Jest's face as she tapped in time with the others, and flung her arms wide when they did.

The gardener had asked if I would invite the radiographer to the launch party, on the grounds that the radiographer never got out to see people, and this way she might *meet someone*.

She sees people all the time when you have friends over, I'd said.

Yeah but then she's always doing her chores. Or she disappears when we get drunk, and we're always drinking.

She's not my responsibility.

Well, no, but would you be kind? It would mean a lot to me.

Hence the radiographer was now sitting on a bench seat on my side veranda, and party protocol meant I should exchange a few words with her.

Hi, how's it going? I said, sitting up the other end of the bench.

Good, good. Thanks for having me at your launch.

I'd like to say it's a pleasure.

She laughed. I read your book, she said, my friend had an early copy.

I had no idea you'd be interested.

I read. I like fiction.

I only ever see you read gardening or sheep manuals.

You don't see me when I'm alone at night. She paused. In Israel, she said, there's a saying about how stories get written—and here she said some Hebrew words—

Yes?

'*It was, and it was not.*'

I looked her in the eye and it was impossible to tell whether she was making a friendly comment on the nature of fiction, on the composing of fiction, on the unreliable narrator, even, or whether she meant it as a quiet buried taunt about the state of my relationship with the gardener. Or was it more subtle even than these, a comment offered in camaraderie, on the state of both our relationships with the gardener. Not that she kept her face deadpan, there was a note of cheer and a twinkle in the eye, but then many of her earlier taunts had been delivered with seeming cheer and a confected twinkle which may now simply have signified irony.

We talked briefly about sheep then I went inside for a vodka.

The gardener was standing at the drinks table chatting to some woman I didn't know. She didn't introduce me, but seeing me, excused herself from the visitor and said to me in a low voice, come with me, and walked me to my bedroom, where our only company was a pile of coats on the bed. She shut the door behind us and started kissing me, as if about to seduce me, when I broke away and said

What's this in aid of?

Do I always have a motive?

As far as I can tell.

Goodness. I wanted the privacy to tell you that I love you.

I see. What is it you love about me?

Well, I have to say it's your wrinkly neck and your arrogance.

I got up and went to the lounge room and picked up a postcard from Bird, who was in Perth. I handed it to her to read, then went out to my guests. The gardener was no doubt four or five drinks in, the stage where she usually wanted to have sex. It didn't matter to her that I might be ignoring my guests, or that someone might come into the room—perhaps that even heightened it for her.

Years later in Davo, when I read in a biography of Philip Roth about an orgy he went to in Berlin, I thought of the gardener; it was a scene she would have enjoyed. The biographer describes the bodies everywhere, and how Roth, in going upstairs was *bitten on the ankle* by one of the copulating bodies.

5 The Farm

Ghost towns

Every day real estate agents called John or Mick drove me around small farms for sale, including those near ghost towns like Majorca and Red Lion. At first, travelling across the country, it was only the flatness I saw, and in the paddocks near the road, ancient rusting harrows. In some places there were no trees in paddocks lasting five kilometres. Wheat country, or rye or oats, the men said. Shadows no longer had soft edges, the light was at a lower slant to the ground this far south and the heat was more intense, the cold colder. Hours inland. The climate is like a person you constantly have to contend with.

There was no actual town of Majorca, Mick said. I asked if he had heard of a Majorca in the Mediterranean. He hadn't. The dry, dry smell of the air, with its hints of grasses and stubble. We got out and walked around—empty shop windows, grasses growing in the cement footpath, silence. A notice in one window said there had been eleven pubs and butcher shops there during the gold rush.

The land I wanted was uncannily as hoped for, at the dead-end of a dirt road. Surrounded by scrubby bush and other small farms, it sat in a haven of silence. Most of the locals were not really farmers but blockies.

It looked like all the original bush was gone and this was regrowth. Very few big trees. The front gate was already open and Sal and I drove in. There was the big back lawn—the previous owner had done a lot of mowing. I would be getting sheep for that. Seventeen kangaroos grazed the paddocks—I had seen them jumping the fences.

The front paddock had the house and garage, and a tank on a high wooden stand. A gate led to the back paddock where a huge dam glittered in the sun and near it one huge gum tree—the only big tree on the place. To the east was a fourth long paddock. There was no town power or water.

The agent had showed me the paperwork and asked me to *pace out the boundaries* to make sure the dimensions on the paper were roughly right. Sal and I did this with a lot of glee. The glee was a thin top layer over the humus of the knowledge that the gardener and I would never live together; it was glee nonetheless. We counted our paces to the twenty acres and laughed in the wind.

The Annandale house had sold and I moved into Majorca about a month later.

For the first time in decades I didn't need to work for a while. The land was dry, it was January. There seemed so few birds in the country, but maybe I didn't get up early enough. A man came to explain the solar setup, amps and ohms and the battery bank. The inverter. All this was in a tiled lobby when you came in. I was in no state to remember anything and wrote it all down and pinned it to the mud wall.

A removalist truck arrived with my books and bed and table.

Living at Majorca—endless uninterrupted time and time alone—was my first real experience of solitude. I now had time to wander at will, or to sit and read deeply all those books I had collected, taught from, read quickly.

The quiet was broken up now and then by visitors from Daylesford and from the gardener. She said with a shy look that she had a crush, she hoped I would not mind, on a woman from Amazon Acres (a place she had often mentioned in glowing terms), a person called Mei-ling. She had fallen for Mei-ling because Mei-ling's aim in life was to spend *all her time gardening*.

Oh? was all I could manage.

Though she said she still loved me, and I was 'the main woman', she was already having her fling with Mei-ling, who was now enjoying the perfect vistas of the farm.

What are you doing here if Mei-ling is at your place?

Oh, she said, I brought you some seedlings for the vege bed.

For a moment bizarrely I felt a twinge for the radiographer, who had gone through the worry that her friend might decamp to live with Glenda, then me, followed soon after by a perhaps even deeper worry that her friend might decamp to Amazon Acres, seventeen hours north. This empathy was momentary; most of the time when I thought of the radiographer I imagined her being blown up and landing in little pieces on some droughty ground, her body parts falling into big cracks in the earth.

After Mei-ling there would be others, over the five years I lived at Majorca.

I had just finished unpacking the books and scanning my favourite authors, when a farmer came to the door. It was Mr Kenden the dairyman from the end of the lane who wanted to run his dry Friesians in my top paddock where currently there were only the stumps of dead trees among the grasses.

And how have you been keeping? he said.

Very well, thankyou. I like the quiet.

When autumn comes on you'll hear chainsaws, he said, mildly.

He told me that country people went to town on Fridays, so that is when I went.

In addition to Emma Bovary and Charles Bukowski and Joan Didion and Renata Adler I became interested in the irrigation shop, the dimensions of ag pipe, types of joiners, tap spindle extenders. I was determined to have my experience of country life.

One winter morning I dressed warmly and went into the top paddock where I saw the cows coming towards me out of the mist, their breath rising. Just coming to see who was there.

The empty farmhouse

I recalled the empty farmhouse on my father's old farm, Clunybegg. My friend Hazel's father had bought the place to run his dry cows on. It was school holidays and Hazel and Barney and Linda and I rode our bikes the sixteen miles to the farm, where we planned to stay for a few days. Mum was bringing our food in the car, and all the kids.

The house was small wooden place without electricity, with the kitchen out the back in a separate building in case of fire.

The trees, the quiet, the smell of the air. I thought about Dad and his Mackie ancestors. That was the only time I got to be on the Mackie land. Later Mum produced a handwritten book detailing the trees that had been in their orchard, six plum, two apricot, three apple and so on.

When I bought the farm in Victoria I heard Dad was gobsmacked. He had done everything he could to get away from seventy acres of dry ground down a dead-end dirt road outside a small town; here was I heading towards it—for what possible purpose?

On the phone he told me about Arthur's Seat, an area of land near Clunybegg. How there wasn't enough water, and they were dynamiting the creek to sink a well. Once they had a certain depth, his father and uncle had tied a rope around his waist (he was nine) and lowered him, with the dynamite, into the bottom of the hole, where he had to plant the explosive then lead the wire up as they hauled him out. None of them had handled dynamite before.

Dad and his brother were up at 5am in the frosty New England climate, chilblains to the knees, and went down to get the twenty cows to bring to the bails, milk, and put the milk in the separator to make cream. Feed the milk to the six pigs. The cream cheque was less than the Widows' Pension.

When Dad's father died the women tended to stay in the house, so the boys, my father and Allan his brother, did the farm work. My father was 14. I am a product of his desire to finish school, *to go on with my writing*. Allan was nine and thus had to go to school but helped on the farm when he could. Dad hitched the horse to the plough and ploughed while Allan walked behind him dropping corn seed into the furrows.

Years later we visited Uncle Allan in the nursing home where he sat in his wheelchair in his room, and we sat ranged around him or on the bed. He had met up with other old men who'd been in kindergarten with him, and talked about their long lives of knowing each other.

Then he talked about his young life on Clunybegg. He said he had a pushbike to go to school. His mother drove a sulky. I asked if he remembered anything about the farm. Yes. One day he was bringing up the cows by himself, Allan said, when he 'chased them hard', and made one slip on the rocks, crossing the creek, knowing it might break its leg. The cow had to be shot, he tells us, a mischievous glint in his old eye. Meat for dinner, he said.

Mudbricks

For a long time, I worked on sealing the mudbricks of the main house. I set up my stereo and wired it on long leads to sit just inside the French doors so the speakers could easily be brought out onto the pavers near the lawn. There were no near neighbours. I could have Joan Sutherland and Marilyn Horne screaming ecstatically across the orchard.

On Fridays I went to town and stocked up on food and bought more irrigation gear, poly-pipe, elbow-joiners. I bought a hardback foolscap Farm Daybook. A list of things that needed doing to the car, a more detailed explanation of ohms and amps and how the inverter for the solar panels worked. Things I had to multiply to work out whether I could turn on another light. Phone numbers for woodmen.

A dust shroud on the road told me Mr Kenden and the dog had walked more cows down. He let them in the gate and waved.

Bird called from Perth and was sussing out the performance poetry scene. I got the impression that things were a bit quiet in Perth.

Ben's letter

That night I sat at my fuel stove in the kitchen, a stove that I loved like a person. Maybe it was no accident that recently the firebox burned out, and had to be replaced. I stared into its new blank heart, and reached for the newspaper and the kindling.

In the end, and even near the beginning, self-pity is boring. I got up and roamed around the room, staring at things on the wall. The Armenian icon, its gold leaf glowing, the saint's face serene and almost severe. If religion has become aesthetics is there any point to praying? Yet did it matter if I didn't know the saint? On the kitchen wall a photo of my sisters, who I stared at for some time.

Then I looked at one of Ben at seventeen in his first suit.

On the bench was a recent letter from him: He was now nineteen and travelling in America with Uncle Vlado (Joe's brother) who owned a nightclub in downtown Cleveland. I picked it up and reread it. 'Pass on my news to all the family, I don't want to write ten letters the same. Uncle Wally took me to Las Vegas and Reno where he won a lot of money and I lost a few hundred, not to worry because it was Wally's money. Then Wally took me overseas to Berlin where we hired a Mercedes and drove south into Yugoslavia where our other relatives live. Wally and Srechko took me to see their old farm. Mum, the house was only two rooms. We visited Uncle Aloys and his wife, who gave us their home-made cordial.

'Then we drove south to Italy for a day to see the world cup soccer match with 80,000 other people and sang a lot of soccer songs and I had a great time because on the way I'd made an Australian flag and when I waved it the other Australians at the match about twenty of them came over and sat with me and sang and shouted ...

'Back in America my new girlfriend Jerri picked me up and we drove across the southern states including to Graceland. We visited Elvis' grave and bought some souvenirs which were all about Elvis and ate food from the takeaway places which was the type of food Elvis liked when he was young and singing *Love Me Tender*. We drove to Florida and I was having such a good time I didn't want to come home. But my visa is up in a month so I have to decide whether to get a job here for a while, or go to uni with my American cousins, or to come home.'

We talked on the phone at four in the morning.

Vanguard

On a whim one day in town with Sal, I bought a 1954 Vanguard Ute with a wooden tray back, and a chrome kangaroo on the bonnet. It cost 1200 dollars. I don't know whether I was missing Dad, and his first truck. The mudguards' big round shapes. I cannot imagine what made me want to drive it to Melbourne but I did that, several times.

Back home at Majorca, Sal was there and we planted vegetables and looked after the existing orchard and read *The White Album* and shifted the lawn panel to follow the sun. We drove around the paddocks picking up fallen timber for the open fire. The fireplace in the lounge room was wide enough to fit quite big logs. I didn't want to be chain-sawing. Living in the country can be so noisy, but I made it as quiet as possible. I bought in truckloads of firewood but it was already in rounds and I liked getting the axe into it. A noise I could bear. I was learning how to read wood and cut it—whether to go with the grain or across it, and then, the different types of wood, their different smells when burning. Things that are being forgotten.

Friesians

In the early days of the farm, before the parties started, it came on to winter and I again had three weeks alone, no visitors. No one camping at the dam or in the orchard. No sulks, no bitch-fights, no one sneaking around the tents at night and getting into bed with the wrong woman. No dog-fights. No flat tyres, or utes out of petrol, or gangs descending on Centrelink, just the solitary life again. Heaven, in its way.

I looked at the trees for two days and then started to unpack my books and notes which had arrived from Annandale. Was any of this stuff useful? Did I need that much Bukowski, or every thought of Gertrude Stein? In each case it seemed I did, still. Here was a box of UTS (University of Technology Sydney) teaching notes, negative capability explained, the third person plural, the unreliable narrator, Foucault on Foucault. A discussion about whether free indirect style was the invention of Flaubert as so often claimed, or whether it really came from Jane Austen.

Another box of books, heavy theory. And now I recalled coming out onto the street after my last class at UTS, after six years, and doing a massive brain-dump onto Broadway. I remember thinking, 'Have *that*!' to the traffic. I would never need to understand Derrida again, or the enduring mystery of why Lacan thought women were the phallus. All the same I reread Baudrillard on 'The Precession of the Simulacra', twice. Maybe three times. Kristeva on abjection. Extracts from Walter Benjamin's *Arcades*. I had washed my brain with a few ideas and now it was time to deal with the firewood.

I could see Mr Kenden's Friesians in the top paddock, now being hand-fed. I rugged up and went out and found the axe. Chopped half a ton of wood and stacked it at the end of the house. Then I could hear Mr Kenden hooting at the top gate, his way of letting me know Goodbye.

That winter I often went out at first light in the frosty air and climbed over the stile into the Friesians' paddock. It was chilling cold, I had my beanie down to my eye-brows. I stood there, waiting. By now the cows knew me. Slowly through the mist their faces began to appear, their soft eyes, their whiskery mouths huffing out warm air. They let me go in with them, being sniffed by them and walking with them. Then, standing still. Their massive shoulders in their black and white coats.

A Phone Call

Then one day a call from Bird, who was thinking of leaving Perth; the performance poetry scene there was too small and she was over it.

Well you got my number so you probably know I bought some land, I said.

Weird thing, she said, two days ago I was looking around this house where I'm staying, see if they had any fortune-telling gear, only thing I could find to use was a Bible, so I open it at random, asking the pages "Where should I go?" and the page says "The Land of Ham".

She arrived on the bus days later and I picked her up in Ballarat. Backpack, two plastic bags of kit, a bicycle. Her makeup was Nefertiti or hinted that way and she had reapplied her lipstick recently. The high hair was gone and the shaved part. She wrapped her arms around me, leaned her head into my neck and we stood still for a while. Bird was the only person I ever met who was able to hold a hug for minutes, rather than seconds. These long hugs and the wildly changing hair, the vintage frocks and the privacy of her personal life were the hallmarks of Bird.

Once at the farm we walked round the place and last of all the bottom paddock with the dam and the one big gum tree. That week we drove the ute paddock-bashing for firewood and on the local dirt roads to the tip. Bird called the ute Greta and was already making good finds at the tip that caused her to be known later as the Tip Queen.

She was staying in my second bedroom but I said I didn't really want to live with anyone.

She asked if I had any money left over from selling Annandale.

I said I did. I wondered whether she would like to build a mudbrick cottage in the dam paddock.

She said she would.

We examined the paddock and she chose a spot. I was glad of her, so glad of her.

By then it was so cold we were wearing triple layers and wore our beanies to bed.

We went for a walk and asked the neighbours if they knew who had made the mudbricks and built my house. They explained where Brendan lived, what his gate looked like, on the road into town, a tin crow on the letter-box. An ex-priest, they said, he was now the local mud man.

We drove Greta to his place and Brendan came out and laughingly admired her, patting her maternal curves as fondly as he might a wife. He suggested we make a rough design for Bird's cottage, and go to the second-hand building materials yard and buy the windows and doors, then he would build the place around those dimensions. He could do it for about twelve thousand dollars. Bird raised her eyebrows at me and I nodded. We shook hands with Brendan, and as if to seal it, also shook hands with his wife and three children and his brother-in-law who would help build the place. We could come over in two days and learn how to make the bricks, he had a claypan on the place, and the frames for the making. We could hardly believe things were moving so fast. Whooping, we drove home. Underneath the whooping, huge bells of sadness.

The Witch's Cottage

Once established in the biggest shed, the garage, Bird designed a one-room mudbrick cottage, a rectangle with a bay window looking on the dam and a loft bedroom.

We began visiting the second-hand building materials yard in town, where she bought windows and doors and French doors. She was dressed in frayed jeans, a satin vest, boots, and lipstick. The men at the tip competed to give her discounts, and began to look out for things she might need, and put them aside for her in the shipping container that was their office and drinking den. She had no qualms about going in there with them and doing deals.

With the measurements of the windows and doors she bought or was given, Bird edited the plan around them.

In Brendan's front paddock, we were making the mudbricks, while in Bird's paddock a man with a trencher was digging into the clay for the footings.

'Winter's among us,' Brendan said to me one early morning as he stopped at my gate and I climbed up into his truck. I think that was all he said all morning.

He was bringing more mudbricks for Bird's house. We swung into the bottom paddock at the open gate. Gloves and boots and your breath showing.

We worked hard, making slurry, rendering the bricks already laid. Lifting the mudbricks into place onto the slurry and laughing at how inept we were at first. Brendan had told us over lunch he'd been good at Latin, and been sent to the Vatican on a scholarship, but had then fallen in love. He encouraged us with Latin quotes. He said the Ora pro nobis was not from a mass, but from some other sacred music. We worked in the wind and the rain, worked till we were filthy.

At times that winter I silently cried for the whole morning, while rendering bricks. They all knew the situation. Kindly no one spoke about it.

Bird often went to visit the gardener; I didn't go with her. They were good friends. In sisterhood theory, I was also friends with the gardener. And even with the radiographer. At Radclyffe, Bird also met the gardener's ex, Glenda, and immediately got a crush on her. In fact they seemed well-suited.

We didn't get much post but one day a letter arrived from New Zealand with a cheque from Lenny, Bird's father. With rising jubilation Bird squirmed in the passenger seat of Greta as I drove her to town. As she hesitated, the men in the second-hand car-yards said things like, What can I do to put you in it, lovey?

One Saturday we got in her ute, who she named Barry, to go to the tip. Sal and her friend Trudy were in Greta. Trudy was up from Melbourne with good cheeses and fish. She was tall and quiet, and years before had been Sal's lover. They were both dark, and tall. Trudy had a round face and gleaming eyes. Like Sal, she eyed off my books. She took down a copy of Leonardo's Notebooks and when she left, I opened it at random. It was a paragraph titled 'Of Sobbing'.

The Tip Queen

It was maybe our tenth visit and though we had got Bird good stuff, armchairs, a table, this time we were searching for kitchen cupboards. And here they were, sitting right way up near the shipping container where the men hung out. Whether they were being paid by the council or had set themselves up to run the tip, was unclear. If there was a good stereo, they took it. If there was something Bird was on the lookout for, they kept their eyes open. This day they nodded at her as she drove in and parked and we ambled back to their shed. The kitchen bench sat on a pile of rough timber.

I hope you weren't proposing to *sell* this to me, Bird began, imperious in her lipstick and moleskins.

Jayden, c'm'ere, one of the men said to his boy. Do you think we should give this bench to the girls?

The boy looked us up and down and nodded.

Good boy, go and finish sorting the bolts now—the man turned to Bird, Looks like it's all yours, Janice. Want a hand loading it?

We got our thick gloves on. Jayden came back and said Frickin freezing, looking sideways at his father to see if he could get away with it.

By this time Bird was camping in the cottage and once the kitchen was in, living there. We had the phoneline extended to her house.

Next day, Sal cruised in the gate and swung to a slow stop on the claypan in front of the house. Her new car was a '69 Valiant Regal pillarless coupe, iridescent green with a cream vinyl top. Bird and I came up to admire it. We stepped into it and Sal drove us slowly through the streets of our nearest ghost town, where blond grasses came up in the footpaths and the sun glowed on the previous century's red brick houses, solid in their silence. The gold rush was over.

Pulling the plug

Once Mei-ling had returned to Amazon Acres and Zoe was on the scene, I gave up giving in to my desire and collected everything the gardener had given me, clothes, her letters, a small figure of a witch, tapes, jewellery, photos—put them in a cardboard box and sat it on the claypan at the front of my house. The place where everyone parked when they came to visit.

Coming through the paddock to Bird's house I saw Glenda's car and Glenda working with her, building a firepit. Glenda had brought some big stones. Her little boy was with her, and she had brought some smaller stones for him to add and he was diligently helping them. Bird was in her element it seemed when she was with a single mother who had a male child. She had talked before about this pattern in her life. The woman she stayed with in Perth, same. At any rate we lit the fire and they brewed some tea. It was obvious that Bird and Glenda were now an item. I shook my head and silently wished them luck. I told them I wouldn't be on with the gardener any more, and had put the things out in a box so I didn't have to see them around the house.

Is it really over Ham? She loves you, you know that, Bird said.

Yeah, I'm done. Let her enjoy Zoe, or whoever.

Glenda was looking at me over her teacup, not saying anything, but her look of complicity was enough fuel for the afternoon.

Well girls, thanks for the tea, I'll be off.

The following morning the box was gone. It seemed that Bird assumed she was doing me a favour, and told the gardener the box was there. That night the gardener apparently had come over, and when my light went out, climbed the gate and took the box. She never mentioned it and I never saw those things again.

Weeks later while looking for a particular picture of Ben to put on my kitchen wall, I was ambushed by a photo taken at Balmoral, the early days of the gardener and me, the wind in her hair and the sea behind her. I knew for my health I should simply get rid of them all, the ones of her or us.

I took the Balmoral photo and went to the outdoor fire where I put a grate across and held the picture till it took the flame, then set it on the grate and watched her burn. The surface celluloid bubbled along her right forearm, then her shoulder and then her face, the flame moving across her cheek as it burned her up, then the sea behind her, then the seagull over the sea.

What was left sat curled on the grill. It still had a frail integrity but soon enough a breeze came through and when I next looked, grey filaments wavered in the moving air, and I was sure the next time I came outdoors it would be gone.

It took years before I removed all the photos of the gardener from the several albums she was in. There were stages of burning.

I had wondered if Bird and I would spend our nights at each other's firesides, but mostly we stayed alone in our own houses; that surprised me, that we both liked being remote and solitary. Bird did have company—Glenda, who came to visit in a smart car. Glenda for some reason now had money. Yet many a night Bird would have been alone like me and staring into the coals in her pot-belly.

A Possible Murder

One night I woke to a terrible screaming sound, like a woman being murdered. It was three am. Bird's car engine sounded in the front yard and I grabbed a dressing gown and ran out. We drove along backroads towards the sound.

Are you sure you want to do this?

Bird nodded grimly. Someone has to intervene, she said.

Then the gulping and screaming seemed to move and be coming from a different direction. No one else's lights were on. Eventually we drove home—I was lost by then in the backroads but Bird knew where she was. We drank cups of tea till dawn and then went over to Geoffrey's house. Geoffrey was an up-the-road neighbour. He was in the yard with the dog.

Hear that last night? Bird said.

What's that?

Screaming sounds. Like a woman being murdered.

He laughed. Girls, that was an owl. The Powerful Owl.

Wilful and Proud

We had a lot of parties, people came up from Melbourne, people I didn't know. Bird had befriended them through the gardener. Women from Daylesford turned up with a band from Melbourne, The Screaming Harpies, and stayed for a week. The Harpies were in the house, with the French doors open. I couldn't understand their lyrics but I was never one for thrash.

One day the phone rang and it was the publisher of *Surly Girls* saying there was a ticket for me at the Qantas desk at Tullamarine, and could I be there by 2pm the next day.

Return ticket to Brisbane, paid for, the woman said.

What is this about?

The hotel is also paid for, (she named the hotel), it's near the river which is near the convention centre where you'll be going on Wednesday.

I'm going to a convention?

Surly Girls has won an award.

I arrived in Brisbane still somewhat mystified. I walked along the riverbank till I found the convention centre but they wouldn't let me in because I was with Cath, a friend from Daylesford who had moved to Brisbane and who was wearing shorts and a T-shirt. She explained to them that I was one of the guests of honour and they checked my name and let me in, but rejected her. I said I'd invited her, so, rather unwillingly, they let us both in. They made her sit at a table on her own and put me with people who turned out to be prize-winners in other categories. I didn't know them though the woman next to me turned out to be Jessica Anderson whose name I knew. However she was deaf so we couldn't converse. Everyone had put their books on the table so I did the same. I watched the last people coming in, including a man in a suit who came straight over to our table and sat next to me. I said Hi, and introduced myself.

You don't know who I am, do you? he said, smiling.

Sorry, no. Should I?

Who did you think I was when I came in?

I thought maybe a footballer or a lawyer.

Ah, he said, well, I've been both. But right now, I'm the Premier of Queensland, and my name's Wayne.

OK. Well, hi Wayne.

And I'll be handing out the cheques for the awards.

That's great, thanks.

And you'll need to make a thankyou speech.

None of this was really explained to me, I said, but I can think on my feet. What is the name of my award and how much is the cheque for?

Here he referred to a sheet of paper he took from his inside pocket, and said, It's the Steele Rudd Award, and (I thought he said) it's for two thousand dollars.

He reached out for my book and opened it at random. It was possible he would find a rude lesbian part so I was cringing a bit, but he had good manners and when he came to that part he politely closed the book and smiled and introduced himself to the person on his other side.

I don't know at which point the food arrived, but I watched Cath at her solitary table eating everything in sight, and grinning at me. I grinned back, and began mentally preparing to say that I had read and appreciated Steele Rudd, and, because he wrote about the country, I thought he would be glad that I'd be spending my prize-money on irrigation gear so I could water the vegetable beds from the dam on my farm.

When it was time to speak, I thanked Wayne and his government—by now I was able to refer to him as Mr Goss, as I'd heard another prize-winner do that.

Cheque in hand, I signalled to Cath, and we went off to the toilets where I opened the envelope to find the cheque was for $10,000, and we squealed so loudly a person a few stalls up came along and asked if we were all right.

Back home I went straight to a car-yard and bought a good second-hand Toyota for ten thousand dollars, eight thousand more than I had ever spent on a car.

Eventually Centrelink encouraged, I think was their word, Bird to do a course, and they gave her the TAFE leaflet. She ran her finger down the index and without looking said 'I'll do that', and maybe she really was that wilful and proud, or maybe Doll Drone had sneaked a look at the list, and she read out 'Welding and Forging I'. She had made me come into the interview with her, fearing they would force her into a job, and presuming I would help her think of some way to go on living her life. In particular now she wanted to build a big tin shed for her workbenches.

Lenny her father in New Zealand was so proud on the phone hearing she had topped her Welding class, he sent her money for tools. With what gratitude she slung her toolbox in the back of Barry. We were looking for an anvil. It was in this ute we went for drives, stopping at abandoned farms and lifting up broken harrows and draught-horse traces and other good cast iron and putting it in Barry, the Bird silent. Later I found she'd been imagining the harrow as a coat-rack and how she would burnish it. I think I had that coat-rack for years. I have some things that belonged to Bird, I think we all do, all her friends. Clothes she bought us at op shops that were the perfect fit, decent boots. She was the kind of person who remembered your birthday and your shoe-size. I think her father Lenny had been a snappy dresser. One of those men who went to the races.

I suppose it was his hat Bird always wore, a man's hat. It suited everything.

One summer afternoon we drove to Cairn Curran to see the birds on the water there. It was quite a way with the dust and Tracy Chapman and Tori Amos. Bird was talking about how you could get a poem out of two words if you had to. And sometimes, she said, you could even combine that with an idea, or use the two words to express the idea, and have it as a book title.

Manufactured Consent … she said, Don't need to read the book.

Yeah, I got it. This is why voting in a democracy is a bit of a con.

Yeah, but you gotta vote, she said.

Don't worry, I always vote. I stared out at passing sheep.

She admitted to a fascination with putting just two words together. 'Negative capability', she said in the car as we drove home, I could never get a handle on that. Is it Keats?

It seems to mean something like 'Don't overthink what you're doing and thus ruin the life in the writing.'

Years later, alone again, I came across the phrase 'performing gender' and thought of Bird and how she would have liked how it *already said* everything, you don't need to read the book. I thought also of Sister Immaculata and Mother Abyss performing gender. But it applied to everyone really. Bird seemed to understand theory without having read any but my guess is she quizzed her friends who were studying: didn't need to read those heavy books with all their abstract language. Preferred her welding manuals. These were her constant reading. How to do a butt weld. When to use the oxy.

Unpacking at Davo in my new house—among the photos of the building of the witch's cottage, a file card drops out. In Bird's handwriting

STEERING (SLOPPY)
BRAKES (NONE)
FAN BELT LOOSE
RADIATOR GLUGGY
GREASE AND OIL CHANGE?
ENGINE MISSING AND CAB FUMY
DASH AND INTERIOR LIGHT
HEATER
TOWBAR

Yet Barry lasted for years and was always fixable. I may have given her the money for a new timing belt.

Welding

Despite her Welding qualification, Bird did not earn her keep and on principle never made one commercial object even when Glenda's uncle who had greyhounds offered her good money to build dog-cages for his trailer. Bird refused the work, and when the uncle asked why, she said she was busy, nothing personal, and he asked what she was working on and she showed him, a piece that came off a deconstructed crane on Cockatoo Island, a huge circle of rusted metal, and said she was going to make the sun.

A tall blonde called Lindy appeared on the scene, a girl from the nearest small town, who had heard from friends about a woman who lived in a witch's cottage at Majorca somewhere, and she had driven around the backroads till she found it. Entranced with our lives, she started wearing Blundstones and bought a ute. Though heterosexual, she was especially entranced with Bird and they formed a sort of team, scouring the countryside for metal. Lindy then took Bird to the old butter factory in town—now empty—and Bird fell in love with the big spaces and the old machinery. They rented the place and began to work in there. Lindy was learning to weld, and now had steel-cap boots. Once when I talked to her at the fence I asked what her childhood was like and she said, Oh you know, I was a stubby girl.

No? I don't know about that, I said.

You know, bring your big brothers a stubby when they want one.

Lindy took her apprenticeship seriously and the work went well for many months. Glenda was often there with them, sweeping out, helping make the factory into a private gallery for the three of them. Found objects began to appear on shelves, and there was now room for whole harrows which sat on the concrete floor rethinking their purpose in life. Glenda dusted the harrows. For months they were happy there.

One night Bird came up for a bath and we sat by the fire after and talked. She was really pouring down the beer.

Something wrong?

Ham, Lindy has decided she's gay. She told me this afternoon. I started to be glad for her but then she made a confession, she's on with Glenda.

What?

Yeah.

I shook my head. There really was nothing to say. We sat in silence for a good half hour, drinking steadily.

The next day she came up to cut my hair.

I've lost Glenda, *and* Lindy, and worst of all, the *butter factory*.

Now and then she went to Melbourne to some poetry event and performed. I don't know if she was still being Doll Drone then, or whether that was an earlier, discarded personality. I think it was Doll who went to Mexico, and went to the parade for Day of the Dead and danced among the ghouls, wearing her fifties outfit. I had a postcard from there, full of puns, but I've mislaid it. I have retained the jar she kept her tea in, from its niche in the mud-brick wall. Those niches she spent days chiselling out, her overalls covered in dust. At night she read my books: Rimbaud and Frank O'Hara and Elizabeth Bishop. 'The art of losing isn't hard to master.'

Saille

A green ute drove in and I saw it was Saille, a good friend and ex-lover of Mase. She was a Scot with pale skin and deep black hair and green eyes and always polished boots. She was studying at the uni at Ballarat and had fallen in love with her Derrida lecturer a woman with a child but no husband, and the woman had fallen for Saille so they were now an item but privately and only off campus.

Cup of tea?

She nodded and I bent to her dog and spoke to her.

Something I wanted to ask you, I said. Where did 'Saille' come from?

A footnote in Robert Graves' *The White Goddess.* Listen, I came over to ask a favour. My Melbourne house is folding up—could I pay some rent and come and live in the garage? It's got that north window, I could put a desk under there. Got a deadline on an essay.

What's your topic?

Desire. I can do it as a photo-essay.

OK. Well if you need a poem at any point I can recommend a sonnet by Sir Thomas Wyatt.

Oh yes?

'They flee from me that sometime did me seek

With naked foot, stalking in my chamber.'

Saille sat forward and looked at me. Do you know the story behind it? she said.

Yes. Wyatt was in love with Anne Boleyn, and she was in love with him, but Henry VIII decided he wanted Anne Boleyn and *sent for her.*

A good distance

Saille moved into the garage the next weekend, first sweeping the dirt floor then putting a big carpet down on the dirt. Bird had found her the carpet at the tip. The new name of the building was the bunker.

Not long after this, Mase asked if she could come and maybe stay. Her landlord in Hepburn had put the rent up.

I asked her if she was happy to live in the meditation hut, which was in the top paddock with the Friesians. Very happy she said. We negotiated a small rent. In fact I soon stopped taking rent because Mase understood all the machinery including the pump on the dam and the inverter in the laundry and she mowed the house lawn without being asked. So now there were four of us sharing the place with the resulting economies of scale. Very fortunately none of us were currently on with each other.

We lived and moved as a group, two cars with seven people and their dogs would set off for Mollongghip near Deep Spring for a party, or to have our hair cut. We lived on a backroad 5 k from the nearest ghost-town and 15 k from the nearest town. It was a good distance.

No one went to work. No one talked about it; it was assumed you were not working and could make yourself available at almost any time—for a picnic, for building a chook house, for going to the tip, for killing rabbits. We did not mark time, except in heatwaves, or visitors, or Fridays for town. Decisions were not made by individuals but by the group. If Saille said she was going to a friend's farm to pull cabbages, we went with her.

Parties

We planned a Taurus party since so many of the people we knew were bulls—Bird, the gardener, me, maybe six others. Sal came early and helped me weed the vegetable beds which were in the view out the back to the forest. We sat on the lawn under the tennis-court sprinkler. We didn't have a tennis-court, just the right sort of sprinkler.

At the time of the Taurus party, Sal and Trudy drove into the yard in a borrowed ute with a huge papier-mâché bull Sal had made over a wire armature, strapped into the back. We took it out and put it near the bunker's outside fireplace, where it stood to greet the guests.

The parties became more frequent and many people brought animals when they came, often to visit the people in the sheds. There were dogfights. There were fights among the women; I tried to stay out of that. Everybody smoked, Drum rollies and cannabis, with the occasional infusion of skunk from Melbourne, so strong that people were having epiphanies at the dam. Meaningless because by the following day they couldn't remember them. Now and then my sense of responsibility kicked in, and I took a walk to make sure people were drinking enough water, had someone with them, and were not passed out in the creek. Though since the creek was always dry it was an OK place to pass out. I woke there myself several times. Most people drank. I think we all drank. Some visitors were ex-junkies, at least I hoped they were ex. Some were good singers and were in bands. Many of them were good cooks and helped me with the parties. Now and then I went to Melbourne to do a reading, this was the early 90s when I still thought performance poetry was an important part of life, part of the way you lived.

Our first fellow

After *Surly Girls* won the award I began to be offered work doing a semester here or there, or Writer-in-Residence for three months. I went away to earn money and my friends minded the place, checking the batteries and the tank, driving around Maryborough in the Vanguard and being hailed by old men from around the district who admired and remembered Greta and knew her history, her previous owners.

It was the second night of a three-day party when a professor of English rang from a Canberra university and asked if I'd be their first fellow. He sounded very pleased, 'our first fellow.' Phoenix went by the back door wheeling a barrow of firewood. Fires were going outside with various things happening at each fire, some in other paddocks, and I couldn't concentrate well on the phone.

Hearing my silence the professor raised the amount being offered—'Would a thousand a week be suitable?' I turned my face away to smile at the mudbrick wall, crumbling under the icon. A thousand? The power of hesitation, once learned, never forgotten. 'Yes', I said gaily, 'that would work!'

The sobering effect of a decent payment and for what? Sitting in a chair writing a book about a statue coming alive. Giving a reading from this book to a few people before the wonderful snacks. Running some workshops on point-of-view and free indirect style. Things I can't even remember now. I mean, I could give you examples of free indirect style. But do I have anything to say about point-of-view? I recall a session where a young man asked how to put a story together. We talked about the conventional story, rising action, climax, and so on, but I pointed out that most of what they were writing was actually memoir. That week, I was reading *Maigret's Memoirs*. And someone, Simenon or Maigret himself, asks if there could be … 'some discussion of what is called the naked truth, which convinces nobody, and of "organised" truths which are truer than life'.

At the goodbye party one of the lecturers said to me, 'Where were you when Livio rang to offer you the fellowship? Were you far away?' Er, I didn't say, I was deep in the rural lesbian ghetto. Ah, I said, Victoria.

Then the airport and returning to the farm with enough money to buy animal feed and fencing and live for six months. I could tell by the cars in the front yard who was in residence or visiting, Bird, Mase, Saille, Sal, Trudy. I was greeted by six dogs. Later, the quietness of dust falling off the walls.

Bird's Loft Bedroom

It hadn't occurred to me that Bird might be going to bed with Trudy. The upstairs of the witch house was now finished and Bird was sleeping in her loft bedroom. Was Bird sleeping alone in her room? Or was Trudy there?

I certainly had no knowledge of what went on in Bird's paddock, such was her discretion.

Years later I was at Sal's in Melbourne when Trudy came to visit, and during conversations about ancient nights and a party we'd had with fires and boats and drama, Trudy said 'Oh yes, that happened when I was on with Bird.'

Trained by my milieu not to react to sexual information, I sat still.

Though briefly, sadly, Trudy said.

Yes, Sal said, Audrey told me when she was on with Bird it lasted from Darwin to Perth, three weeks.

Yeah, about that. Trudy had the courtesy to laugh.

Not that I wanted bourgeois coupledom, I did not. But I was enough older than these women that I found their world way too random, or perhaps it was my nature, I wanted relationships to last, at least for longer than three weeks, at least till you got to know the person, to see if you could make something of it. That was my thought. And though my life had turned into serial monogamy, each time I had hoped the lustful situation might develop, expand, acquire contexts and some mutual history, acquire a comfort level and an understood mutual humour, grow into something I could recognise.

This information from Trudy meant Bird had possibly had many partners and kept it very quiet. I had to reset my notion of her. By then I had known her for years; it meant that in our time at Annandale her love life must have happened off-stage or with people who came to our house late at night. It altered my view of the house, with its late visitors who must have left before dawn, or stayed in her bed till Ben and I had gone out.

Black Lincolns

It was some time after Bird settled in to her own cottage that I bought five Black Lincoln sheep, whose wool was almost a dark purple, a seven-inch wool, good for carpets. We carried long sticks as advised and ushered them into the back paddock with the dam. I went down to visit them, going slowly, but they ran off each time.

The sheeps' noses had the same aristocratic Arabic curve as the ones at Radclyffe, and as if they knew their nobility they often stood in profile on the grass near the house. All the visitors enjoyed them. Two of them were pregnant and both had twins. I took the mothers extra food, a lucerne mix, spread on square pieces of corrugated iron, as instructed by Mr Kenden. And something else. Molasses.

The radiographer rang and in her nice voice asked how I was doing.

Coping, I said, and hung up.

Then the sheep started to droop and swell up, something was wrong. I called Brendan. I remember thinking as I went outside it was a perfect day, the dry air, the silence, the gum smell of the forest, the fine high blue of the sky. The sheep stood near the bunker where Bird and I had herded them earlier that morning. Their guts were swollen. Brendan got out of his truck and examined them.

I've been playing them, 'And sheep may safely graze,' I said.

Well, it was never less true. Brendan stood up. They've got pulpy kidney, he said, probably from being suddenly put on different feed.

No one advised me about that.

Don't assume they'll tell you everything when they sell you sheep.

Is this because I'm a blockie?

Everyone's a blockie round here except the Kendens.

But where I bought the sheep –

I know where you got them, I made a few calls. Don't let it put you off getting more sheep, but ask more questions, get some sheep books, do the reading.

He went to his truck and got a big knife that he had recently sharpened. It shone in the morning sun.

Are you going inside? he said.

No.

He took a sheep by the scruff of its neck and stepped behind and around it, his legs on both sides, and reached under the sheep's chin and pulled her head back, exposing her neck. He parted the wool and reached beside him on the ground for his knife. In two or three strokes he cut her throat while I watched her staring eyes. He lay her aside and began on the next one. When they were all down I pointed at the hard clay of my ground and said I would need to get in a digger to bury them. But he thought it would be better to take them into a clearing in the forest and burn them.

No, burn them here where I can keep an eye on them.

I waited a while and said, How can I thank you for doing this?

No need.

I did buy more sheep and this time with more research. The same breed, but from a different place. Three of the ewes had been covered and were pregnant when I bought them, and when they had twins, as expected, I knew to put out extra feed for them. Slowly they came to the fence with the house paddock and watched us gardening or chopping wood. The lambs frisked up and down the fence, with each other and separately, kicking up their back legs or leaping off all fours so seemingly joyfully that they made sense of the Lamb of God, all that imagery, Christ, we were meant to be happy.

Samba

We heard from one of the Harpies that there was going to be a samba band playing in Castlemaine the next Sunday. It was 40 k away—we usually went there for the pictures. The band would be playing in the main park. We made a picnic and about ten of us went to listen. The music came on slowly with a weird lilt in the drumbeat, a sideways movement of the hips. We stood at the edge, dancing, our arms lifting. I was trying to hum the beat, was it syncopation, or a combination of syncopation and accent. Later, I couldn't understand or recall the beat.

The band had finished their set and were relaxing under the trees with their kids. I sidled up to the bass drummer and said, Talk to me about the samba beat.

She took up the big furred drumstick and hit the drumskin once. Under her breath, she began a chant, She-BOOM she-kaa, She-BOOM she-kaa, and on the BOOM we were already swaying our hips. Now that I had it in words, I got it.

Doing anything later? I said.

Maybe, why? she laughed.

Want to go to that tent for a coffee?

Why, is this a date? Coz I have a girlfriend.

No no, this is so I can quiz you about how a band works.

She looked at me to see what my neutral tone meant—was I being ironic? I was not.

OK sure.

Drums began to accumulate in the lounge room at the farm; a bass-drum, someone had said, would be essential. I drove to Melbourne and Sal came with me to a drum shop, where we bought a djembe, a tambourine, then, eventually, a bass-drum. I had received the money for a grant, and thought the drums would be a good investment in getting a book written. Someone already had two cowbells.

We practised on the drums every week, sometimes three times a week, with whoever was there. At Mollongghip we were sitting under the trees in a circle when a familiar car drove in the gate and the gardener stepped out and produced a bottle of tequila and passed it round. That kept us on a better beat for a while.

Co Ping

Back at Majorca, Sal came from the Vic markets with a Chinese drake handsomely white and strong. We went through the house gate and down the track between the long beige grasses to the dam, glinting silently. I had the drake in my arms and for some reason he didn't struggle but sat peaceably against my chest, surveying his new realm. We squatted on the clay bank and I set him on the water where swallows were dipping for insects. He swam around merrily, gliding with little swirls.

He immeasurably improved the dam.

Along with the sheep he would come to the fence of the house paddock and walk up and down inspecting our doings.

The gardener arrived with milk (she had called in at Mr Kenden's) and potatoes. Her role was now that of a friend and incidentally Lady Bountiful.

I didn't want her around too much but Bird did. Mase and Saille were also friends with the gardener and visited back and forth.

Bird and I walked round town on Centrelink days, through the second-hand builder's yards, whispering the samba mantra, She-BOOM she-kaa. Looking for materials to build a chook-shed, Mase's new project. A neighbour had offered us five Isa Browns. Mase was in Melbourne a lot, then at the farm, looking more and more haggard. I don't know how she knew how to build a chook-shed; I had no idea. There was a lot of digging to start with. We had to lay wire under the ground because of foxes. Radclyffe gave us six chooks. Two were large white hens with fanning black neck feathers, great-looking, but a tendency to go broody. Sussex.

Another day the gardener arrived and said she'd been missing me, again with the shy smile she was known for, a smile I now saw as cover for a predatory instinct in her, an instinct that had now become as practised as an understory in a big story, a kind of girding foundation that moved the action forward simply by being a structural component. And over it all, what was visible, the shy smile, the quiet voice, the professions of love, the new girlfriend, the importance of remaining friends with exes, the continuing love for exes and the continuing it seemed desire for the odd fuck. Just here and there on an as needs basis, I saw.

How goes the fling with Mei-ling? I said, aiming for a neutral voice. Or Zoe?

Oh, Mei-ling hasn't visited for quite a while. However, the gardener said brightly, putting her beans on my bench, her lettuce, and as if speaking to a friend who had no sexual interest in the speaker, Zoe was coming over later and that could be fun.

Does Zoe have a girlfriend? I said.

I don't know, that's up to her to sort out. By the way, if you don't have a name for the drake yet, how about Co Ping?

I shook my head and smiled, the drake would have been discussed at Radclyffe.

Courtesy of you-know-who? I said.

Who else? She laughed.

The name was too good. The drake became Co Ping. In one sense we were all Co Ping.

Badde Manors

It was a hot February and time for Mardi Gras. I'd driven north with Bird, ten hours with two short breaks, bringing a carload of drums. I dropped her at her friend's place and went to Gleebooks. David Gaunt was still there. It was comforting. I bought a *London Review of Books*, then went a few doors down to Badde Manors. My haunt. The same banquettes and laminex tables, the same window at the side where you could get gelato. I sat at my usual table reading.

After coffee I was walking up Glebe Point Road when behind me I heard a deep voice say, 'Mum.' I turned around to see my son, grown from a boy into a man. We hugged and walked along together for a while.

You came up early, he said. Isn't Mardi Gras next week?

Yeah. I like to get to Glebe first and walk from Badde Manors to the harbour, past Gleebooks, The Post Office, the Pudding Shop, the Valhalla.

Well, I'll walk with you, he said. I didn't know you liked Glebe that much.

Yeah.

I knew that for him his six years at Glebe High School were not too happy. I knew he only pretended to have done his homework in a free period, and that he didn't read the novels that were set for English. Couldn't relate to any of it, couldn't wait to leave.

I know it was different for you, I said, Glebe.

Glebe High School was a *torlet.* (imitating the way some kid pronounced it.)

Dear me. Why didn't you tell me more at the time.

Did you tell your parents things?

Ah, no.

Last time we had a reunion, there's about fifteen of us that get together, one girl said the experience of Glebe High School in the 80s was like the Vietnam War, to us, in the sense that we all left scarred. There were kids shooting heroin in the school toilets, and by age fifteen most kids were getting stoned on cannabis on a daily basis. Some kids suicided.

One of the teachers was an alcoholic, one went down for being part of an armed robbery, one propositioned a girl and her brother beat him up and he came to school next day with two black eyes and a missing tooth. A lot of the kids came from Housing Commission homes and some were selling stolen goods on behalf of their parents. Old-style Sydney crims who lived in the inner west, different from your experience of the inner west which was the arts community. School was just a reflection of the area at the time. Some kids were unable to break the poverty cycle and ended up as single parents living in Housing Commission homes.

The pig in Albert Street

I asked whether he might now tell me a bit about what happened at weekends when he went to visit Joe. He had studiously not talked about these visits; I imagined he had also not spoken to Joe about our life in Annandale.

What did you do on those weekends? I said.

Sometimes we went to see the Eels play. Or— did I ever tell you about the black pig in Parramatta?

No, tell me.

Do you remember the house where Dad lived in Albert Street? Well one Friday I arrived and there was a black piglet in a pen at the bottom of the yard. My cousin Geoffrey used to go hunting for wild pigs on people's properties, and had captured this piglet when he shot its mother. He gave it to Joe to raise up because Joe always talked about the pigs of his childhood. Anyway I was just a kid and I thought it was a pet so I named it Piggy. We fed it scraps and sometimes Dad got corn that was a bit old from the fruit shop man. Piggy was quite smart and he would follow me around the garden.

They say you can train a piglet like a dog, I said.

I wouldn't be surprised. Anyway he grew up into a quite big pig. So one weekend I got there and no Piggy. The pen is empty. Dad, where's Piggy? Turned out Dad had taken it to the Yugal Club and butchered it and cooked it and shared it with his mates and partied on, and the fridge was full of parts of Piggy. I was quite upset but Dad didn't really notice. I said, Dad, how could you do this? Why didn't you tell me what you were going to do?

Why, you were going to stop me? Joe said.

Why didn't you tell me at the time, son?

Mum, what could you have done.

I didn't know what to say. We walked on and I moved the topic back to Beni Bizarre and the magic shows, and we remembered various tricks he had.

Mardi Gras

In the crowd of the sweating parade I stood between Bird and Sal. We watched the floats and bands and gangs of dancers, and just past eX de Medici with her tattooed clients, we heard drumming and came on the others from home. We'd been joined by another samba band, some women from Sydney. The amalgamation wasn't really working because we wanted to do our own thing. But sisterhood being what it was then conceived to be, that wasn't really possible, so we went on together and when it came our time to move we were playing to the same beat.

Unlike last year, when I was so preoccupied with Heather dying, this time I was able to pay attention to Mardi Gras and what was happening. A swarm of Misses go by, Mis Alliance, Mis Taken, Mis Anthropist, Mis Nomer, Mis Er, Mis Ogynist, all fabulously dressed. I left my friends and began to almost swim up and down the length of the parade, through the floats of the dancers and the singers and the beginnings of the corporate floats, AIDS organisations, families who support gay children, past the little old lady (or a small man dressed as one?) who carried a sign saying 'New Zealand', past Fabian dressed as Mother Abyss, and her adherent Sister Immaculata, all the Sisters of Perpetual Indulgence, till I reached the tail of the beast, then back up through them all to the samba band where Ruth handed me back my drum and in front of us I saw Sister Mia Culpa who had joined us and was dancing with an old friend from Glebe, Mickie, who danced as if she were liquid, almost, and when she paused for breath I called, Hey Mick, who are you tonight?

I'm with the Sacred Harlots from the Temple of Isis, she called through the din, but I've lost them.

Now with the other band competing with us, I learned to play *across* the beat. My second instrument was the cowbell and it was a great thing to belt that out across Paddington. I passed my son with his friends in the crowd and raised the bell. He gave an ironic cheer.

The parade finally filtered in to the showground and the Hordern Pavilion where the party really began. I was dancing within the big crowd and the pulsing beat from the high bank of speakers near the front of the pavilion where you could really blast your whole body, your clothes, your flimsy clothes, your silk shirt, blowing around your body under the assault particularly of the basses. The MC a drag queen of note broke in now and then to encourage the bacchanal, to invoke, to taunt, to sexualise, 'you *know* you want it!' Then this year as every year it seemed, losing people. I lost Bird in the dancing and danced with many strangers, people I would never meet again, whose histories I didn't have to know or bear.

And it happened that by the time I found Bird it was almost sunrise, certainly the air was getting lighter, and the words 'relight my fire' now seemed to refer to the dawn breaking low across the grass of the ground outside the gate and where we now walked uncertainly and in an altered, augmented group across the park to where we'd left the cars. In these dawn or pre-dawn walks there would be an atmosphere of untouchable serenity.

Visit of the Professors

It was not long after the lambs were born that we had a visit from the professors. Saille's girlfriend had told her their faculty would be hosting a conference held every year for the study of Australian literature, the ASAL conference.

Do you have the program?

She handed it over and I scanned it.

I know two of these people, one at Sydney and one at Macquarie. I've studied under them.

Do you want to go to the conference?

Nah.

We should invite them here to the farm.

Yeah, feel free.

The weather was good, so we decided to eat outdoors. We built a fire on the claypan in front of the house, with stumps around it for them to sit on, and good champagne. It was winter and the air was nice and sharp. Bird made a barbeque and we baked the spuds in the coals. One of the professors, Liz Webby, was getting tired I saw, so we shifted proceedings into the house and the armchairs at the open fire. I offered them sherry which seemed right and we started in on it. Bird sat on the floor, expressing an ardent love of learning by resting her head on the leg of Professor Webby. I sat opposite, convinced that if the professor objected to Bird she would be feminist enough to move Bird off her leg, but this didn't happen. I put another log on the fire, and across Bird's head, the professor kept up a conversation with me about Elizabeth Harrower. How I admired her verve and her forbearance. The Bird was not quite asleep.

Messy

It took me a while to understand that when Mase said 'messy' she meant drugs, so my question, 'How was it in Melbourne?' drew a headshake and the reply 'messy' which meant heroin. Saille had been with her so maybe Saille was messy too. I gave them a look and said, Listen, if you want to stay here, don't ever bring heroin to the farm. Or really, since that was the unreliable narrator stepping in I fear, I gave them a *look* which meant just that, and hoped they understood. They stood there with deadpan expressions, like thugs or businessmen.

Another layer to the underbelly of the life here that I had no knowledge of, was the actual amount, as distinct from the perceived amount, of sexual activity. We may add to this the layer concerning the reasons behind a person giving their serious attention to hard drugs. With Mase it had been her uncle, a crude attribution of blame, but let's say her uncle didn't help, her mother's brother. He owned the house Mase's family lived in, and rented it to them cheaply, and in return he took, let us say took, Mase from the ages of nine to thirteen. He did it in his boat which he kept in their backyard. Mase did tell her mother who didn't believe her, couldn't believe her, and as soon as Mase finished school she left town and hitched as far south as she could: Melbourne. It had been hard to concentrate in school, she had no work skills and knew no one in Melbourne. One night at Flinders Street Station she was picked up by a guy who wanted to take her to a hotel and pay for her. Although or because she was tall, boyish, handsome, androgynous-looking, she was a successful hooker for a while. Of course, she shaved her beard when she was a prostitute.

I wished she had not told me about the uncle. Or rather, I didn't mind knowing, which helped me understand her, but I did not want the details. If I were fully compassionate I would want to understand him, as well. It is the details that have lived with me in the years since, images scored on my brain, of the many varieties of sexual abuse that have occurred to my friends. One was raped by a taxi-driver, and was now a successful writer. One was offered a lift home from a nightclub by two seemingly OK men in a two-seater sports car, and while one drove the other one who had sat her on his lap, raped her. From this encounter she had an STD which she somehow kept under control. As much as one could.

Sexual abuse also seemed to be a major cause of women deleting their pasts and changing their names. Often they had no surname. In the case of Phoenix the 26-year-old forestry worker from Clunes there was no family history. When Bird asked her one night, 'Where does your family live?' Phoenix said, 'Agh, I couldn't really say.' No one knew her backstory.

Afterwards, I found this aspect of Phoenix made her easier to be with. Some of the others I knew too much about. And it got to the point after some years that I knew more women who had been sexually abused than those who had not. This changed later when I moved. And for many years now, if someone is about to mention a few unpleasant events from their childhood, I stop them, my hand goes up. Please don't tell me.

Many women who are promiscuous have filthy histories, in my experience. I never knew a prostitute who did not have a history of sexual abuse, in some form.

There was also a layer of people who had not actually been raped but had been mucked around with and sexualised in some other way, often by other children. Some of it was simple curiosity perhaps. In my home town, in the case of the children from down the road who showed me in my cubby what f-u-c-k- meant, never spoken, only ever spelled—these two girls, who were then nine and seven, had older brothers who may have given them *a spelling lesson.*

The Festival of Petrol

The residency in Armidale would happen the following semester, so there would be money again. We decided to have a big mid winter party.

Coming back from the tip one day I saw near the bunker some people sitting on logs around a fire, doing something with sticks. The chooks had been let out and were grazing around their feet. Making torches, Mase said.

I got out of the ute and brought over a life-size shop model I'd got from the tip, and stood her near the proceedings. With a terrible impassivity the model watched Mase and Sal and Bird wrapping and tying cotton rags around the tops of sticks. They had tested the first one by dipping it in kero and setting it alight.

We were going to have a festival at the solstice.

Preparations went on for months. One Friday I walked through the paddock to Bird's shed and showed her a design for a metal coffee table made of square steel tubing, in effect a stovetop for placing over a fire. In Daylesford at the vintage shop I found a 20-litre black metal urn or samovar with a brass tap—this lived at one end of the metal table. Logs and chairs accumulated round this fire which was near the bunker. We sat here at night and drank.

The day of the festival I was cutting up oranges for the mulled wine with Sal while Tracy Chapman sang *Fast Car*,—this was when it was new, thirty years ago, before it became muzak at Coles. Then we half-filled paper-bags with sand at the dry creek that ran into the dam. We set them on paths Mase had mowed through the paddocks and put tea-light candles in the sand and folded back the rims of the bags a few times. Lit at dark, these would make warm glowing tracks.

I was aware that I was enjoying the preparations to a degree that the party itself could never match.

A truck came in the gate with a ton of wood. And the men seeing our preparations joked around with us about rumours in town of witch covens in the bush. Is that youse? Yeah, we said, laughing, must be us. They wanted to be shown around the place but I wasn't sure of their motive and I started to say we were busy, but Bird leaned forward and said to one of the men, aren't you Hoag's brother? From the car repair? He nodded. She turned to me and said, Hoag used to own the next-door place way back.

They had seen the mud house built. So the men went about marvelling at her witch's cottage where inside she had chiselled out mudbrick walls to make internal shelves where her spices were stored. They said the last owners must have replaced the pump at the dam, it was different from their day. We talked about pumps and what could go wrong and how to notice when things are about to go wrong. And this was my experience of men who came to the farm to deliver things or do jobs. They were unfailingly kind and helpful and the man who explained to me the solar and showed me the battery bank and explained its intricacies was also good with laptops and Word.

The Harpies would be on the lawn of the main house, hooked up to power. The samba players would walk through the paddocks drumming that hip-swinging beat. The party was at midwinter and was supposed to be a Festival of Light, but we changed the name I now can't recall why to the Festival of Petrol. Perhaps we thought it was all very well to say we were making our own light from the sun with the two panels, but three grey days in a row and you pull the generator; likewise, the garden was near the house, not down at the dam, so water had to be pumped to the vegetables and both orchards, requiring us to pull the pump. Maybe the pattern of pump and generator noise in a country otherwise so quiet, often, also, so still, was enough to make us realise, Festival of Petrol. Even getting water to the bath and kitchen meant the automatic turning on of a small pump that worked on a high tank at one side of the house.

People began to arrive early afternoon, parking in the claypan in front of the house and wandering to one of the fires where they knew people. I didn't know everyone and didn't mind as long as they controlled their kids and their dogs. There were torches burning at the main gate.

At the fire near the bunkhouse the samovar was filled with mulled wine. We had bought half a sheep from the radiographer, though I had not invited her; the deal was done via the gardener, who arrived with the lamb cut ready to cook, and cakes, and greens from her garden. Some of the meat we made into big casseroles and the rest was barbequed on the first night.

Gallons of mulled wine disappeared and joints were lit. Drugs provided by the gardener, who was enjoying the party and very attentive to me. Just on dark I showed some of the kids how to light the candles in the paper bags without burning the bags. They were diligent. I found the kids a lot more reliable than the adults when I needed help. At some point we walked down a lit path through the paddock to Bird's house where the back window (not yet installed) was a space, and we could see through it a table and chairs, where a play was now going on. Bird had written the script and had in the past weeks chosen the two actors and had them rehearse. It was Beckett on drugs, Beckett as lesbians, Beckett with bitch-fights. Bird had been reading Godot and adjusted it for our situation, though keeping some bits of his dialogue, which was appreciated by the more literate members of the audience.

There were slanting references to the misdemeanours of people in the crowd, how A had fallen in love with B, who later left town, how then C arrived and fell in love with A, and then later left town. C had got work in the town where B was now living, and since they all moved in the same circles, they met: C then fell in love with B. The problems funny and otherwise caused by the circular economy of the sisterhood.

I looked sideways at the lit faces of Sal, Trudy, Bird, Mase, Saille, Phoenix, Ruth, and I felt an incredible calm. After a break, we followed the kids to the dam where on cue our wooden kayak came out of the rushes, Mase paddling evenly, a lamp someone had rigged above her, and behind her sitting in the boat a person dressed all in white and veiled. Beside them gliding, the smooth white shape of Co Ping. No one made a sound. No one knew what it meant. It didn't mean anything, was just a piece of dam magic.

The following morning most people were still there. They appeared in the blue air from tents and the backs of cars and trucks, carrying breakfast food to the fire where the first cigarettes and joints were lit and the day began.

On the third day of the party the die-hards were left, sitting on woodblocks at night around Bird's outside fire.

Sal was fiddling with the fire tools and seemed to be speaking to herself. 'The king sits in something town, Drinkin the blude-reid wine', her voice getting louder as she remembered the words, 'O whaur will A get a skeely skipper, tae sail this new ship o mine?'

She then started to improvise words relating to our situation, the sheep, the party, her lost tobacco, and the words altered till they became, at least in the refrain, 'Wheer's me Doctor Pat?'.

Café in Ballarat

For reasons unknown to me, the gardener had invited me to go to a café in Ballarat with her, for an outing, she said. On the journey there, about an hour, we talked about gardens and music and surprisingly she didn't mention sexual encounters, her other loved topic of conversation. We watched the countryside glide by, the mammalian hills to the south. A lot of the country was bare, but now we came to a treed area.

The gardener remembered that in the second year they were at Radclyffe she had offered as a sop to the dole office to design and co-ordinate a program of tree-planting, to source the young trees, to choose the bare country where they would go, to make sure the trees were native to that area. She would apply for a grant to cover the costs and asked Centrelink to provide the labour. They agreed and she worked hard at it for months; they had planted ten thousand trees.

These, she said, waving her hand out the window.

At the café, once we ordered, she leaned forward and said, Your party was wonderful.

Yes, I enjoyed it, I said. Thanks for your help.

And I've brought you here onto neutral ground to tell you something. I've fallen in love with you again.

In Christ's name, I said. Just stop it.

I mean it.

I sipped on my tea and waited for it to be over. I had nothing to say on the drive home.

Help from Geoffrey

Some weeks later I heard a racket in the chookyard and rushed out just as Bird was arriving from her paddock. Co Ping had flown over the chookyard fence and was stalking the chooks. He got one pinned against the shed and jumped on her, holding her neck in his beak, and started raping her. No sooner had he finished than he began to stalk another chook. Bird and I looked at each other.

Go with nature? she said, red in tooth and claw? Just what happens. Lions eat zebras?

I don't know. I was shaking with the cries of the current chook. Co Ping seemed twice their size.

Or, she said, kill the rapist.

Let's talk to Geoffrey. He told me the other day he was going to kill some roosters this week, I said.

Let's grab him, anyway, she said and we got a cage ready and went in the yard with a blanket and pounced on him. So entranced was he by his current love he didn't escape in time. We left him in the cage watching the injured chooks. Our question was whether the chooks felt it as an injury or whether they were used to roosters doing that and thought it was normal and were perhaps even turned on by it.

But the aggrieved squawking, I said.

You know how much noise some women make, Bird said. And 'aggrieved' is an example of the pathetic fallacy, I think. Or anthropomorphism.

Bird was making good use of my books on literature.

Our thoughts came to this: we had to kill the beautiful drake because we couldn't stand the noise of him raping the chooks.

Over to Geoffrey's we went and found that he was having a killing day the next morning. Come early, he said, six o'clock. Before the flies. Next day we put Co Ping in a smaller lighter-weight cage and took him across.

You've really thought about this? Geoffrey said.

You do a few roosters first so I get the hang of it, then I'll do Co Ping, I said.

No one handles this knife but me. I've told the boys that and I'm telling you the same. (He had four sons).

Why don't we watch you kill a few roosters then we'll take Co Ping home and do it there.

Where are you gonna do it?

On the chopping block.

I hope you're not thinking of using an axe.

I said nothing.

An axe would be a mistake. It might take three blows and all the time you've got the eyes of this terrified chook staring at you.

Duck.

Duck. The neck is even thicker and stronger. Are you gonna eat him?

Bird looked at me. If we were proper country people we would eat it. We weren't proper, I could tell from the look in her eye.

One of Geoffrey's boys Nathan had come up and heard most of this. He looked at us and said imploringly, You can't kill something you've given a name. Can you Dad?

Geoffrey said, Not normally, no.

Why don't we put him on *our* dam, the boy said.

Because you'd have the same problem we had, Bird said.

What problem is that? The boy looked at the duck and said, He looks so nice.

He is nice, Geoffrey said quickly, leaning forward, but you'll just have to accept that he has created a problem for the girls and they need to kill him.

Then I think you should eat him. Kill him and eat him, said the boy definitely. He turned and went back to the house.

Look, Geoffrey said, you could go back home with your duck and sharpen a knife if you have a good steel knife and a sharpening stone. That's one way. Or you could simply let me do it right now, and let me know whether you want it gutted, etc. Are you going to eat it?

No, we said together.

I'm gonna do it right now, Geoffrey said, and went to the cage for the duck.

As soon as he had Co Ping pinned down on the chopping block with his knee, he took out his knife and, holding his hand over the face of the duck, began to cut. A horrible honking came out from under the hand and the duck writhed and clanged, its honk now more strangled and gargled till the neck was cut through and a hissing came from the severed neck. Blood poured onto the wood. Geoffrey stood up and held the duck by his feet so the blood poured on the ground into some sawdust he had put there.

Do you want to bury him?

Yes.

I thanked him and he handed me the duck by the feet and Bird picked up the head and the cage and we left.

Thistling

Though the gardener and I were no longer on together, we now and then, as friends, worked on each other's places. The next week she came with poppy-seed and spent a day helping me finish built-up beds near the back door and plant the seed and water it in. We still liked working together and it was less painful for me than a complete and utter cut, though which method takes longer to heal is moot.

At her place now I never went near the radiographer's area. One day I was across the road from their place in a paddock they rented, helping the gardener chip out Scotch thistle. While we were thistling under the hot sun, the gardener turned to look at me and looked at me so tenderly—as if we were still lovers—a look I had to ignore since it had no real meaning—in my terms—when I suddenly *saw* Tommy in her—the tan skin and blue eyes, the athletic build, the love of hard physical work, the brown dog nearby, the stopping for a smoke and a drink from the thermos. The realisation hit me so hard I sat straight down on the ground. I did not quite sit on the thistles. So, so. It wasn't really about her. Or the seeming depth and power of it was perhaps reverb from Tommy. Knowing this didn't help. The feelings were there, willy-nilly. I struggled to my feet and went on working.

6 TOMMY Part 1

The station-wagon travelled south on the New England Highway, Dad driving, Mum knitting, six daughters strewn in the back. I was fourteen, of an age to be conscious which towns I liked, and I waited for Murrurundi. Then I waited for the smell of the sea at Maitland. Our destination was Stockton.

Violet was sitting benumbed in her breakfast room. It was August. We'd driven nine hours to reach the punt queue, we crossed the river and went along the road beside the sea. She was numb because a woman from over town was claiming to be Pappy's first wife and claiming Violet's house. Pappy had died a few weeks before. And in fact there was a first wife, which Violet said was the reason she and Pappy had to pretend to be married for fifty-seven years. She was telling my mother in a monotone about the woman over town, who as a Catholic didn't believe in divorce, and who had two children. And Pappy having created this family sailed into a pub and began to flirt with the barmaid, Violet. We are the result, so cannot complain.

I was living in my childhood bubble, not quite hearing the content of distressed adult talk in Violet's kitchen. They didn't tell kids anything. I could see that Violet had been crying and was now more or less reduced to a statue. I had seen the earlier statuehood of my mother when she could not find a way to deal with Dad's outbursts of temper or his rants about certain people in the town. It seemed being a statue was in the family.

You kids get outside, my mother said.

The house was a low-slung place with a hip roof and a wooden veranda where Violet had stood waiting for us. You entered these houses via the lanes. I looked through the screen of the back door and saw Violet get up to go about some chore. She had on an apron with a bib to save her dress. Behind her solid and reassuring figure I could see the dark shadows of the house and the open front door to Mitchell Street going past and the sand dunes and the bright sea.

I'm going to the dunes, I said to my sisters.

When we came back inside there was a woman squatting on the floor of the breakfast room cleaning the lino. She stood and gave me a direct look and a shy rather private smile. The sort of smile a fourteen-year-old boy might give you. Her eyes were blue, an unfair blue, I would say. It was hard to look away. It was hard to tell how old she was, maybe thirty.

This is Tommy, Violet said, from down Cardigan Street.

Tommy was married with two kids and while the kids were at school she came around to help Violet. She was slim, about my weight, and tanned.

Tommy held out her hand and I shook it. She was silent and looked at me as if she recognised me. My sisters were running around in the yard. I could hear their wild cries.

It's really Laurel Gordon, she said, but my maiden name was Thomas. No one ever calls me Laurel, she said, still holding my hand. I could hardly look at her—the air seemed electric.

Violet leaned in and said, Tommy used to go night-fishing with your grandfather.

She found her voice cracking on the word grandfather. She was crying because Pappy had died so soon after he retired.

It was three shifts at the steelworks and then … nothing.
She worked her hands in her lap.

Violet was at the beginning of a thirty-five-year widowhood, though she didn't know it then. I was at the beginning of a lifelong attachment to Tommy but I think I knew that. Everything about her already made sense to me—the squatting, the slim build, the trousers and shirt. The athletic body. The direct look.

When she left I walked with her to the back gate and she said, come along the lane and I'll show you where I live. Then you can visit me sometimes. How long are you here?

Two weeks.

That's good. If you hear tapping on the boards of the middle room—is that where you'll be sleeping?—

Yes.

—then get dressed and come out the back door.

That night my father commented that Tommy looked like Katherine Hepburn, and Mum and Violet nodded.

Very like, Mum said.

Movie star looks and married to a drunken fisherman, Dad said.

Sunrise

Tommy drove me down to the bottom end and out along the breakwater into the sea and parked. She didn't speak much. Just the necessary things. Butted against the side of the breakwater was the metal skeleton of a ship called the Adolphe, wrecked on

top of six other ships, she said. There was a reef near the harbour mouth which had caused the wrecks, and they'd built the breakwater out to the Adolphe.

No one else was there. The hull was like an orchestra, different notes booming or pinging from where you stepped on the skeleton. I started with a hand line she'd already rigged, and she showed me how to swing it in circles beside you then lean back, keeping the spin going and then, once facing the sea, on the outswing, let it go.

The first burst of laughter was because I couldn't get the cast right, and hooked myself. The hook was caught in my trousers, behind me. About the third time I got it, and cast quite far then began to wait. I wasn't sure I'd have the patience for all the waiting. She showed me how to rebait the line, then while I held the line at the cork, she tugged on the other end and said, Feel that, that's a nibble, play it carefully; feel that, that's a bite, wind it in.

She caught a bream and two tailor, I caught nothing, didn't even feel a pull on the line. Her fish gleamed in the bucket of water and swam uselessly in small circles.

At her house she would hold my hand while giving me a tomato or a handline. Meanwhile pretending nothing was going on.

At night she walked me to Violet's back gate and gave me a short hug and a kiss on the cheek. Really, I was on fire and she, I could see, was being restrained, careful, almost mean.

A school of tailor

At her place I met her son and daughter who were in Primary School. The girl, tall and rangy like her father, Jock, who I'd seen in the back shed making a net, though we weren't introduced, and the son small-built like his mother.

A week later in the car Tommy lit two cigarettes and handed me one.

I'm too young for that, I said, and she put it out, but I wanted it.

The sea was flattened by a westerly coming off Kooragang Island. We drove south a mile to the breakwater. I put my hand in my pocket, where Tommy had tucked a freshly-ironed hanky. It was still warm.

The hull clanged its deep notes over the water. We had barely set up and cast out when the water to the north began to swarm and seethe in the early light. A big school of tailor hit a few seconds later and we were pulling in fish at the same time, grabbing cloths from our gear bags and holding the fish by the head with the cloth, so we could pull or cut the hook out of their mouth. Normally then we would straight away kill and gut the fish but since the school was passing through we had no time for that and put the fish still alive in a hessian bag and rebaited the hooks and cast out. And again within seconds we both had good-sized fish on the line, swinging and struggling to get off. There were holes in the metal of the deck and several times one of us lost a fish down the holes or the fish jumped or slid into a hole but was still on the hook so we brought it up again and I saw Tommy wasn't worrying about the cloth any more but putting her shoe onto the fish's back and bending to get out the hook.

From the moment it hit, the school kept coming. In the end we didn't rebait the hooks but simply removed the caught fish, cursing and yelping as they swung about and hit our bodies or the iron uprights of the ship, put them in the bag, and cast out with an empty hook—the school was so thick we were jagging them through their sides or even near the tail. Our glee transported itself into the resounding deck and I at least was squealing as each new fish hit the line. The sugar bag was nearly full and writhing around so I put my foot on it.

Then something in the air changed and the school passed

around the breakwater and went south. I was covered in blood and scales and had again a hook in the pants of my jeans where a wild cast earlier had gone around me and I had just grabbed another line and gone on fishing. I looked over at Tommy—we were filthy. We started to laugh and gulping lungfuls of air we counted the fish—twenty-three. Normally, she said, we might get three or four.

Back at the house we cleaned and gutted them—I could see Tommy's mind working over how she would talk Jock into letting her use part of the big freezer in his shed. They would not all fit in the fridge even if I took a lot home to Violet. Depending on Jock, we might have to give most of them away. But when he came in and she showed him the tailor in his freezer, he said, Good, Bloss. What time were you out there? About ten to five, they hit, she said. She looked quite proud and he put his hand on her shoulder. He was over a foot taller than her, six foot six. Kid here caught some, she said, and he looked at me, right in the eye. He did not quite smile.

Later that day while Tommy was elsewhere I was cleaning gear at the yard sink and got up to go inside when a shadow overtook me on the back step—it was Jock leaning strangely close to my ear and saying, Want a naughty? I had never heard it called that but had some idea what he meant, and even that he possibly didn't really mean it but wanted to say it to me to see how I'd react. Without thinking I said firmly, No thank you and turned and left for Violet's straight away. Kicking myself all the way back—why did I say thank you? How stupid was that, in my politeness. No *thank you.*

I was cleaning myself at the tubs in Violet's laundry when Tommy came into the yard and said, What happened? I had to fudge my answer so as not to implicate Jock in case Tommy took that to mean either that I had flirted with him or that I shouldn't go to their house again. I was already thinking ahead, but not in any logical way, just by instinct. Protecting my access to Tommy. And in fact I went straight back with her, by which time Jock had gone to the Boatrowers Hotel and would be gone till eight or nine. I felt creepy about him but he never again acted that way and we both went on as if it had never happened. And with what I now know about alcohol, maybe by that night he didn't even remember he'd said that to me.

I finished cleaning the mess of the lines and getting the blood and scales off. Tommy had kept two of the fish for our dinner and had already done the vegetables. Her daughter Shelley came in with her spelling book and I helped her while Tommy cooked the fish the way she always did it—first flouring the fillets, then getting a pan of fat very hot and cooking the fish fast, turning them only once, pulling the flesh away from the neck bone with a fork to see if it came away easily which meant it was ready. Salt and lemon. Done quickly and still tender.

Cardigan Street

We knew Jock was coming because you could hear him from up the street, crooning to himself or haranguing as he came along, having an argument with an unseen assailant.

I was at the small kitchen table having a last cup of tea with Tommy, talking about nothing. His dinner was on a plate over a simmering saucepan where it had been for hours. Tommy and the kids always ate dinner by themselves, and the kids were in bed when he came home.

Though she had not spoken much about her background, and deeply resented questions about her earlier life, I knew Tommy had been a nurse up at the Mental on North Stockton. On the mantelpiece over the fireplace in the next room was a photo of her squatting on the lawn in her nurse's uniform, and the photographer must have squatted too, Tommy smiling into the camera. A shy reserved sort of smile. A white cap in her hair. There was a photo of Jock with his cocky on his shoulder, a previous cocky, and school photos of the two kids. Everything was a bit dusty—she wasn't interested in housework. The ironing board was always set up in the lounge-room and every day she ironed a fresh shirt for Jock to put on after fishing, to go to the Boatrowers and get plastered with his mates. He always wore good pants and a fresh-ironed shirt. We discussed the tide. Jock's cousin George came down the path for a haircut and she sat him in my chair with a towel on him and I moved onto the back steps in the sun. She passed me the local paper to sit on and I did the crossword while they talked as she moved around his head. Only now and then was I aware of their voices, 'he was the skipper', 'in that mesh size', 'on the slip'.

Tommy had married into a big family where she was very much accepted and loved. Jock had seven or eight siblings, mostly men, all tall. These men were all more or less in love with her. She had no one—had grown up in an orphanage in Singleton. There was one uncle, who may or may not have been her older brother.

Jock also had many cousins, most still on Stockton. Tommy was tiny compared to these men, maybe five foot four, and they had such big frames, they loomed at the door. George was six foot four. He was accused of taking lobsters from Jock's pots off the north side of the Newcastle breakwater. At least, someone had, and George's boat *The Dreamer* had been seen there at four-thirty one morning. Jock's boat was called *The Lobster Queen.* They drank at the Boatrowers Hotel opposite the fishing fleet, but after being accused and denying it, George drank at the Gladstone.

Late on a night when Jock was out checking his crab pots, Tommy talked about her earlier life, the orphanage, then changed the topic and became frosty. Angry.

Another night for an unknown reason she spoke. We'd had a bath and she had washed my hair. She talked about working at the Mental, and when I asked what they did with the hard cases, the really raving mad, she said they were chained to the wall and hosed down.

She looked at the expression on my face and said, It wasn't their fault. And this was the days before drugs.

So now they drug them?

As far as I know.

In a few days my parents had sorted out the legal problem so that Violet did own the house. Most days they were over town doing some sort of business and my sisters were playing Monopoly. Lining up their houses and hotels. I hardly saw the family.

Next morning it was fine and sunny and at eight o'clock it was hotting up. I had breakfast with Violet and asked how her night was. She said she wished I would watch TV with her sometimes—my parents and sisters went to bed at eight o'clock. There were good shows on. I said I hated TV, sorry, really couldn't bear anything about it. She said every night after the last program she prays for all the sick, sad, lonely and bereaved people.

What are you doing today? she said.

Probably go down Cardigan Street.

Oh well, go then.

Down the river Tommy told me the land we stood on was mostly ballast. It was made of rubble from the San Francisco earthquake. No one ever said, I'm going down the river, but I'm going down the ballast. Ships had dumped the rocks and parts of crumpled roads and buildings of San Francisco along the river, and loaded coal to go home.

From where we stood, Tommy said, gesturing with her chin, on the Newcastle side in the early 1900s you saw high-masted sailing ships, waiting for coal. Jock had told her that.

The hook knot

On the back steps Tommy opened her tackle-bag to check the sinkers. She made them in a metal mould in the shed which nominally belonged to Jock but he was out in the bight fishing in his trawler at that hour.

Nets hung from the rafters over trunks of tools at the foot of workbenches full of things being made. Up the end was a big freezer. Jock made sinkers too: they stole the lead from people's roofs or found it on the road where it had dropped off the wheel rim of a car. I was always on the lookout for lead.

I watched her hands as she taught me the hook knot. Once she had poked the line through the hole at the end of the shank on the hook, she turned it and formed a figure eight, then fed the line back though itself, through the eight: into the top hole of the eight you went down, and from the bottom hole you came up, so when you pulled on the line to tighten the knot, there would be no undoing.

There are other hook knots, but she maintained hers was the strongest. She showed me how to rig a line for tailor, bream, and flathead. The different size and shapes of hooks. Other lines in her bag were rigged for the different fish. She gave me some gear and I went to Violet's and in the big back yard I practised casting. I played with the gear for an hour in the sun. The whizzing sound as you spun the line around your head. Violet stood at the yard sink in her dress and slippers and apron, watching me.

Catch anything?

Not yet.

Want to try it in the water.

I will, tomorrow morning.

You should tell me when you're going out, so I know where you are.

Violet, I'm fourteen.

That's what I mean.

All right. If you see my bed's empty at five am, I'll be on the Wreck.

Jock tripped on the dog's chain and swore, or half-fell into a chair. He snorted and swore and was restless while she put the dinner down in front of him. Resch's lager and VB and Dr Pat rollies, he smelled like the pub, and never spoke much. His days started at three a.m. Some food went to the dog. The dog's name was Blossom and for some reason Jock called his wife the same name, 'You there Bloss?' and Tommy replied as if he had said 'Tommy'. At first it may have been that Jock called her Blossom to distinguish her from his cousin Tommy. When he said 'Bloss', Jock may even have been flirting.

One afternoon Tommy told me that the men on Stockton called us 'the boys'. They had noticed us going fishing, we were a thing.

Women on Stockton did not fish. Tommy had a full kit and fished almost every day. There was a tide chart on the fridge. Women were not allowed on a boat. It was bad luck. She hired her own boats from Mr Lindstrom who lived up the river. That strip of river was where I learnt to row, to cast, to be silent, and to smoke.

Unable and untrained to think about my situation or its possible future developments, I rowed, taking the next day, or next hour, as my limit. I was more interested in the tide or the bait than anything to do with my own future.

I rowed, and Tommy watched what the water was doing.

Tommy's parents

Tommy was singing *You Never Can Tell.* We'd heard Chuck Berry sing it on the jukebox at the Royal. She was dancing around her kitchen. Later, I asked her where she had grown up. I knew so little about her. I was conscious of being so much younger. This time though, she went quiet and then did talk—but in fragments and without explanations. So when she told me about her father, or the man she thought was her father, it was an unusual circumstance and I now think she must have been drunk or vulnerable in some way.

Grew up. Well I can tell you every Saturday we wrapped our hair up in a kerosene towel.

What? Where was this?

In the Home. And that son-of-a-bitch, supposedly my father, tried to give me threepence, can you believe it, at the railway station, tried pressing it into my hand. I let him put it there then I threw it on the track and started hissing. I turned around and showed him my teeth.

Tommy now sprang from her chair and turned to me to demonstrate what she'd said, 'You bloody up-jumped never-come-down son-of-a-bitch!' She leapt about the kitchen, opened a drawer and began brandishing a knife, laughing at herself and hissing and swearing.

Son of a bitching bastard was a comment on Jock when he whined once. No whining, was her rule, and no skiting. But you could swear till your mouth fell off and it was just good for laughs.

About nine Jock came in, not merrily drunk, not rolling drunk, but blind drunk, and tripped on Blossom's chain which was anchored to a chair and fell with his face down in the kitchen. We somehow got him onto the lounge in the next room. He was breathing but either unconscious or asleep. Tommy didn't seem bothered and was quite tender with him but later said, Look at Jock's long eyelashes—he looks like a cow, or a girl. Let's put some lipstick on him and see how he looks. She went in for her makeup kit (I didn't know she had any, had never seen her in any) and wanted me to help her but I wouldn't. I watched her do his lips, then blue eye shadow on his inert eyelids, powder on his nose. She was laughing and adding a new element, sipping on her beer and puffing on the cigarette and considering her handiwork. He did not move the whole time. Tommy turned to me. I can't wait to see what he says when he goes to shave in the morning. She laughed again and came back to the kitchen and sat, and now her voice went quiet.

You know, he can't swim.

What? So he must be frightened every day, I said unnecessarily.

Maybe only in big seas, she said, puffing on her Viscount. Want a beer?

No thanks.

What about a shandy?

I'm too young to drink.

Yes. You're probably right. She poured herself another one. She was tanked up now but holding it well.

She named the winery she thought her father was the heir to, up the Hunter Valley. A well-known winery. He had made no contact with her mother after he found out she was pregnant. She (the mother) was eighteen.

But somehow he knew Tommy existed, and what she looked like, at least, enough to recognise her on the platform.

When I was two years old, she said, my mother died, I don't remember her. She caught pneumonia. My grandparents raised me till I was nine and when they died someone took me to the home. Maybe Brother Wal.

So is Uncle Wal your brother?

I call him brother. But he's my mother's brother. He gave me away at the wedding.

Yeah. I notice no one gives the men away.

Yeah.

You could give Jock away.

You're a very funny girl. Come on, I'll walk you home.

Many years later it occurred to me that the mother Tommy had lost had been like me, a dark-haired adolescent who was a good swimmer. There were times I swam in dangerous places such as the water under the Wreck, where there might have been sharks. We threw burley there to bring the yellowtail, then caught them and cut them up for bait. It's possible the sharks might have come after the yellowtail, but I didn't think of it at the time.

Often we tried outsmarting each other physically, taking risks and laughing.

She walked me from her back lane into another lane and up to my grandmother's back gate. Kissed me at the gate. Pretty chastely. More or less chastely.

I never saw her read a book. I never saw her read. She flicked through the Advocate to see what was on special. She harboured a great hatred. I would turn up and say, Anything happening? And she'd say, Nothing, nought, nix. Then she'd give me a little sideways grin to indicate we might as well go fishing. As it was back in time, we caught a lot.

I realised I'd done nothing with the other kids all holiday and made myself join a game of Monopoly. But I didn't care who owned the hotels. Soon it was time to go back to Inverell and school. I found it hard to care about Julius Caesar or why trigonometry was important but I sat with my books and studied—it was the only thing I was good at.

The following Christmas holidays we stayed with Violet for the whole six weeks.

A lovely dog

Tommy's in Jock's shed, or *their* shed, with her hammer—her tools are kept separate—putting another hole in Blossom's collar.

Behind her in the wind on the high clothesline, Jock's blue King Gee overalls fill and deflate and refill, dancing or almost fighting against the sky.

On the back steps now, Tommy began filing her nails with a builder's file from the workbench in the shed. She was using the file gently, as if it was the correct implement. I stood there watching her and after a while she said, Move over and put some shade on me, it's hot already.

This is the kind of thing a servant does, I said.

I wouldn't know, she said. There's tomatoes on toast on the table ready for you.

We went inside where the kitchen was so small the table only fitted two or three people.

The dog rested her snout on Tommy's foot and went to sleep. A westerly had come up and was blanketing BHP dust over Stockton, turning the white-painted weather-board houses a dark red brown. When you took a wet cloth and cleaned the clotheslines, it came away black on the cloth. We all breathed it and no one took any notice. Violet lived to ninety-two.

On Tommy's sink I could see two whiting and a garfish and something horrible-looking—was it an eel?

What's that?

Yeah I'm gonna make soup. Jock likes it.

Do you eat it?

No. I cook it for Jock and his brothers. Don't tell Jock I give some to Big George.

I won't, I said.

Good girl. Tommy took my hand. I looked at the shape of her mouth.

Later the dog got up and sat a little distance from Tommy, looking at her expectantly.

Oh you're a beautiful thing, are you not, Tommy said to the dog, smiling and softening her voice to tender affection. You are a lovely girl, there's no doubt.

The dog wanted to go for a walk but sat quietly bearing her praise.

In the middle bedroom at Violet's I tried to sleep. What would a kiss really feel like? On the riverbank at times, alone, my mouth and nose tingled from the desire to be kissed. In my mind and the muscles of my face I felt it many times, always at the river for some reason. I couldn't imagine kissing any of the men or boys I was likely to meet, but that didn't bother me. And in fact Tommy had a boyish look. I just knew we would have to keep it quiet, if anything happened. This was unlikely.

That night I dreamed I was flat on my back in a paddock. Tommy had gone to the shed and got her tools and pegged me down with tent pegs. I couldn't get up and go off and be my intense and private self but had to stay there, open to the public gaze. And the public had to put up with me: I couldn't get up. It didn't matter too much to them, just that I was a fixture.

The tip

Next afternoon we drove north to the local tip. Drawers from dismantled bunk beds lay strewn with girly underwear, music boxes with tiny broken ballerinas, and cushions with the stuffing swelling from them. Two Aboriginal girls were working through a pile near me and looked up and quickly down again. I could see through the trees their parents sitting on the ground at the edge of the tip. They had a fire going. The atmosphere was calm and mild, swallows scooped across the piles. You could get a working fridge and decent bed frames. The face of a stripy nylon gollywog looked with its glazed expression from a washing machine.

Behind a broken radio I bent down to a small leather bag containing three hand lines, a tobacco tin of sinkers in various sizes, ditto hooks, including bream hooks and a few ganged tailor hooks and tiny ones for the yellowtail, a small pair of pliers, a rag, a knife. Someone had died. I didn't care. I now had my own private gear. Stockton was such a small place she would have known whose gear it was, who had died, but she never said.

Her tact was the advantage of her shyness; the disadvantage was a prickliness, a willingness to take offence, or misunderstand things, perhaps because she was often drunk, but held it well so you'd never have known. She never slurred her words.

We had cleaned all the gear and packed it ready for an early start on the Wreck the next day. Our preparations were done. Someone had given Tommy a butternut pumpkin and she was making a bacon bone stew. The smell of the onion being opened filled the air and she chopped methodically, enjoying it, crying a bit and laughing. Bastard, she said. When the sweet spud and parsnip went in she turned it up and went out to deal with Jock's overalls. She had to wash them every day otherwise you had the laundry stinking of fish, and scales everywhere.

The stew was boiling furiously when she came in. I had not turned it down but had been doing the crossword in the paper. I made a point of not touching things in her house or changing things since one time when I cleaned up and it was not appreciated. At that time her moods varied from exultant (when we were on the Wreck and the tailor hit) to ordinary tenderness to a black and sullen anger.

I put the Herald crossword on the table. One across. Habitual criminal, ten letters. Hmmm. Six across, Large-scale book or film, four letters. Could be epic or saga, wait on that. Seven down, Assumption, seven letters, hmmm. Eight down, Sent settlers to a new land, nine letters, colonised, therefore epic. As I was writing in the words Tommy came up the steps and encountered the fumes of the stew and immediately stepped in front of it and said, I always belt the Christ out of it at first.

She was making the stew for Audrey her sister-in-law.

Audrey was tall like her brother, and wore lipstick. I didn't want to sit around with them talking babies but when I came in Tommy had got my new gear out of the car and was showing Audrey the flat sinkers in one of the tobacco tins, traces and swivels in another. A perfect find, I heard her say, she just came across it. Audrey made appreciative noises and may have been indulging Tommy, who as far as I knew was the only woman on Stockton who fished. Audrey would probably have had no interest in fishing though she loved a feed of crabs. She'd had two pregnancies and each time developed a thing about blue swimmer crabs.

Tommy said, Old mutton-face, up Roxburgh Street, what's-'er-name, near the butchers, let me think, you know, relatives of Sylv's husband, aargh! Every one of them like a haunch or a backside, fat cheeks,— Daphne! Audrey said.

I best get this girl back to her grandmother, Tommy said, standing up. She kissed the baby and Audrey and signalled to me. I picked up my kit. We weren't really going to my grandmother, or not yet. We went to the riverbank and as the sun sank over the BHP I remembered the crossword and took it out. One across, I said, Habitual criminal. Without a pause Tommy said 'recidivist'.

Kiss me properly

It was the end of the school holidays and we were packing to go back to the hometown for my last year of school. After dinner at Violet's I lied and said I was going onto the beach for a while, and turned the other way into Cardigan Street and went the two blocks to Tommy's back gate. It was almost dark. Jock had brought his birds into the shed and put them out of their cages and on the bench where they walked up and down among his spanners. He was sitting on a stool watching them and singing some incomprehensible song. His lamp was on.

I went silently down the path to the back door where Tommy was expecting me and held out her arms and kissed me on the cheek. I could smell she'd had a few drinks. Kiss me properly, I said, and I felt her turn me and walk me backwards to the sink when she stopped and turned her head aside. Perhaps thinking she ought not do this. I reached out and turned her face to look at me. We were the same height. She relaxed her stomach against mine, leaned forward and kissed me, properly.

Very soon I said my goodnights to Jock and the birds as I passed.

The letters

Back in Inverell I applied my mind to 'Prufrock' and 'Five Bells' and a novel called 'The Passage', set in Queensland. In the science club under instruction from Mr Graham, also my Sunday School teacher, I made a crystal set radio. Our local station 2NZ started transmission at five am when the announcer said 'Yodel-odel-o, it's five am on your country rodeo radio.'

They played *Wa–ah– o, I get around, get around round round—*

and *I shoulda known better with a girl like you*—and *Ooby dooby, ooby dooby*. 2NZ sponsored Little Patti and Col Joye and the Joy Boys to do a concert in Inverell. Little Patti was 14. We weren't allowed to go across the river and anyway it would've cost money. My parents talked about going to Newcastle to live.

Every Friday I received a letter from Tommy. Flathead caught, high tides, some weird thing the kids said, Jock's cousin Hinkler coming in for a haircut. Blossom sitting on the mat in the sun. Jock's cousin George had stolen Jock's lobsters again from the pots off Fort Scratchley—obviously a recidivist! No luck at the Wreck this morning. Best if you come back soon.

The circus

One summer into the general lassitude of days passing with nothing happening, to the point where we were digging up the road with sticks looking for coins, I heard a noise across the river on the common and saw a circus arriving. I got up slowly and extracted myself from the others and went down the road to the bottom bridge and across to the caravans and trailers, the smell of lions and elephants, the circus hands doing their chores and young men beginning to put up the big tent.

I went up to a young woman practising her gymnastics and waited till she was upright. I asked her where the boss was and she pointed to the biggest trailer. I knocked on the door and a man came out. Cartwheeling, standing on my hands and doing multiple somersaults I asked for a job. He shook his head, You can't just join the circus, he said, where are your parents?

They're dead. I live with some people who don't like me.

Still we can't just take you on. The people who work for the circus grow up in circus families.

I slumped to the ground and began picking the grass.

And you can't stay here while we're setting up, circus people only. Sorry, but you should go home now.

I was determined to see everything and pretended to go home but hid behind some trucks that were backed on to the river, and waited and watched everything for a few hours. Particularly the women. So far I had not met any woman I might wish to become, (and until I met Tommy, who I somehow *recognised*), my only model for existence was the women from the circus. Some of them I noticed had their own trailers. The smell of hay and summer air was opened up by the weird calling of the elephants who had been chained to big stakes in the ground. Some of the chains were quite long.

Finally they sent the gymnast to ask me to move on. It took me a while to get over knowing or guessing that my parents would not afford tickets to the circus and I would never get to see it. The circus people would do their show and then leave town. I fantasised so much about leaving with them that I started having dreams about it. At this time I threw myself into more serious attempts to learn piano but without success.

Books

We had no money except I think two shillings a week for pocket money, when they were flush, that went straight into a money box. In high school I saved up for a push bike and a pair of strap-on roller-skates. For months at a time I went to live with Aunty Mi and Aunty Pearl. Their street was bitumened and had a footpath which was better for skating. I was like an only child there, away from the noise of eight people living in a small house. I went home to collect Tommy's weekly letters.

Aunty Pearl made raspberry coconut slice. They had a strict routine about who lit the fire. They never asked me anything personal, or told me anything personal. They wore home-made dresses to church on Sundays. Wesley might have been a Puritan but his hymns are the best.

As a child, looking through the index of the hymnal out of a terrible boredom with the sermon, the words that mystified me were the ones that followed the first lines of the hymns. After 'Jesus, the children are calling', it said Rickmansworth; after 'Joy to the World!', Antioch; 'Judge eternal, throned in splendour' was Rhuddian, 'Judge me God of my Salvation' was Blaenhafren, a word I specially liked, and used to recite to myself to try and sleep when my parents were arguing in the next room. *Blaenhafren.* I see now these are the names of the tunes. I don't know why I didn't realise it at the time. These mysterious words took me to a place where I understood nothing but was free to play around with possible meanings.

At home there were three or four books including a medical book and a Bible. I think a novel called 'Ride on Stranger'. Essentially I didn't read as a child. I did have books, once in high school, but kept them stacked as a barrier on the floor in the doorway of my sleepout. I didn't want other children in my room. Perhaps I tried reading the books but couldn't really understand them. I understood *The Passage* by Vance Palmer, or 'Prufrock' in Eliot, but I had no idea about the irony in Jane Austen (our diet at home—from Dad—was sarcasm) and I cared less about who would marry who.

I didn't want a normal life. I was attracted to a wayward life, but didn't know where to find it.

Taking the pledge

Dad's mother Lucy came to lunch after church some Sundays.

She'd grown up in the city. Her father was a drunk. At somebody's funeral he recited the whole of the liturgy for the dead, in Latin, wavering on the edge of the grave. Lucy grew up and joined the temperance union and made her sons take the pledge. Dad remembered taking the pledge. He pretty well kept to it.

Once her husband died, Lucy had to raise four kids and run the farm. She'd grown up in Leichhardt, and knew nothing about farming, had fallen for the farmer when she was sent to Inverell to be one of the first 'hello girls' on the Inverell telephone exchange. They married. Good Church of Christ people. No drinking.

At the Mackies, Dad's family conversations were mostly slinging off at other people. There was no concept of discussion or alternative points of view. Church was compulsory. Dad and his mother were happiest not at the delights of this world but at the vanquishing of a foe. Slights punished, harms repaid, stories of why a particular neighbour or congregant is beneath notice, Dad's lip curling in contempt under the hawk nose.

They had ruthless honesty, high expectations, and the tendency to think other people were probably stupid.

Dad became an atheist at seventeen when he left home, and he and the family never mentioned religion to each other again.

Some days Dad was a seething cauldron of hostilities. At the same time, in a different mood, he was physically warm, able to hug you, at least when you grew up, and even sentimental, able to cry. Stood on his honour and was overproud as they used to say. Fatherless, he had to be the man. In his adolescence he endured whimpering crying sisters. Weeping women. Women who did not help at all with the outdoor work, even to chop the wood. Maybe that is why he liked my mother. An accomplished wood-chopper. Also, she didn't cry.

Mum said she did not think the Red Cross Younger Set existed today. But that was how she had met Dad. One weekend the group had gone to visit their sister organisation in Moree. Mum and her friend Helen were 17 and 18. Dad was 23, one of the older members. She hadn't met him, though she knew of his family. At

the river bank on Sunday a picnic lunch was provided by the Moree hosts, and afterwards they played cricket. One of the Inverell boys, as a token of his affection for Mum, rubbed some Bathurst burrs into her hair. As she was trying to get them out, Dad came along and helped her get rid of the rest of them. They stayed together for the afternoon, and after tea, boarded the bus back to Inverell. Dad put his arm around her shoulders and she put her head on his shoulder, and they sat like that all the way home—only realising later they should have sat up the back. Later, during the courtship, when Dad visited her at Aunty Mi's, if he leaned against the dresser, she would lean against him. Soon enough, he proposed.

Tools

While still young, Dad had made himself two large wooden toolboxes, these were always in the back of the truck. C & A Mackie on the door. Now and then he took the toolboxes down and sorted and cleaned everything, the plane, the drill and the drill-bits, the ordinary hammer, the ball-pein hammer, chisels, the cold chisel, the tools rolled up in the pockets of his old calico apron.

My mother's tools: an axe, a spade, a fuel stove, a copper and a wringer, cloth nappies, a hose and a yard-sink, a laundry tub, soaking buckets, a Singer treadle sewing machine, piles of cloth for toddlers' overalls for winter. Indoor and outdoor brooms. Knitting wool and many sizes of needle rolled in a needle bag. A rosewood desk Dad had made her, in the back sunroom he'd built onto the house. An adding machine. A phone. Barely used, but useful. Later, a stereogram. 'The King and I'. 'Oklahoma!'

My father wasn't good at managing anything, lost his temper easily. Got on with his work. Gave apprentices such a hard time one of them topped the state in his exams. Uncle Allan was his joiner, made the windows and doors. Kitchen cupboards. They both smelt the same, of timber. And well after my father died, when Mum and I visited Uncle Allan and Aunty Joyce in their sunroom and Allan was old by then and sitting in his chair, I leaned over to kiss his head and he smelt the same. I stood there bent over sniffing him for a while. The last whiff of Dad—genetic, or timber in the pores?

At fourteen I sat the bursary exam and only one other student sat for it. We both won a bursary intended to help buy books etc. Mum and Dad traded in the Customline and used my bursary to put an extra payment on a two-tone blue Fairlane. We rode round town. Their one luxury.

Although we went for Sunday drives, we didn't need to visit people as there were so many of us and our cousins next door, nine kids for games. We had our own world down near the railway and the river—which to us was a green-lit willow-strewn area of tracks and water.

When we saw other kids had ponies or pianos or went to swim squad, we knew not to even ask for those things. It wasn't a topic. But neither was being poor. We didn't discuss any of it, just lived.

Not much happened in Inverell. One night I climbed up the tankstand and onto the roof and sat there looking out at the town and said under my breath, 'Dear God, the very *houses* seem asleep.' Nothing stirred. I think it was about four am and I couldn't sleep for a kind of excitement. Wanting something to happen. Waiting till I could go back to Stockton and be with Tommy.

Making the piano

The music teacher was Mr Duck Chong, who played us *Peer Gynt* and Smetana's *The Moldau,* and talked well about classical music. Then one day he played Handel's *Largo*. I was able to borrow the sheet music and copy it out. By laboriously working out the notes from Every Good Boy Deserves Fruit and so on, which Mr Duck Chong had taught us, I tried playing it on the piano in the school hall at lunchtimes. But when people came into the hall I felt self-conscious, and stopped till they went out, then went on, working out the chords in the bass line. It was frustrating.

Dad's mother Lucy had moved to town years back and she had a piano. I asked if she would teach me. She held the sopranos together at church. Both her daughters sang well, and she had taught them piano (but not the boys).

My problem was I had nothing to practise on at home. At the weekend I made a paper keyboard of the whole 88 notes which was furled and in a rubber band when I wasn't practising on it. When I opened it out I put weights on the ends of it. Here I could play whole songs, first the treble then the bass. I never worked out how to put the bass and the treble together.

Later I glued two sheets of art paper together and drew up just the middle area of the keyboard with a pencil and ruler. On this paper I practised all the scales, night after night. B flat, I could still play you the scale.

Lucy's choice of songs began with *Home Sweet Home*, but it was syrupy to me—I probably wanted Bach but I didn't know he existed. Her sheet music was scales and finger exercises, and songs like this, and since she had a rule I couldn't move on to other songs till I perfected this one, I learnt it by ear which meant in her terms I had no discipline and couldn't stick by her method.

I didn't realise that getting the fingering right was vital, and she didn't insist on that or talk much about it, so I fumbled and failed and stopped the lessons. But I think now she was right, I had no discipline. Several times in adulthood I have bought a piano and tried again to learn but could never pick up sight-reading well enough to keep the tempo.

On the radio I tried the ABC but one of the parents wanted 2NZ because on the ABC the announcers *sounded like the Queen.*

There was a blurry line between Roy Orbison and Cilla Black, or the Beatles. I didn't pay much attention to the radio. I kept the crystal set on a chair by my bed. "2NZ your local rodeo radio! And now we'll start the day as we do every morning with *The Redback on the Toilet Seat* by Slim Dusty." I tried to pick up other stations but couldn't hear them for static. I probably didn't dare play the ABC.

My room was a sleepout off the big room where three of my sisters slept, and in another room were two more sisters. We stayed out of our parents' way pretty much. They were busy. All the yards were big. We had sheds up the back. In the sheds were cubbies, one with a smaller back room behind a hessian-sack door. Passwords. 'White elephant' was a popular password. We rarely saw the adults except for meals or if it was raining hard.

We were pretty much unsupervised. We lived as Tarzan and Jane, designating a choko vine as our jungle. How we got to know about Tarzan and Jane I don't recall. We weren't allowed comics. Dad thought comics were low. In the same way, he disapproved of rice.

Mum asked him to take her to the Show but he was unwilling. He was so unused to having or spending money he couldn't really bring himself to say yes. She insisted, saying they needed to have *some fun* and he gave in. But he wasn't able to enjoy it, she said, because it was *costing money*. So that made it hard for her to enjoy. Naturally, we kids knew nothing about them going to the show. She told me much later.

I went on practising on my paper piano and humming to myself in the sleepout. At least I had privacy. Before I was given the sleep-out, the only way I could be alone was to hide.

One school holidays Tommy and her kids arrived in Inverell for a few days. I remember nothing about this visit. Truly nothing. I know it happened because there is a grainy photo taken on my camera of a barbeque in the bush somewhere, Tommy holding aloft a sausage in tongs, a fire behind her, her kids nearby, double-exposed with another shot of the same bush and in the fire smoke, some of my sisters. Where did they stay? How long were they there? I don't know.

That year I was finishing school. Since the rest of the family had already gone to Newcastle to live, I had been billeted with a woman Dad had done shed extensions for. I don't know why I was put with her and not one of the aunts. I didn't know her. I just accepted it at the time. Another thing they did somehow on their budget, was buy me a plane ticket to Newcastle for the day after the last exam.

This was when I really started smoking. Lighting up a Viscount and studying Gerard Manley Hopkins and listening to the radio.

Living on Stockton

Mum said Tommy would collect me from the plane. Exams over, Inverell behind me, I stepped onto the tarmac and into her arms. She said my parents were doing well over town, and would visit me on the weekend.

As always in her kitchen Tommy asked me to sit in the chair that was in the sun, and made tomatoes on toast, saying which vine she had got the tomato from or its type, cherry tomatoes, gross lisse, others I forget. Then we went outside to check the beds, hers were up near the fence, parsley, tomatoes, rhubarb, and Jock's in the lawn near the shed. His climbing beans on their frame, his cabbages forming hearts.

I picked up my suitcase and walked up the road to Violet's. She said she didn't mind if I lived with her while I was at College, but it seemed a bit mad—I'd have to get the ferry over town then a bus ride, when my parents were in town and near the college. Too crowded, I said.

My parents were living across the river in a suburb called The Hill. My younger sisters were doing well at the Infants and Primary School or in a selective girls' High School with Latin and French and a revered hockey mistress. They were going to have a different sort of childhood.

Violet stayed up late and I had a few hands of cards with her before we went to bed. She was drinking Royal Reserve sherry and gave me some. It was good. Something in me, too deep down for me to know about, understood I could never have Tommy. I went on the back porch and smelled the night wind. It was 1965. I had a lot of my life left to live, a non-Tommy life, and I tried to imagine it. Drifting in on the wind was the smell of wedding food being prepared for the daughter of next door.

On Stockton we knew the time of day by the steelworks' sirens. They worked three shifts, morning, afternoon and dogwatch. Pappy had been a boilermaker, and in the end, old enough to not have to work dogwatch. Violet kept house. I fossicked about and found three old photos.When I showed the one with the beagles to Mum, she looked at it in silence for a long while, then said, 'I was lucky.' She had talked to her brother Norm about his childhood.

When Mum was 12, the family photo includes three dogs but does not include her. These may have been hunting dogs. Two beagles and a foxy. They could afford by then to feed three dogs, but still June is not sent for. They do not go to get her. Possibly still thinking that Mi and Pearl would be too bereft. On the back of the photo: 'This was taken at Taylors weekender/the sun is in our eyes/I am holding a bunch of xmas bells.'

In this photo, I think they're digging for worms, for bait.

Uncle Norm had wanted to go on fishing boats but had been made to do his apprenticeship at the BHP as a boilermaker and had then gone to Sydney to work on boats. My cousin Steve in his turn became a fitter-and-turner at the BHP. Violet was glad of this and wanted to make sure someone from each generation was doing his time there, because it meant it was easier for others to be taken on. Years later when I was back living with Violet again, my husband worked at the BHP as a boiler-maker's mate.

It was before sunrise and the dunes were cold and clean. Two trawlers were working in the bight, I couldn't see their names … the Rebecca. I walked back towards the river, past Betty Skews' house, and went in Tommy's back gate. The birds made a comment as I went by their cage. Cockatiels.

Tommy gave me a kiss on the cheek near my mouth and pointed to the chair that got the morning sun.

Next morning early we went upriver to the whiting spot. Tommy pulled in to the yard at the front of the bait shop and we got out.

Mr Lindstrom was a dwarf and lived in the small house he had built for himself opposite the mangrove flats, and kept the bait in two long freezers. A wooden stepladder leaned against each freezer and often he spoke to you from the top of one of these ladders. Sometimes he sat on one of the steps while his customers worked out where they would fish, and what bait they would need. It was a subtle process whereby in our case Tommy would quiz him mildly about what was going on in the river, or offer up information from Jock, in return for information Mr Lindstrom may have had from earlier customers, who may also have relayed something from their uncles or cousins concerning which side of Walsh Island etcetera. Sometimes he almost whispered and Tommy had to lean forward. He would recommend one thing or another depending on the wind and tide. There was a windsock in his front yard. We had hired one of his long rowboats and went across the road to the jetty where the boats were moored. The tide was in and they were rocking at the end of the jetty where often they sat on the mudflats. Tommy had gone out to the end of the jetty and got in the boat where she was storing the picnic. Mr Lindstrom took my thin hand in his pudgy one and held it softly. He looked at me as if he knew everything that was going on. There was a breeze. His white hairs lifted and settled again on his head.

Tell her to take you up to Fullerton Cove, he said, to the whiting hole. She knows where it is.

It was this kind and understanding look which sustained me for years.

Down the Royal

The Ladies Lounge at the Royal Hotel looked out at the river. Often while Tommy and Sylv were talking I sat at the piano fooling around. I played the treble and then the bass; it's an area of musical blindness I'm not proud of. They wanted me to play honky-tonk or ragtime but I had no music for that. I was still learning Handel's 'Largo', or as I later learned, 'Ombra mai fu'. There is a section where the treble goes down to meet the bass, which I could play together.

I was drinking shandy but not liking the sweet taste, then taking sips from Tommy's glass while she was talking to Sylv. They were talking about where they might get jobs when the kids got older and went to high school across town.

Tommy took a breath and began
They say we should work
like the normal folks do
how can we work when
there's no-o work to do

Because she made it into two quick notes, the word 'no' had a sort of yodel. She always looked at me when she sang this note. 'No' was an important word between us. Many things I suggested, particularly more physical intimacy, received a No. Or, somehow by implication, Not till later. Later could then be infinitely deferred, or acted on as desired. Until many years later, it did not even occur to me that she could have looked away, because that No also had a tone of seduction in it, a kind of challenge. I don't suppose I even knew what flirting was at the time. But she could have walked away from the whole thing. Or I could have. Then again, I was a child.

A barmaid they liked came in and cleared away their glasses in a little stack up her arm and wiped down the table. She leaned in dangerously close to my right cheek. I could smell the mixture of shandy and sweat and fish, but perhaps the fish was on my own clothes. I looked across the table and under the breast at Tommy who winked at me.

Sylv leaned over and said to me, are your parents expecting you back over their place soon?

No, I've moved in with Violet.

And what is their opinion of that? said Sylv, taking an interest.

Well, they've hardly been over to see me.

One less mouth to feed, Tommy said, and started to sing again.

Tommy's Uncle Wal put his head in the door from the main bar and sang with them—'Hallelujah, bum again'—and disappeared.

Mame nonsense

Coming down the back lane I watched the spaces between the houses where I could see long thin strips of sea grilling in the sun. At Violet's back gate I could smell she was making chicken giblet soup. I took my fishing bag into the laundry and made room for it on the shelf. I would have liked to take it indoors. Violet was standing at the radio, which was on the fridge, listening to the weather report. A southerly was blowing up in Sydney and would reach us later tonight. She turned and wanted to know where I'd been.

Up the tip, then down the bottom end.

Out with Tommy again.

We set the table and I realised I'd have to do something about Violet's jealousy so I got out the cards. She wanted to know whether I had found a job, and I said Not yet. (I hadn't looked.)

Your parents can't be giving me money for your food and keep, she said, they've got five other kids at school.

I know. I'll look for something. I just now finished studying.

Studying is sitting in a chair, she said. Sounds like a holiday to me.

My head needs a rest I said. Are you aware that's a left bower you've just put on?

Why do you think I put it on?

Oh.

How do you propose to rest your head?

Reading. Mooching around.

Violet put her voice almost into her cards and said I woulda thought reading would keep your head busy. Why do you want all that stuff in your head? Mame nonsense to me.

Mame? I thought. But that was what she said.

Letters came to Violet's address saying I could have a

Commonwealth scholarship and go to uni, (four years with a Dip. Ed.) or a Teacher's College scholarship (two years and you'd be working). Without anyone saying anything, it was clear that I should start at College. It was over town so I'd be living at my parents again at least for a while. In the meantime I had three months, a whole summer.

Punt

Sitting in my chair at Tommy's was a squat man having his hair cut.

This is Mick, our best man.

I said hello and sat on the back step sunning myself.

And what do you do, young lady? he said to me.

I'll be going to Teachers' College in a while. Till then I'm reading books and fishing with Tommy.

Yes I've heard about you, he said, smiling.

What do you do, Mick?

Engineer on the punt.

Oh! I like the punt.

Then next time you're on it, find out if I'm on shift and come down below and I'll show you the engine-room.

I next saw Mick at the Royal. We heard from the front bar that the Serena, Jock's sailboat, was winning in the twelve-foot race outside and we all went out to watch him come round the final buoy. Mick turned to me and said, inclining his head to Jock, 'When he's not in boats, he's in boats.'

You should talk, Tommy said to him affectionately.

Once on the punt I crossed the deck ahead of the cars and asked after Mick, yes, he was down below. They pointed me to an area behind a store of lifejackets where I went down a metal ladder to the engine room, a spacious area. In the centre was the big diesel engine, taller than me and four times as long. I could see

Mick waving to me with an oil-rag. The moist air was throbbing with the regular beats and puffs and sighs of the pistons. The sign from the skipper changed from slow to full steam ahead, Mick touched various levers and stood back. Sometimes he talked to me but mostly had to concentrate. It was strange he was running the engine but could not see the water, it was all under the surface.

Talking to Mick

When we berthed on the Stockton side he was coming off shift; he waved to the man replacing him, and offered me a lift to Violet's. We sat in his ute talking. At least, Mick talked. He wasn't married and maybe lonely. I was interested in all his stories. He was one of the few people—men or women—on Stockton who actually wanted to talk. Most were so silent.

He spoke about how he'd grown up in Maitland and come to Stockton every school holidays to stay with his grandparents, and had always thought he'd live there as an adult because it was his holiday town, his childhood freedom.

And do you live here?

Yep, further up, towards the tip.

Yes. I see black people at the tip scavenging.

Woromi. You know Stockton belonged to the Woromi people.

I didn't, no. It's horrible our ancestors just took the place over.

It is horrible. He paused and looked out at the sea.

The Woromi Aborigines lived on the southern beach near Lynn Oval, he said. My grandpa talked about them. Beach fires, flints, oysters and fishing. Stalking wallaby. They were there till the 1870s at least, the young ones growing up during the time of shipbuilding. On a walk round the suburb you'd see and hear sawyers, timberyards, shipwrights. Boats on the blocks or up on the hoist, ladders under the hulls, ropes and blocks, men working at barnacles.

Mick waved his hand and went on. Gantry cranes, mobile cranes on barges. Dry docks. Buyers looking. Chandleries. People discussing net sizes.

The sun came through the windscreen and in the warmth and the soft drone of Mick's voice I heard him say that way back in 1840, there was a textile factory on Factory Street and Stockton was a suburb of spinners and weavers. Did I know that?

Go on, I said.

So, let's see—there was also a mine that went out from Stockton beach under the sea for a mile.

We sat in his ute imagining that.

Then he said, The coal under Stockton was Newcastle's best, the Borehole Seam. It lasted maybe ten years before a flooding when I think eleven men drowned, and then the mine was closed.

And then?

Well, after the mine disaster Stockton became a residential suburb. People helped build the dyke that grew into the state dockyard site.

What was there before the steelworks?

Walsh Island before that, let's see, it was a market garden and a dairy, and the farmers rowed their produce to market across the river to Stockton or to Newcastle.

Summer

Three or four times a week I went fishing with Tommy. She gave me a river rod, which was also good on the Wreck, and taught me to cast, practising on their back lawn.

Violet had by now got used to me spending so much time with Tommy and may have felt she couldn't complain because I was bringing home fish every day or two and she (Violet) didn't like bought food, always preferred what you could get from the bush or the river or the sea for nothing.

The best fishing was at Easter. You could tell from the smell in the air when the mullet were running, and the sea was writhing with them. The moon was brighter then, too. They travel close to the surface, jumping and flicking all the time as they move to the sea to spawn. You couldn't catch them with bait but threw an empty hook into the school and jagged them. They had a muddy taste and we didn't eat them much but gave them away or Jock used them as crab-trap bait.

One weekend Mum arrived with some of my sisters and we had a hand of euchre with Violet. That is, the sisters and me, Mum didn't play cards or games of any sort—she was raised a Methodist.

I was enjoying the summer, and avoiding getting more work. Violet always had the radio on low while we played cards. It excited her to trump someone with an ace, particularly a black ace on a high red card. We played for hours in a dreamy kind of state, not really talking about anything, with the thump of the surf in the background and the radio. Mum asked after Tommy, and I said she and Jock and the kids had gone to Mungo Brush camping for a few weeks. I didn't say how strange that would be for me, to be thrown back on my own devices. I had to act like I had a life of my own.

Mum had brought a box of my stuff over and when they went, I unpacked it in the back bedroom. Among the gear was my crystal set—I was surprised to see it, Mum had thrown out most of my things in a complicated manoeuvre I admired years later when I thought about it.

After dinner I said my goodnights to Violet and in my room I turned the tuner on the crystal set. Before I could get to Violet's station I came to someone playing piano music but not a large triumphal classical thing—it was moody, had a gentle sort of atmosphere—classical but a bit hesitant. The announcer said it was a Gnossienne by the French composer Erik Satie, written in the 1890s. The manuscript had no time signature, no bar lines, and his tempo markings said things like 'lightly, with intimacy', and 'don't be proud'. I was thrilled that everything I had been learning about written music could be thrown away. It was one of the big lessons in life, even though it was only seconds sitting near a radio.

Secret stuff

Tidying the wardrobe in the back bedroom to fit my things, I found a tiny Mass book and asked Violet about it. She said Oh yes, it was hers, but she had put it away because Pappy didn't want her going to mass.

Did you used to go to mass?

Yes, we were raised Catholics, the Murphys, I thought you knew that.

No, you never mentioned it.

That's why Pappy couldn't divorce his first wife, she said. She was a Catholic too and wouldn't divorce him.

Do you know her name?

No.

Or where she lives?

Over town somewhere.

So your wedding ring, I said, touching her hand and the rose gold ring which so seemed to be a part of her hand.

We just had to *say* we were married. She was crying now, crying for Pappy, and I would have to stop. It now occurred to me there was no wedding photo on the wall, and the cause of this was not poverty.

Did they have any kids?

Pappy said they had a little boy, but he died. She waved her hand at me, across the front of her head, and I said Sorry, sorry.

But I knew that these tiny bits of information, roused from silence by the Mass book, would have other hidden bits accrued to them. For example, I thought that Pappy probably had a daughter by the unnamed first wife, and that she was still alive.

In the wardrobe I'd also found a long flat suitcase which revealed ribbons, medals, an apron, and a leaflet with the rules of the International Order of Oddfellows. I hadn't known Pappy that well. He was on shift or away a lot, up in the bush shooting, or over on the beach fishing. Or he was down the bottom end at the George Washington.

Near the end of his life, he wrote in my autograph book

'To the Sea'

You are so mighty
and my ship is so small.
Have mercy.

I tried to have a conversation with him but you had to choose your time of day and I blundered and he stormed out to the shed. Or maybe it was nothing to do with me, that's even more likely, and some internal struggle he was having caused him to turn and cross the lawn. I think I wanted to talk about books, and I knew he was a reader. I don't know where he kept his books, just somehow I knew he read things.

In the end though, he wasn't really an Oddfellow, but pretty normal if you were a boy born on Stockton—go fishing, find work, get a tin of rolling tobacco, start drinking, get a boat, get some girl pregnant, drink while fishing, work shifts, threaten your kids, bash your wife, put on your ironed shirt, go down the pub. In that sense not odd at all.

When Pappy finished working Violet gained great comfort from the house. I didn't know then about their earlier life living in a tent. She only spoke about the past unwillingly, and then would cry, so my mother and I stopped asking her. It was hard to find out much. Years later we found out about her real mother.

In the sewing machine drawer

In one of the drawers of the sewing machine looking for elastic I found a photo of a family in the bush camping. The younger Violet, dark-haired, thin, stood in front of a tent, holding a child against her apron front. Two other kids either side of her. A campfire, blackened pots, 44-gallon drums.

I knew from my mother that Violet had followed Pappy round places in the bush near Inverell in the Depression when he was an itinerant worker. One time the men were framing up scaffold they would use to build a wool shed. Violet was living in the tent with three kids under the age of five, washing nappies in four-gallon drums, the fire constantly going and the oldest child, my mother, June, learning to mind the younger ones when Violet was over collecting kindling or stringing washing on a line between the trees.

I also knew from Mum that Violet had finally gone to town and found a place to board: two rooms at the front of the house of the Miss Rolfes, seamstresses, who lived in the back part of the house. At a certain point in the hallway there was a curtain, and behind this was the area of the Miss Rolfes. Violet was allowed to go back and use their kitchen, then take the food to her rooms. The Miss Rolfes got very attached to my mother.

Much later Uncle Norm, Mum's brother, remembered that there were threats from the authorities that he and his brother would be put on the state. By this time Violet was in living in Maitland in a shed near her parents. She was pregnant again. Pappy was still working up north and still drinking all his pay.

June was safe in Inverell with the Miss Rolfes, who had come to Maitland on the train to rescue her. But Violet had nowhere to put the boys or herself. Then somehow Pappy must have relented and come to Maitland and found work in a mechanic's garage and they lived in the back shed of the garage. This shed had electricity. When finally Pappy got taken on at the steelworks they were able to afford the deposit on the house on the beach at Stockton. They settled but didn't bring my mother there; it was thought it would be *too hard* on Miss Rolfes to take my mother away.

My mother was getting a better life where she was, and everybody knew it. She lived with the ladies till she was married. At times from the age of fifteen she went on the train to Stockton to visit Violet and the family. Violet never hugged her and found it difficult to meet her eye. But my mother persisted. Once the family had moved from Inverell to Newcastle, Mum visited Violet every Sunday. It was a ritual.

I never saw Violet touch Mum. She (Violet) never hugged us either. It just wasn't the way things were done.

Fern Bay caravan park

It happened only once that a person in Violet's family spoke openly about their past. It was many years later, and the person who spoke was Uncle Norm, who by then was 85, a year or so younger than Mum. He was living north of Stockton at Fern Bay.

My main memory of Norm was as Uncle Grunt, sitting on Nana's back veranda drinking himself into an acceptable stupor. Norm and I had both lived at Violet's when we left our marriages. Violet never turned anyone away, on principle.

Norm had six kids and couldn't cope. Went to Sydney and worked on boats, lived in a shed in someone's back yard.

We drove into the caravan park after putting Norm's secret number into the boom gate pad, cruised down the narrow streets to his shaggy area of caravan, annex, and car.

We had brought pies and lamingtons. The only thing in his fridge was beer, but he seemed to be lasting OK. He was tall, wore shined boots, and drove a Fairlane. He sat on a bench seat in the annexe to his caravan. We ate our pies in silence and opened the lamingtons. I encouraged him to talk.

There are also large gaps in his story. After years of silence, he was now talking about his early days. Not in any articulate way but muttering, considering, talking in a rush then not at all, or throwing phrases over his shoulder, 'as far as that goes'.

So many things had been covered up in various families, so many actions were areas of shame, that most of the adults in my world rarely spoke about their personal lives. The talk was all jobs, weather, tides, what the kids were up to. Only later did my mother begin to talk about her life and why Violet had given her away to be raised by two sisters in another town. Among the men, silence.

The exception, but not till late in his life was Uncle Norm.

What I know about Uncle Norm

The Rejects, the gun, the dead baby, the steelworks, the boatshed, his kidney operation, the way he gave up smoking, the caravan park. The Fairlane. His good boots. His boating books. His Stockton Historical Society magazines. I knew he hadn't seen his wife Betty for a long time. He left when the kids were small. Only some of the kids were still talking to him. The grownup kids. The boys in their 60s now still lived at home with their mother in the Commission house in Edgeworth. Or maybe West Wallsend. No-hopers, he's ashamed of them.

Ben called Normie Uncle Grunt because he rarely spoke in words. If he was sitting on Violet's back veranda a certain grunt meant he wanted his mother to bring him a stubby from the fridge. Other grunts meant hello or goodbye. I never saw him sober but he was rarely falling-over drunk. Once he was bloodnose drunk but didn't seem to realise his nose had been bleeding and we were all too polite to mention it. When he first started coming to family events he arrived drunk and sobered up as the party went on.

Then when he turned eighty-five something happened and he

started to talk. I asked him where his memory kicked in. At the age of five, he said, he had started school at Bulahdelah. Pappy was working as a motor mechanic. It was 1935 and they lived in a tent and had a garage or shed for the repairs. Before that Pappy was working on the silos at Binigai near Moree, where they had also been camped. They carted water from the river. Pappy made ironwork for the formwork for silos. These were rail silos for wheat. The wheat came in bags—hundreds of trucks would be lined up waiting to unload into the rail silo.

Norm didn't get to grow up with Mum but got to know her as an adult, maybe in their fifties they got to know each other a bit. Now in their eighties they have lunch at the Stockton RSL every Sunday. He goes in all the raffles. The meat tray, the chook, the bottle of bubbly.

Over his schooner he remembers the tent in Bulahdelah, and where things were kept. The tin meat safe. The table and the kero lamp. Mattresses on tarps.

Later Pappy was taken on at the BHP and they bought the house on Stockton over the road from the beach in a time when houses were cheap. The three boys played jokes and fished and tried to stay out of their father's way.

Norm was the oldest boy. 'I copped all the beltings.' In the school photo they had no shoes, but everyone was in the same boat. All the fathers went rabbiting. When Norm was sixteen he stood up to Pappy who had come home from the Gladstone Hotel and was hitting Violet inside the house. Norm was on the back veranda and 'the door banged and she come sailing out of the house with two black eyes and a busted nose.'

Norm went in and towered over his father who from that point did not beat up his wife. But Clanka and Carl, the younger brothers, have the same story, so perhaps as each brother grew up and left home, the next brother had to beat up the father to protect Violet.

June came down to Stockton once when she was fifteen for the Christmas holidays and stayed with them and finally got to know her brothers. They were shocked at first they had a sister. After that she went back to Inverell and went to work as a legal secretary.

Like his father, Uncle Norm served his time as a boilermaker at the steelworks. He still went fishing—at that time beakies came in a swarm. Garfish. He fell in love with Betty and they had seven kids but he didn't stay around for long—he was working shifts and drinking, she was drinking, and one baby died.

He got up and went into the caravan and brought back a cutting from the Herald showing the 1946 end-of-year results from Tech when he was studying to be a boiler-maker. He had topped the class. I asked if he could tell me something about his working day—what was it like?—had anything special or unusual happened at the steelworks?

See, they had these huge ladles, he said, bigger than a car, suspended over the vat of molten steel. And the ladles come and dip into the steel and swing away to pour it into moulds for iron bars or whatever. Men that worked there had high heat protection clothing, asbestos suits, masks, goggles, big asbestos gauntlets, steel-cap boots. One day as the ladle swung away this man who was working right nearby fell—or jumped—into the vat.

So—

So he would have been vaporised. I think he jumped, but anyway. It was quick. Then the wife applied for insurance, but she had a lot of trouble getting the money because there was no body. So they couldn't prove anything.

He sat silent for a long time and we said nothing.

After the BHP Norm went to work on boats in Sydney. When he retired and moved to the caravan park, he became part of a group of men who call themselves The Rejects. They are proud of this status and intend to remain that way. Most of them like Norm had been married a few times and have kids all over the place but they prefer to live alone. All the old men who give him the short wave when he drives out have a good car in the carport. They live alone in caravans but drive Fairlanes and such, V8s, that handle well whether the driver is drunk or sober, and corner well even in bad weather. They have a Men's Shed but Norm doesn't go there, he is a reject even from the rejects, and this makes him laugh.

During the kidney operation my mother visited him in the hospital every day. One of his daughters who has remained in touch with him and who is a nurse, Sheryl, did the same. Sheryl survived her childhood because when she was sixteen her boyfriend's parents took her in and basically re-raised her. Taught her table manners, and how to receive love. Sheryl had to speak of this quietly because Norm was in the room and although he had industrial deafness he often heard things he wasn't meant to hear.

The doctors removed one kidney which had cancer, and he came good and went on drinking. He was eighty-two then, still tall, and always dressed well. The doctor spoke to him about the drinking and he cut back to a few schooners less and went onto light beer. It took him ages to get used to it.

He'd been drinking a bit more because he'd given up smoking. It happened like this: he'd been smoking since he was nine, like all the boys on Stockton, and one day in his seventies he was driving to Sydney and had to stop and have a cough. And he coughed so hard he vomited. And when he got to Sydney he went to a pub he knew and gave the cigarettes and the lighter to one of the men at the bar. Went cold turkey.

For a while, between wives, he lived in the boatshed on the back of Violet's block. This was in the sixties and he didn't talk then, and was always heavily drunk. He is the only uncle who eventually talked about what life was like in that family. Uncle Carl never spoke of it, nor the middle brother Clanka, that is, Uncle Ron, a fisherman, who we didn't see much because he was kicked out of Nelson Bay for drinking and rabble-rousing, and ended up in Mooloolaba, making a good living fishing for spanner crabs.

When my mother turned eighty she had a big party at a bowling club. Her six daughters were there. A woman who resembled Mum more than any of us was there: our cousin Vicky. I hadn't seen her for thirty years. She was Clanka's daughter. Clanka wasn't there: he had died of leukaemia years ago, some time after picking up a faulty electrical lead on a wharf and getting a mighty electric shock. It took quite a while for him to die, he was strong. The third brother Carl had been a long-distance truckie and had died of bladder cancer, they said from smoking. He didn't drink and was Violet's favourite child for that reason. They all smoked, but Carl smoked all the time to keep awake on long haul drives. He told me to smoke 'only tobacco'.

Vicky asked what I was doing with my life. I said writing, and teaching writing.

Like, what, she said.

Well, fiction. Non-fiction. Scripts. Poetry.

She shook her head.

What do you do? I said.

She helped her husband run his building business, she said, up in Nelson Bay.

Where are you teaching? She wanted to know. I said I'd just come back from Darwin. She'd never been there and wanted to know what it was like. I tried to describe it. Later I said to her, No one in the family ever asks me what I do for a living. You're the first. She asked if I remembered on Stockton her family visiting us while we were staying with Violet and Pappy in the Christmas holidays. I said no. She went on, So there would have been nine kids. Pappy chased us off with the kangaroo gun, and ran after us waving the gun because we were being noisy in the back yard. Yelling at us. You don't remember?

I stared at her. I had no memory of the situation or the gun. Very early I became oblivious.

I mean no doubt we were, Vicky went on. We ran away from him across the road into the sandhills and onto the beach and headed for Nelson Bay.

In her memory we kept running for quite a while, as he had followed us over to the beach, yelling at us and waving the shotgun.

No, I don't remember anything like that, I said. I asked my sister Linda, she also didn't remember.

Later on during the party, I saw Uncle Norm sitting alone and went to sit by him. It was the time he had a blood nose and hadn't noticed; the blood had dried on his cheek. You were often not sure if he was awake. The party was wearing on and he was beginning to sober up though he seemed to be sitting crooked on the stool. I asked if he knew whether Pappy had a gun.

'Had a gun? I'll tell you what happened.' He leaned forward, looking at me directly. 'One night we three boys were eating dinner at the table and Carl was excited, telling some story, probably made up, being entertaining—Pappy told him to shut up. After a while Carl forgot, went on with his story. Pappy got up, went in the front bedroom, got his shotgun out of the wardrobe. See, he laid it down on the table across all our place settings and said "Anybody who talks I'll shoot."

Were you quiet after that?

Pretty quiet.

Vicky said he had a gun in the shed.

That was the rabbiting gun.

Was he a good shot?

We ate a lot of rabbits. And sometimes kangaroo.

And you never liked him?

I never liked him.

The cage

Once Tommy and her family were due back from Mungo Brush, I went looking for her car, but no luck, so I caught the bus to the waterfront and the ferry to town to visit my sisters and parents. Trisha and Barbie had the bottom bunks, Gwennie and Kathy the top ones, and Linda and I (when I was there) the single beds, everything put away and very neat, and in the other flat (Dad had put a door between the two flats) Mum and Dad had their area. It was a Saturday, most of them were out but I had a chat to Mum. She'd got work cleaning houses and Dad was working for a building firm as a supervisor. I stayed the night and left early next morning.

Back on Stockton I couldn't see whether Tommy was on the Wreck, her car wasn't in its usual spot. I decided to walk up to Violet's from the ferry. Bobby Ferris's sister's ferret cage was standing on the footpath, empty. She had taken the ferret into the pub—to sell it? To shock the men by suddenly producing something from up her sleeve, and get a good laugh?

Then a car slowed beside me and Tommy's voice said, Fancy a ride to somewhere darling? The men on the street had noticed and were laughing quietly.

I got in the passenger side and she did a U turn in the main street. She threw me a smile, the car window framing her. I turned my head and watched the river going north. I knew I had to prevent myself from enjoying this smile or giving it any meaning, or any credence at all.

How was the holiday?

Good. The kids like camping. Jock still wakes at three every morning.

She put two cigarettes in her mouth and lit them, gave me one, held my fingers for longer than was good for road safety. On the carpet at my feet were some sticks and newspaper and matches, a billy, some bread, cheese, two apples. I leant down and picked up a toasting fork, made from twisted wire.

Your grandfather made me that, she said.

Further north along Stockton bight we turned onto a track she knew, got in amongst the sand hills and started collecting driftwood. There was no banter now, no quipping, just a concentrated look now and then.

She reached in her bag for two tin cups and a tripod contraption made of metal that went over the fire and had a hook dangling from its centre for the billy. We made toast with Pappy's fork. I realised she had known there'd be no fish today and the purpose of the afternoon was really a fire. I had stopped wanting her to kiss me, at least for now. The look was enough, maybe it was better. It was a neutral look, not enquiring, not inviting, not ironic, not longing, not guilty. The expression in her eyes had no content and in this way it was a paradox, because it was also filled with content, unspoken, but the stronger for that. Anyone could speak. Anyone could crack a joke. Silence was harder. She went to the car and came back with an old sleeping bag. We sat on that and talked about nothing. Later we lay down together and she tucked herself around me and we went to sleep in the spring sun. I was surprised that I was able to sleep, but we slept soundly.

College

I took up my scholarship and started Teacher's College, but soon it was only in theory that I went there. Long days of practising Modified Cursive with the edge of your chalk on a blackboard, followed by a sort of italic script, at an even closer edge of the chalk, had convinced me I'd be better off fishing.

Violet had no money and neither did I. At least, she had the Pension, and lived well within it except that I had arrived. I never asked her for anything, and provided the Coles money and fish two or three times a week. Tommy had got me a job selling old ladies swami silk underwear in Coles over town. It was excruciating.

A college friend called Pinky had an older sister at uni who loaned me books, and now I really began to read. I had won a poetry anthology in the annual awards at high school for coming first in English in my final year of school, but it wasn't till college when a man in a pub told me about a poet called Charles Causley that I saw a way forward with words. I didn't want to write like Eliot or Kenneth Slessor. But Causley, and later Larkin, made sense of how I might go on. And then Bruce Dawe.

Tommy didn't read books and Violet's eyes were too bad to read. My parents read in bed at night, library books, but I never knew what they were because the books stayed in their room. Most people I knew did not read and I knew no one who thought of being a writer.

There were two enduring mysteries during my time at college. One, where did a person find other writers? Two, were there other women who felt like Tommy and me?

My parents had built a block of four flats and lived in the top two; Dad had cut an adjoining door between the two to accommodate the family. I tried living there for a while.

I sat on the top bunk in the kids' flat one afternoon and tried to imagine other women like Tommy and me. She didn't seem to know any, had never mentioned any, and I had never met any. What were we even called? While my sisters were at school I wrote Tommy a letter, saying honestly how I felt, and asked what were we called, and what could we do about the situation. This sounds logical enough but it took me an hour and was still incoherent. I gave up and folded it into a small square and hid it in my part of the cupboard, in a hockey sock that I no longer wore. I realised I could never ask her these things, it would only embarrass her. That is, it only worked while we never mentioned it. I pushed the underwear in on top of the sock and forgot about it.

A week later I thought Dad must've had a hard day at work or even fallen off a roof as he looked so black when I walked in. Black in the mood I mean. Finally after staring at me like a lunatic for some while, he said the college Principal had rung the house and asked to speak to him and told him it was common knowledge that I was having an affair with a fisherman on Stockton, Jock someone, and that I had denied it. Dad's face darkened and he said, How *dare* the Principal assume he can interfere in the private lives of his students, how dare he ring parents rumour-mongering, let him organise the teaching of the curriculum. Mum came in and tried to calm him down, and at no point did he ask me whether it was true. I felt that he had defended me, and thanked him silently.

Sharks on the line

One Thursday I spent the whole day with Tommy fishing with rods off Nobby's beach—no luck and I have never had any luck on that beach, though I've seen people catch bream there. Tommy was in a good mood and singing some dirty song. She talked about fishing off Stockton beach with Pappy a few years back, when they had each caught a shark in one night, and gone home covered in blood and guts because they'd tried to clean them on the beach, on the hard sand, with the big knife Pappy had, and wash the guts back into the sea but the tide kept trying to take the sharks back from them so they took them by the gills and dragged them across the road and down the side path into the back of Pappy and Violet's house, and started again at the back tap, all this in the middle of the night with a lot of suppressed laughing because they'd been sharing a flask of rum on the beach while waiting for anything to happen and not a bite for an hour and a half till suddenly both sharks hit within minutes of each other and they were both letting the lines run out so they didn't snap, then later running backwards up the sand and reeling in and whooping at the same time as they realised they had sharks on the line.

The lobster feast

On Saturday when Jock went to the Boatrowers, Tommy opened the fridge and removed a lobster she'd taken from her husband's catch the day before. She was beckoning me with the lobster's feelers. At the bench she showed me how to open the lobster, laying it on its back and beginning at the tail make a neat cut along the gut to the head, and open the shell away. She sent me out for a lemon and squeezed that across it. Then ground some pepper over it. Now she took a round segment from near the tail and held it to my mouth. With her other hand she was feeding herself and looking directly in my eyes as we ate. The flesh was moist against my tongue. It was as though every sweet flathead fillet was a preparation for this craving in the mouth. We set to and devoured the lot, grasping legs and cracking them open and sucking out the flesh. We ate the lobster's brain. We upended the shell and drank the juice.

Tommy wrapped what was left and put it in the bin out of sight. We sat down again and her face seemed to set in its lines like a statue. Sometimes this had happened at night, when she was tired. She sat very still, without speaking.

The hit

I came in from college one Tuesday to find Dad pacing in the kitchen. He asked me to follow him into the big kids' bedroom. Now he had his hands among the things in my underwear drawer, and pulled out the hockey sock and took out the letter. His hand was shaking and his colour was high. He lifted the letter in the air over my head and went at me: what is the meaning of this? This, this, disgusting, he seemed to crumple in on himself then raised himself up and whacked me hard in the face with the back of his hand. I went down onto the nearest bed, on my back, and when I came to, he was still glowering and ranting. I pretended to be out to it for a while longer when I felt liquid in my ears—my nose was bleeding. Recalling that the carpet in our room and the lounge room was new, and a pale colour, I stood and lurched towards the back bathroom, and had the satisfaction of dripping blood all the way. I cleaned myself up and he told me to tip my head back to try and stop the blood. Eventually I did that and soon Mum came home and said, What's all this blood? My father went back on the boil and said, How would you feel if some woman was putting her finger inside you? Mum thought about this, and said, I might like it. She put the kettle on and went about making dinner. I retreated to the bunkroom where I found the letter on the floor, squeezed into a twist, and tore it to tiny pieces and flushed it down the toilet. Dad cleared off for a few hours—we didn't know where he went. Neither parent mentioned this scene to the other kids when they came in. We went on with dinner as normal and Dad turned up during the meal as if late in from work. It was only now that I started registering that my mother had defended me. I looked at her gratefully but she kept her face neutral, a thing she was practised at doing and perhaps not even conscious of, at this point.

The next day Sunday I got the bus down Darby Street and walked along Hunter Street to the ferry wharf. I saw the coloured page in my autograph book where Dad had written a quote from Shakespeare: 'This above all, to thine ownself be true'. I liked his writing. I'd tried being true to my self and got a whack for it. From the bow of the ferry I could see the twelve-footers racing and we were almost among it. There was a fair breeze up and I could see the blurred S of Jock's boat name going by. I couldn't remember the name. He was at the buoy and going under the boom to make the turn. Peter was with him, leaning out over the gunwale, learning. I turned my attention to the inside of the ferry. It was about half full, no one else on my long seat except to the left a woman at the far end. I looked at her but she didn't look. In front two kids were playing along the seat.

Then to my left I heard a snorting sound and looked to see the woman jolting and jerking, really as if some demon was in her body—I thought she must be having a heart attack. And then I thought maybe it was a fit and now she had calmed down, but it was a pause before the next crushing contractions, flinging her body sideways, and loosening her false teeth. She was dying in front of me and I was transfixed—yet I knew I should get up and—do what? Attempt to comfort her? She might not want a stranger at her death. Her brown handbag seemed to wait at her feet like a small dog. Her body jolted again, the heart giving out a huge current, then she sat still for the rest of the ferry ride, her teeth resting on her lips. Her body moved only with the current of the boat. Should I then have gone to sit next to her, held her hand, or put my hand on her shoulder.

I was almost the last passenger to get off the ferry and the woman had not moved or got up and the deckhands were beginning to notice her.

I walked north from the ferry shed for half an hour and down the track to Tommy's back door but it was shut. Blossom came out from under the house and looked at me but no humans were in sight except Jock in his shed. He tilted his head a centimetre or so when he saw me. I knocked and waited. Nothing. I went looking for her at the riverbank and then the beach, nothing. I walked far enough south on the beach to see her car wasn't parked at the breakwater that led out to the Wreck.

The icy treatment

When I came back and knocked and coo-eed eventually Tommy appeared from somewhere further in the house and lifted her chin at me and said, Sit down, sit down, in such a tone that I knew the visit would be short and there would be no plans for the Wreck that afternoon. In a cold and polite tone, she asked what I'd like to eat instead of giving me tomatoes on toast; made a cup of tea for me but not for herself. What's wrong? I said. Nothing's wrong! she said, and stirred her cigarette in the ashtray. Nothing's wrong.

No come on, I said, this isn't fair, what's wrong. I waited.

Nothing's wrong, she said in a monotone. Maybe you'd better get a boyfriend.

A boyfriend! Why would I want a boyfriend!

Her hand went up, I can't hear any more of this, she said.

All right. Can I finish my tea?

Finish your tea.

It was clear some decision had been made, or something had happened, that I would not be told about.

Squalls in the stomach, surges in the bowel. I couldn't feel my feelings, but my legs were trembling. Finishing my tea, I picked up my tackle bag from under the chair, nodded and left.

Back at Violet's I picked up my rod and rigged it for the river, had lunch with Violet—How are things down Cardigan Street? Fine, good, all well. How's college going? Good. Are you learning anything? Not really—and walked over to the boat harbour. It was early afternoon, not a good time to catch fish but now I was burning with indignation and hurt pride—how could she think I would want a boyfriend, and why would she diminish the love I felt for her? Of course I was sixteen and not able then to think of it from her point of view. For instance, I couldn't imagine wanting a man. That came later.

The feeling that I didn't exist, or if I did, it was only in a ghostly form, returned. The river itself was real, the sky, Kooragang Island, but I wasn't there.

In the following months, between these times of non-existence were moments and even sometimes hours where I did again feel my existence—or if not exactly that, then the sensation of the river wind on my face, and the noticing of the tide, would make me forget for a while that I was nobody.

That afternoon, fishing alone for the first time, my mind dissolved under the power of the sun on the water and slow pelican flights from the tops of poles to fish they had seen, or shadows of fish. I stopped thinking about myself and had a great sense of relief. After the third throw I felt a jolt in the rod and the reel was spinning; something had taken the line and was swimming swiftly upriver with it. The tide was coming in. I clicked the lever over and started to wind in against a fish that was really fighting, swerving and diving with the bait. It was a good rod and the line had plenty of breaking strain. I pulled in a good-sized flathead, and not long after I caught another one, a bit smaller but enough to feed three men.

Months later when it seemed unbearable I called in with some flannelette shirts from the op shop and she was milder.

There was no more flirting. There was simply getting through it. The eyes did not light up but kept to the surface of the beer or the table or the Form Guide or the cigarette. There was occasional humour but it was kept tight near the lip.

I continued to visit but ironically it was Jock who was now friendly to me. He did not go so far as hello, but came out of his shed and grunted or nodded at me. When I first went there I wondered why he was too ignorant to speak properly as I had been taught. Look the person in the eye and speak properly. He never did this. He had no pretences so every emotion was registered even fleetingly on his face or in his posture. And his kindness to me at that time I took for an acknowledgement that his wife was treating me so coldly. He may have wished to compensate somehow, at any rate, I smiled and said good day. And so there was a sort of truce area between the back gate, passing the shed, the vegetable beds, and the back door, where the icy treatment would begin.

7 Canberra And Slovenia

A pressing topic

But back to the gardener. I interrupted that story, perhaps to try to make sense of it. I worked with her—that is, the gardener—in the paddock, in order *to be near her*. Is there something wrong with me? The hardest thing is to try to understand yourself.

It was a hot afternoon. I picked up my thistling tools and said I had to be off. The gardener looked up and smiled, thanked me for coming over. I didn't thank myself, or the situation, or her. I looked up at the cloudless sky and went to my car. Driving back to the farm I thought, This is the last time I'll drive between these two places.

The white dust from the road kicked up by the car rose and stirred in the rear vision mirror.

Soon it would be time to go to Canberra for the residency, and I would be living at my sister Kathleen's house, in among her family and friends. I knew that it was time to get out of the farm: we'd had five good years. I say good.

I parked the car and called my dog and went down the track to Bird's shed where she had the forge going. I offered to pump the bellows for her and we worked steadily for a while.

I had something to discuss with her. Bird knew I needed to get out or I would end up with real problems. Give me another month or so, she said. And, How will you cope with Canberra?

I watched her feeding the forge and kept my eye on the burning glow till I couldn't stand it anymore.

I put the farm up for sale and packed my things. Mase and Saille had moved on, and the last person who'd shared the place with me, Ruth, who had become a good friend, shy, quiet Ruth, was happy to receive Greta. She took Greta to Melbourne.

After I left, Bird stayed, packing up her anvil and forge and tools, and met the new owners who came over to visit on their horses. We talked on the phone. Brendan the mud man was sad, she said. He liked being able to visit us. And the kids loved her cottage with its 'real witch'.

Did you even say goodbye to him? she said.

I dropped in for a hug on my way north.

Yeah. She paused. He's a good hugger.

What's happening with Glenda and Lindy?

I have no idea. I miss Glenda's little boy.

I miss the smell of the air at the farm. Kathleen's a great comfort.

Will you stay in Canberra?

Probably. There are four universities here. Have you decided where to go?

Darwin, I reckon. Barry's just been serviced and I'm on the road, in my mind. I had a goodbye dinner at Radclyffe the other night.

I don't want to hear about it.

OK Ham, OK.

I love you Bird.

Same.

Exhibitions of the metal

She did the long drive from Majorca to Darwin and rang when she got there—had to drop a reconditioned engine in, in Alice. Otherwise all good. She sounded dusty, tired.

Then we were not too good at staying in touch. I knew she was having exhibitions of the metal. Successful exhibitions. She began to win prizes.

Then I rang for her birthday and it went to message, and she didn't call that night or the next few days. I was walking to the phone to ring again when it rang, a voice I didn't know, Bird's first girlfriend in Australia, still good friends, Therese. I had heard of Therese. Her voice went small.

Yes, there was a reason Bird had not called me back.

Bird is dead, car accident, going down to Katherine for an opening …

No.

… she was with her new girlfriend and the girl's mother, they're both OK but the car hit the gravel at 100k when Bird leaned over to do something, car flipped a few times, they think it broke her neck … The last thing she said to her girlfriend was, "I'm trying to stay".

OK. So she's never calling back for her birthday.

She's never calling back, Therese said.

I should have gone to the funeral. I realise that now.

Maybe I didn't have enough money to suddenly get to Darwin but I should have borrowed some and gone. It was just poverty thinking. I heard later from Sal that they had a fire on the beach where her friends read Doll Drone's poems. By then Bird had been cremated and her ashes were sitting in an urn on the sand. Like she was watching us, Sal said. They built a raft out of driftwood and scavenged stuff, and made a mast and tied her scarves to it, then attached to the deck a packet of her poems, a packet of lentils, and the number plate from her now defunct ute. Other things she'd always had about her. Certain shells. A home-made icon. Awards from the Northern Territory government for sculptures she'd exhibited in competitions. Photos of her harrow coat-racks and her metal and bone birds. Then they strapped on the urn and someone in a kayak towed it out to sea.

Let her go, Sal said.

Let her go.

Canberra

I had not known the answer to Bird's question How will you cope with Canberra? And yet I lived there for eighteen years. Most of it very good—differently good. Even semi-pastoral, in its way. Suburbs that backed onto small mountains. People with chooks and wood stoves. Big street trees. Brainy women in Blundstones. Interesting men who knew about Anglo-Saxon poetry or Bach fugues.

Then the bureaucracy, permeating discussions at parties, affecting behaviour and language, but I expected that. I didn't quite expect people being described by numbers, but I got used to that too. 'She's a six now.' 'Gee, that's good.'

Once the farm sold, I bought a courtyard flat in Fox Place in Lyneham, within a short walk of Booklore, a good second-hand bookshop, also near cafes, Tilley's and The Front. I settled there. Ben was in the Australian Federal Police in Sydney by then, and sometimes came to visit as he would be in Canberra doing a course. Eventually he worked in CPP, Close Personal Protection, and because he kept fit and didn't drink or smoke, he was in demand and eventually became part of the team working as bodyguards for Prime Ministers. I would find out he had been with Rudd to Iraq or Afghanistan.

My sister Kathleen and her family lived in Lyneham, and these were the years I really got to know and love her—six years younger than me, and often silent as a child, she was somewhat of a mystery until I shared her life. She was protective of me when I had a series of love situations that didn't work out and then over a few winters I had some bouts of pneumonia and was quite ill—she really looked after me and tried to keep me fit and well. During these years I helped Kathleen and Steve raise their daughter Rosie, minded her a lot, wrote stories with her. She helped me feed my rabbits and chooks, and we walked Otter my dog. Being with Rose was like having a daughter.

We drove north for Uncle Norm's funeral. He had made it to 86, and was Mum's last sibling to die. The next time we saw Mum, she was wearing one of Norm's shirts. In dividing up his few goods, she had taken two of his shirts, and, true to her upbringing with the seamstress aunties, cut them down to fit herself. Still sewing in her late eighties. The shirts were the last vestige of her immediate family.

One day I went into the centre of town to see a woman from the Literature Board who was giving advice to people who were applying for a grant.

I want to write a novel, I said.

Have you written a novel before?

No. I ghost-wrote an autobiography once. I co-wrote an English textbook. Otherwise, all poetry.

Uh huh. All right, well, safer for you to apply for poetry. Any ideas?

Ideas?

About what you might write.

I don't invent topics, if that's what you mean.

How do you write your poems?

I hesitated.

OK. What if you had a sort of unifying idea.

Write to a theme? I don't think so.

OK, but some readers want more than your random poems about whatever.

I thought about this for a while, then said, All right. If not a theme, then what are you suggesting?

How about a narrative. Give it some energy and motion.

Oh, OK. (I doubt she'd had time to read my poems, but I could see the sense in the idea.)

She stood and reached out to shake my hand. Sorry these sessions are so short. Best of luck!

I drove straight home and sat at my desk, scanning everything, most of it concerning *Nike*, and picked up a book on myth. Something made me go to a footnote which said, '*The Kindly Ones*, also known as *The Furies*, are three sisters who live near the gate of hell and punish wrongdoers.'

I imagined them their raising their whips and thought, But what if I brought them to Sydney for a holiday and they got part-time jobs and lived in the youth hostel?

I opened up the document for the grant application and noted my unifying idea. I then gave a few sentences with gruesome details of the life the girls had led in hell.

The rest of the form I'd already filled in, so I emailed it, opened a new document and titled it *The Kindly Ones* and began to write. When I wasn't writing, I read Robert Graves, Brewer, everyone who knew about the Furies. I found out their real names. I picked out one called Alecto to tell what happened.

The thing was writing itself. The postman came with a cheque for ten thousand dollars. The luck of the Furies was on my side.

During this time I had a phone call from my first real friend. Except for a brief school reunion during the nineties, I hadn't seen her for forty years. Sandra, who was now Sandy, had been in my first-year classes in High School. She'd been looking for me for a few years but I wasn't on social media and my name had changed. After a while I recognised her voice and we fell easily into conversation—she would be coming to Canberra soon to a Collectibles Fair at the Albert Hall—could we meet?

She reminded me that we had been so close we shared chewing

gum and walked around the playground with our arms around each other.

I had no memory of this.

Remember I used to visit you on my pony? she said.

Oh?

Well you had all those sisters and cousins and I had no sisters—it was heaven to me at your place.

But you had a brother?

We didn't get on.

You rode all the way from the top bridge to the bottom end of town to see us.

Yes! Do you remember how Ricky was so tame we could leapfrog onto his back?

Oh—yes, I said.

Some months later my cousin Janet began emailing me slides from the collection her father had made during our childhoods. There was Ricky and there were my cousins David and Janet and my sister Gwennie. Sitting on the fence is my sister Trisha, waiting her turn.

I went to the Albert Hall on the appointed day, and while I was speaking to the people at the desk, Sandy, unseen by me, came out from the hall and approached me from behind and wrapped her arms around me. Warm and friendly as she had been in childhood, she took me in to meet her husband and show me their stall of jewellery and vintage things. Blonde and blue-eyed and vivacious as ever, she kept touching my arm and was so pleased to see me. It took me a while to warm up, because I couldn't remember why we had stopped being friends in our third year of High School and I had slowly befriended Barney and Hazel and sat with them instead.

When we went to the coffee room I asked her about this and she looked surprised.

You mean you don't remember the letter you wrote me?

Uh, no.

Well, I was interested in a boy and had started going out with him—we must have been fourteen by then—and you wrote and said, basically, I had to choose—it was him or you. And—it was the year we were all getting boyfriends—I chose him.

I've no memory of writing the letter, I said. I wasn't getting a boyfriend, or wanting one. I do remember feeling different, not knowing why ... Ah Sandy, look, I was probably in love with you and didn't even realise it, or know it was a thing that could happen, no one ever spoke of it then. I'm sorry I was so naïve and intense and sorry it broke up our friendship.

She reached out and took my hand. Never mind, she said, let's be friends now. I missed you! Russel was so pleased I found you. Did you become gay?

I certainly did.

Well, good.

We remembered some of the teachers, and the bachelor headmaster who had brought in a workman to paint a line down the middle of the playground, boys on one side, girls on the other. If you so much as put the toe of your shoe on the line, you were on detention. I put my shoe on the line now and then not because I wanted to get to know the boys, but in protest at the stupidity of the whole idea. The genders were so separated in everything we did, that I wonder how the girls who wanted boyfriends organised to speak to them. But I never had the interest to find out.

Because I kept stepping over the line they made me a prefect in Fourth Year. It was later explained to me that this was a piece of reverse psychology, to make me think I was well-behaved and fitted in. I watched the playground below from my post at the window on the first floor.

I was supposed to watch behaviour on the stairs but I wasn't about to tell other kids what to do. In the strong sunlight of summer I was looking at the shadows of kids in the playground. In time I saved up and bought a small Kodak, and started taking pictures from my window. At the end of my shift I flattened the tail of my tunic and climbed onto the polished wooden bannister and slid down to the landing, navigated the turn, and slid down to the ground floor, where one day I landed in the arms of the shy bachelor headmaster. We disentangled ourselves, both mightily embarrassed. He took me to his office where he punished me by letting me choose a boiled lolly from the jar on his mantle-piece.

A few boys showed an interest in me but I didn't know how to react to them and wasn't attracted to them except as people, their nature or their character. I didn't want them physically, and had no idea what other girls were going through with their crushes on boys and their hormones running. My hormones didn't kick in till I was almost sixteen, my last year of school, and by then I knew I liked girls—that is, I had a crush on my geography teacher who had green eyes and who I walked around the playground with when she was on duty. We talked about music and she invited me to her flat to hear records a few times. She wasn't that much older than us. I think now she must have known no one in the town when she was sent there, and was probably lonely. Still I wouldn't have called it a crush, since I didn't know you *could* get a crush on a person of the same sex. I doubt I knew the word crush. It was never mentioned. I had never heard the word lesbian.

Meantime Tommy and I were writing letters and I couldn't wait to see her again.

At the Albert Hall Sandy and I sat drinking our coffee and looking into each other's eyes the way we used to do.

I'm glad you became who you were meant to be, she said. My daughter's gay. She's living in Paris with her girlfriend.

Right, I said.

That night I was talking to Sal on the phone when she mentioned that Mase had died. Bowel cancer. She was forty-eight.

Had she gone back to Inverell?

Yes, to her mother's.

The mother had never believed her—about what the uncle did—but now the mother did believe her. She cared for Mase to the end. I was surprised and sad that Mase hadn't rung me when she knew she was a goner, but maybe there wasn't time. Or she was past caring.

*

At first it was difficult, but eventually I made good friends in Canberra. I also began to attend to my spiritual life, and I'm still reading Saysana's guru's book 'You Are That'. (My answer is always, What?) Mysterious, slow-moving in me, what another friend ironically—and yet not—calls 'our search for truth and inner peace'.

Saysana was a student at one of the universities where I taught, and he and Jerome and Kenny, all gay, had befriended me.

Later Saysana took me to the Central Coast to visit his friend Matthew, and they became the best men at our wedding. We have adopted them as brothers, since Charlotte has three sisters and I have five, and neither of us has any brothers.

I have wondered how often it is that women from all-girl families have married other women.

It was while I lived in Lyneham that I met Charlotte. I was away at a Writing Teachers Conference in 1996 at UTS in Sydney when I saw her across the room and instantly went towards her, assuming from her look and manner that she was gay—then halfway through our conversation I happened to look at her left hand. Immediately I tried to wind myself down but we were on a roll and gave each other our addresses and said, Come and visit. She lived on a few acres on the outskirts of Sydney. I kept her address in my wallet but never went to visit. She never came to visit me.

Almost ten years later, I was tutoring at a week-long residential summer school in Wollongong when I saw her name on my class list. I went to the room early and she came in before the others.

We've met before, I said.

It was obvious we remembered each other very well. In my mind I took out my wallet and unfolded the paper with her address.

I kept your address, too, she said.

Soon the others came in and I had to pretend there was no electricity in my body or in the room, and act as normal.

We had time off after lunch every day and Charlotte mentioned she'd brought her bike and was going bird-watching down the bike path. We hired one for me and set off. At an inlet some undistinguished-looking (to my eye) brown and white birds were grazing in the tide.

Godwits, Charlotte said. They come from Siberia every year.

Would you like to come swimming with me tomorrow in the sea pool further south? I said.

This time instead of ignoring each other's addresses we decided we'd become friends, since we couldn't do anything about the fact that she was married, had two adult children, and loved her husband.

Perhaps she would have been gay had there been any context for it when she was courting—then again, perhaps not: she wanted children and in some ways was quite conventional. I really wanted her though. Still I was used to repressing, I knew all about that, and we kept it as a friendship for years, writing letters, talking on the phone, visiting each other and not letting things go beyond the bounds of a close affection.

I remember my niece Sophie saying when she met the man she would later marry, 'He's my person'. I felt that about Charlotte, she was my person, but I had to be content with what we had. And that was a lot. We both wrote books and taught writing, we liked the frugal life, and Charlotte had I think five degrees including a doctorate in medieval literature. Useless, as it turned out, except in a spiritual sense, although no doubt it helped get her the job teaching at a private girls' school where she then worked. We rowed out to an island in the lake. I asked her what texts she had read and she quoted *Piers Plowman* —'so I hope to have of Him that is almighty/ a gobbet of his grace and begin in time'.

One time when Charlotte was coming to stay for a few days she rang to say she had been monstered by a dog when riding her bike on a backroad, and had come off and broken her ankle. Later she arrived on crutches. We had been talking for a few months about the possibility of her coming to live in Canberra. It would be a momentous step for her and I didn't let myself believe it would happen.

That was fourteen years ago and she is still my person. Eventually we were married: by then we had moved to Davo and had grandchildren.

When we were planning the wedding her granddaughter Iris said to her, But Granny, who will wear the *dress*?

Well, it won't be me, Charlotte said.

Charlotte's son and daughter slowly got used to the new situation. Jocelyn, Charlotte's daughter, and her husband Martin played and sang at our wedding. I wore a sunfrock and black tights and red dancing pumps, and we asked the guests to wear some item of clothing from an op shop.

The marriage equality YES vote hadn't happened yet, but the bridesmaids had found out if one of you had a British passport, you could be married under British law, on what was technically British land, the High Commission in Canberra.

As we processed in, four of Charlotte's five grandkids waved rainbow ribbons: Elias, Jude, Farley and Iris. Baby Jim was in a pouch on Martin's stomach. Later, Martin played the sousaphone, such a huge instrument that the bell almost bumped the chandelier in the big room of the house where a woman called Menna, the High Commissioner, dressed in a cocktail frock, married us in an atmosphere of great gaiety. She had also married our bridesmaids.

The gay men in the room, Saysana, Matthew, Mr Cha Cha, Kenny, Lewis and others, admired as much as we did our celebrant's blue frock and her savoir-faire.

Charlotte's sister Victoria had made a large cake and iced it with scenes of our life in Davo: the estuary and ducks and pelicans. The grandchildren cut the cake with a ceremonial sword that had come down through Charlotte's family from military men, including her father, who had captained a submarine during the war.

Our fathers had by then died, but both our mothers were at the wedding. Charlotte's mother Zan, who would never have accepted her as gay when she was twenty-two and married Bob, was now at one with the proceedings, loving to us both. Perhaps partly she enjoyed herself so much because it was *political.* Her last protest at age ninety-eight was about the Adani coal-mine.

My mother was wary and found it very difficult to understand but had made herself attend to show she loved me anyway. Still, it really wasn't her scene. In the photos she has a rather fixed smile.

Slovenia 2011

Making room for Charlotte, I was unpacking a box of photo albums one morning in the flat in Canberra. Instead of sorting and throwing out, I travelled far inside myself for a few hours looking at photos of Tommy and Violet and the Wreck and the breakwater. Maybe I was looking for the person I was, before all that I encountered in this world. I sat transfixed, mystified. Just where was the authentic self, before all the stories began, before the restless forgetting of everything as soon as it happened. Before the drift of dissociation.

I picked up an album of the years with Joe, the wedding, my seemingly confident smile, Ben as a baby and toddler, some old photos Joe had given me of his family and the farm in Slovenia. Skinny beautiful eastern European children. A mountain in the background. I rarely opened my photo albums. The consequence of looking in these books was days of feeling numb and disturbed. But at last I was going to see Slovenia.

We were planning three months in Europe and would be visiting Joe. In the last few years he had returned there to live in a flat above the river in Celje, the small town closest to the farm where he had grown up.

From the train in the town of Celje we went to a public square, large and open, where there was a church with the homeless having a quiet smoke on the front steps. They watched people appear and go into the shops around the square. In my memory there were large linden trees but I may have planted them, so to speak. And even now I have to watch myself and the seemingly inborn desire to decorate or embellish a story; the unreliable narrator will crop up and begin to take over my mouth before I've had time to think about it. Now, I'm on my guard. I watch for that persona and make an effort to tell the truth, those bits I recall.

We came up some stairs into a higher street where Joe was waiting, recognisably himself, same eyes. We allowed ourselves a hug. I introduced Charlotte as my friend and she hugged him, saying she had heard a lot about him. He laughed.

At a shady café we sat at an outside table. We had told him on the phone from Australia that we'd be staying at Villa Ainu, outside the town.

I just first time go there, Joe said. I wasn't sure what he meant and looked at him.

Villa Ainu, he said, I went on train, talk to the man.

Oh!

I tell him two friends mine are coming name Susan and Charlotte and are book with him, better he make everything good for them because they are both writers and might write bad review if everything not good. He laughed.

We didn't think it was funny but what can you do, he thought he was doing us a favour.

He had been to a medical appointment as he now had diabetes and sometimes had to eat lollies if he was losing energy. Soon a woman came up to join us and he introduced her as Sonja, a quiet Croatian who was, it seemed, his girlfriend.

He had not mentioned her before, except to Ben, on the phone. He always had bad luck with women, but this time he said, he had it figured out: this woman was deaf and dumb.

Ben took it as a joke and had told us the story before we left, but now in the square of the old town when we spoke to Sonja, she answered in Croatian in a voice which told us she had probably been born deaf and had learned to speak later rather than earlier.

On the bus to the restaurant, I sat with Joe. I could hear Charlotte behind us, telling Sonja things in English and Sonja replying in Croatian or maybe Slovenian. She had no English at all. When I looked around, they were drawing pictures of their families and explaining them to each other.

I turned to face the front again and said to Joe, Do you remember anything specific about our past?

Yes, he said, when you tell your parents we decide to get marry, and I was there, your father said something bad about me, I'm not good enough or no, you will regret, he said, regret.

To me?

Yes. And you said to me, If father doesn't want us get marry, you can choose be with me, and not go home. He waited, then said, You don't remember?

I had defended him. It meant so much to him, since he'd lost most of his own family to another country, that I ought to have remembered.

I turned to him and said Yes, I remember now.

And later as we travelled through even more scenic country with green rolling hills and a distant huge mountain and the smells of summer, I said that seven of my books had been published. Did he know that?

Susan, when you leave I cry for two years then I have to get on with my life.

*

I was hoping Joe had got the keys to the farmhouse where he had grown up. I knew it would be tiny—two rooms. Joe's niece Karmen and her daughter and grandchildren had come in their van to drive us further inland to the farm.

Shrines of the saints appeared in the corners of fields in the hilly country. Protection for the crops. At Joe's farm there was a tree I had only heard about in songs, a linden tree, very tall and wide, which Joe said he had planted when he came back from being a medic in the army. That was sixty years ago, he said, in wonderment.

Karmen gestured to a small two-room white-plastered building, now closed up, that was the farmhouse. It had a big chimney. Behind it, down a hill was the river, from where all their water had to be shipped in buckets. There was no electricity, they had lamps. When it was really cold, twenty below freezing, temperatures unimaginable to me, they slept on ledges built around the big stove. I wanted to look in the windows.

But after saying we couldn't get in, Joe turned and went down a slope to a paddock where his neighbour was ploughing with a tractor. Karmen said the neighbour rented those paddocks from Joe's brother Branko, who now owned the house as his holiday house. He still lived in America.

Only later did I understand that Joe may have turned away from the house because of his shame that it was so small and poor, for a mother and nine kids. We didn't even look in the windows.

He stood talking to the man at the tractor while we looked out at fields of corn and the rich browns of the soil in the near paddock where the man had been ploughing. The man's wife then came across from their place which was behind some trees. She was carrying a bottle of wine and was wearing shorts and a shirt and had unembarrassedly hairy legs. I admired her gumption. They talked in Slovenian while we stood and breathed in the great-smelling air.

Making their own wine, eating their own corn, I said to Charlotte.

I'm with it, she said.

We went to visit Joe's cousin Aloys and his wife. They didn't know we were coming but gave us home-made lemon cordial and two kinds of cake. We were in a covered area outside the house, and I said to Joe—would it be rude of me to ask could we see inside the house? They took us proudly through, a kitsch paradise studded with gruesome crucifixes in corners, one a metre long, made of carved wood, with blood painted on Christ's side and an anguished look. Around the main crucifix were photos of the dead members of the family and we stood here being introduced to them– great-great grandmother Elisabeta, great uncle Aloys.

The room had linen cloths and candles, bowls of fruit, more photos. After you got used to the Christ it was calming to be in the room.

At one point Karmen took me aside and asked whether I had 'a person'. I can't remember what I answered. Perhaps I looked at Charlotte. Karmen then asked whether I didn't like men. I said, It's not that. I do like men.

To someone with no experience of gay people it's inexplicable, and I didn't try to explain. At any rate, many women who are currently lesbians are not only gay, but have loved men, deeply loved them.

One exceedingly fine day we drove up a hill to a castle where at the top of the stairs a medieval fair was in progress amid a smell of animals and fires. Costumed women came up to us to ask if we'd like to try their spindles. Men were standing by fires or a way off, jousting with swords, and some of the women in their long skirts were jousting. Horses stood under trees where they were tethered. A blacksmith had set up shop and was tapping at something on his anvil, the sound of metal ringing out as some heralds and pages arrived at the top of the stairs, waving flags.

A wedding party followed, the bride and groom having hired use of the castle on the same day, and various singers in their retinue were singing them into a broken part of the castle where grass was growing through and you could go up onto a battlement that overlooked a photogenic valley. The priest was a wedding celebrant but she had the sense to wear black. One of the guests waved incense before her as she walked, Nag Champa Agarbatti, I recognised the scent.

When I next looked around Joe was wearing a Viking hat and Charlotte was wearing a sort of jousting helmet and they had been given swords and were holding them aloft, smiling and fake-aggressive and ready for the fight. I watched my husband and wife setting to, stepping around each other, lunging and looking fierce, and was surprised at how muscley Joe's arms still were, at seventy-five years old, and how Charlotte, with her background in medieval literature, was enjoying being a knight.

8 TOMMY Part 2

Boyfriend

I had avoided going to Tommy's for months, and tried to take an interest in college.

It was the summer of love. In Haight Ashbury in San Francisco, people were smoking something called marijuana. I read an article about the effects of the smoke and filed the knowledge away for later. I had never heard of it. One of the boys on the college newspaper was Malcolm Frame, a bright strange man from up the valley, had a shock of brown hair and wore black-framed glasses. I decided he would be my boyfriend. Or perhaps he had flirted with me a bit and I responded.

When time came for a fancy-dress ball he dressed as a king and I was the court jester and we went together. Along with the others from the paper we decided to make Malcolm the lord: we all bowed down to him. I liked it because usually people ignored Malcolm. He took me out a few times but I couldn't imagine kissing him. Even when dressed up for a date he smelled of petrol and engines. I liked him but I wasn't girlfriend material, just pretending. But it got around I had a boyfriend and everyone calmed down about my situation, Tommy included, so I heard.

The shop

Mum and Dad had bought a small supermarket in Darby Street and began working ten-hour days. Dad had never handled money—he didn't own a wallet but took fifteen dollars from the housekeeping jar when he went for a haircut. It was the only time he really handled money. Mum did all that.

He cried, and said he *couldn't go on the till.* Years later he made himself do it, in between bouts of lying on the concrete floor in the store rooms at the back of the shop, groaning with undiagnosed stomach pains. Mum urged him to go to the doctor, but he said, What can they do?

She understood that he didn't think he ought to spend money on doctors, but just wait to get better. She could not convince him.

One rainy day I went to the shop to get fish fingers for dinner and Dad was standing near the door. Pleased to see me, he gave me a hug, when a customer came in and said, Cliff, it's *pouring* down outside! No doubt it was the tenth person who had said exactly that, and Dad snapped.

You don't say! he said, and went into the doorway and looked out as if in awe and wonder. By God and Jesus Christ, so it is, he said, it's raining, it's actually pouring down. June! he called to Mum, would you believe it? Christ Almighty who would have guessed! Would you excuse me? he said to the baffled customer, I must go and check there are no leaks on our glorious merchandise! He went out the back to the stockroom and sat shaking for a while.

I decamped to Violet's for a few months.

Talking to Linda

Across the river, Dad was on the lounge, *hors de combat*, he said. He'd used this phrase a lot in Inverell, too. I barely knew what it meant—out of battle?

I got the lowdown on family doings from Linda in the kitchen. She said it was a relief not to have to cover up for me any more, since she had always backed me up in my lies about the various places I went, when in fact I always went to Tommy's. I said, Sorry sis, I didn't realise. She looked at me and said, It was major. Major.

Where did you say I'd gone?

Just so you know, you've been to the beach a lot, out with Pinky, out with Pinky's sister and her friends from uni, out at the uni checking out the courses (this was true), and at the library. You've been to the Vienna café at the top of Hunter Street, and you've been to a nightclub.

A nightclub? Maybe we *should* go to one.

You already have. I 'confessed' that we had sneaked out one night and been to watch some jazz at a nightclub.

This was plausible, as I had recently bought a clarinet and was having lessons. The false confession my sister had made was impressive—it conveyed a deeper-seeming truth which more effectively hid the lie.

Why don't we do that then, I said.

Why don't we, Linda said.

I don't know why they ask you and not me—they never ask me anything.

Linda thought about this and said, You might tell them too much.

That is, they can rely on you for the plausible lie, I said to her.

Maybe. It might be what they prefer.

Years later, after I was married, Linda told me that when Dad had found the letter in the sock, he had gone over to Stockton the following day in a rage and visited Tommy and told her he *knew what was going on* and that it had better stop or he would go to her work and make sure she *lost her job*. He had gone to see her while Jock was out on the boat, and probably really frightened her.

In all the time Tommy had been cold, this possibility had not occurred to me. Perhaps because my father had so recently defended me to the college principal. Some deeper level of naivety in me must also have expected Tommy to tell me that Dad had visited, so I would have an understanding of the coldness. But since she so infrequently spoke about personal things, why would she have told me? Why would I expect her to tell me?

When I finished college a telegram came, saying I was to take up a teaching post in a primary school in Wentworthville. I rang the Department and they explained it was a suburb in western Sydney. In that first year I met and moved in with Joe, and every holiday we came home to Newcastle.

The factory

In Tommy's kitchen, I told her I was going to marry a man called Joe, and that I was already living with him. His sister, a Catholic, I said, often had the priest around for afternoon tea, was quite upset, was pushing for us to marry.

Tommy affected no interest but then allowed herself to ask what Joe did for a living. I said he worked at Hardy Rubber, a factory in Lidcombe. He took the train to work. She was drinking hard now, and had already had five or six glasses by my reckoning, given her slightly manic mood and the determination to enjoy herself. She lit two Viscounts and passed me one.

What does he do at the factory?

Do you have any Peck's Paste? I said. I got up and opened her fridge.

I took out the little jar and opened it, then took out the washer from inside the lid.

Joe made this, I said. He's the only person in Australia making the washers for these jars.

What, she said, so he stands there, in front of this big kind of—

Egg-slicer, I said, only it's a big machine. He feeds a rubber tube into it, presses a button, and the lid of the machine comes down and cuts the tube into washers.

And does it again and again, she said.

Well it's probably better than working in the Pig Mill at the BHP, I said. Or getting up at three a.m. every day and going to the boat and going out to sea in sometimes huge seas, when you never learned to swim. Or trying to control forty or more active and bored nine-year-olds and teach them spelling rules, when they have a parent in gaol, or they haven't had breakfast, and can't concentrate.

I did not mention hosing down lunatics, as they were then known, in back wards at Stockton Mental Hospital, those ones who were raving and violent or self-harming. Tommy had done that at eighteen years old, the time when she started drinking, and was courting Jock.

Did you know those kids hadn't eaten? She said this to me in a softer voice. Before they came to school?

I looked at the floor and shook my head.

We had moved on from my fiancé, to forms of labour, to hungry kids—obviously we were not going to be discussing the wedding and Tommy would not be coming.

Padlock

I went to see her the day before the wedding, and we sat at the small table eating tomatoes on toast. We were polite and friendly and both hungry. We made some more toast and put Peck's Paste on it, with a second cup of tea. She did not come to the wedding. It was only when I'd had a child and was living back at Violet's—Joe had got a job at the steelworks—that Tommy and I became friends again. That is, it was safe for us to be together again because I had married. At any rate, she treated me better once I had a man working shifts as a fitter-and-turner's mate, and a baby. Perhaps she thought she had wrecked my life (she had said this: 'I wrecked your life once before') yet now it seemed she had not. After all, things were OK. We began fishing again and I helped her kids with their homework. She gave me the same looks, but muted, ironic, and touched my hand sometimes as if by accident.

Once when she had gone up to the back shed for something I went quickly into her bedroom, looking for what? I didn't really know—opened the dressing-table drawer and in a mess of photos found one of Tommy when young—perhaps twenty—photographed out with two of her friends—her beauty shining through. I put it in my pocket and returned to the kitchen just before she came back in. I still have this photo.

The next time I visited Tommy alone, and she went out to get the washing in, I went to the new indoor toilet and passing her bedroom door I noticed a small padlock had been put on the door. Nothing was ever said.

A wife

After the wedding we had returned to Blacktown, where I was now teaching, and I tried to put on the mantle of a wife. It was a category error, I later discovered, but I tried because I loved Joe and unlike my father, he wasn't at the mercy of his temper.

None of the pressure I felt to get married was ever explicit. Joe seemed relaxed and was fun to be with.

I was learning basic Slovenian, and things were affable and friendly. 'Jaz te ljubim, ugazni luc.' ('I love you, turn out the light.')

Then Joe's behaviour began to change. I realise now that he had a war trauma but at the time his actions were mystifying and his need to win and to control the situation came out, having been hidden under his bonhomie during courting and the first months of marriage. He wanted a child straight away. I was nineteen and not ready but didn't know how to talk to him about it. He kept mentioning that my mother had six kids, and it seemed that the person he really wanted was Mum—I was thirteen years younger than him and Mum was only seven years older than him. Perhaps he thought I would be a version of Mum and was frustrated and angry that he kept butting up against this unexpected person—that I was not a replica of Mum.

That I wanted to study.

Soon enough though, Joe and I were living on Stockton in the back bedroom, and beside us on the floor was Ben's bassinet. I was happily breast-feeding him and he was no trouble, a good baby. Joe hadn't yet started on about taking him to Slovenia and never coming back. At night when Joe was on shift I put Ben in his pram and walked him around to get him to sleep. Then at times I called in at Cardigan Street and put the pram where we could see and hear him at the back steps and I went in for a visit. At times Tommy was drunk and playful, but never so drunk that it showed.

She went to work over town, crossing the river on the ferry, and she made the payments on the house from then.

I never saw Jock kind or polite to his wife but they stayed together and she was nursing, or nurse's aide, at Royal Newcastle Hospital, and he had to give up fishing because his back was finished. The fishing families watched their sons buying new boats and installing GPS, driving around in flash cars, and building double-storey houses on the beachfront. The older fishermen were disgusted with their sons having all this stuff, and the easy life they had. Some ability to understand water surfaces and the fish was being lost—GPS showed them where the schools were.

Eventually, Joe and Ben were included in the fishing expeditions on the Wreck. I witnessed Joe's joy at catching a bream. Like my grandparents' generation, he didn't like to buy food if there were other ways to get it. He liked that Violet had a supply of old or broken things to use to fix other things.

Whacka

Years later when I was separated from Joe and living in Leichhardt, I often took Ben to Violet's in the school holidays. We built driftwood castles on the beach and swam when the surf was safe.

One year when I called at Tommy's, her son Peter was there: he was grown-up and had apprenticed with his father, and now had one of the biggest and best equipped boats in the Stockton fleet. He was driving a powder blue Volvo.

We ate lamb shank soup and discussed Peter's boat, what lobsters were worth. The authorities were talking about over-fishing. Quotas were coming in, on the size of the catch—and he might not afford two deckhands soon. Tommy spat at the idea of quotas, and I didn't engage in an environmental debate.

Peter said he might have to let go of Whacka Vial. I tried not to laugh but he saw me and grinned. Oh, there's plenty, he said, and named other deckhands on Stockton—and other mates of his—Sorry Maurie, Whingin' Pete. Stories about Bent Bing, Looney Laurie, things Craze did...

...then there's Eyebrows, he said, name's Wally Smith—alias Bob Hawke—he's growing his eyebrows so they can cover up his bald head. Pop Eye, he said. Big George, Hurricane Harry. Wok Eye, he's got jealous eyes, one eye watching the other, you know—

Mick the Knife, his mother said, Honest Phil the Deputy Lord Mayor.

Seedy Mick, Big Chappo the Log. Big lump of shit. Scaly Tom.

What about Mick, that used to work for you, his mother said.

Worm Bait! Peter says. His mate, Chocka Block.

What about the jelly blubber crowd?

Don't know much about them. Surf club blokes. Sharkey This—Sharkey That—

The talk turned to neighbours and Betty Skews' dead husband's cocky, whose claw was eaten by a fox at Fullerton Cove. When the grown-up daughter visited with her kids and it was time for them to go, Betty's dead husband's cocky screeched from the cage

'Leanne, get in the car.

Leanne, get in the car.'

The high nasal whine on the name turned it into 'Le*Yanne*! Get in the car!'

The following day Peter came again to see his mother. Sometimes he was mean to her or had moved one of her hoses and not put it back and she would be angry for a week. He was rarely affectionate but regular in his visits. He would have a ginger beer, and stood in the door as there were only two chairs at the small table. This day he took something from his pocket when he came in, and handed it to me. It was a seahorse, about as long as your palm, its tail coiled, dry as paper and with holes for eyes and an open flute of a nose. I thanked him and went to secrete it in my bag.

Show me that! Tommy said. She looked at it carefully then gave it back to me. When Peter left, she said in a low voice, He's never given me a seahorse.

Why don't you ask him for one? I said, unwilling to give up mine.

She snorted and went out into the garden where she gave Jock's choko vine, from which he made the pickles, a 'hard prune'.

Loyalty

After six different lawyers, I finally gained custody of Ben, and he came to live with me at the beginning of third class. We lived in the Leichhardt house, which I had bought with my boyfriend, also a poet. It was a relief to have proper time with Ben, though I was also busy with writing and teaching and book launches. I was putting together the manuscript of my first book of poems.

Still, my loyalty to Tommy did not falter. When I needed a week somewhere quiet to get my book in order, it was Tommy that I rang. She found me a cottage in a friend's back garden in Shoal Bay, up north. My boyfriend agreed to mind Ben.

I spent most of the week working on the poems, and in between bouts of writing went down to the beach where a man rented out small catamarans, Hobie cats. Worked off a sail only, yet they could go so fast. He said I would be able to do it and taught me the principles. Almost every day I went and sailed the catamaran which was my first strong experience of independence and exhilaration, the wind, the sun and the lapping waves, the strength of the surf, the speed of coming in to the beach with a following wind.

During the week, Tommy arrived with some flathead and other supplies, and I talked her into staying the night. Although I had the boyfriend at the time, I still wanted her, and she fought with herself about giving in to me, to the extent that she took a shower and let me scrub the barnacles as she called them from her back—for some reason her back had gone kind of scaly—and after we cooked and ate the fish she agreed to sleep with me that night and go home in the morning.

Sleep, she said, emphasising the word.

Yes, I understand, I said.

Yet in the night she did allow herself to touch me, not that I could feel much, after so many years of repression, but something at least had happened, and when I wanted to touch her she said there were areas of her body which were 'frozen zones', that there would be no point. I cuddled into her back and tried not to fall asleep—it would be my only experience of sleeping the night with her and I knew that.

Diary 1986

Tommy is my project. She's like an island I keep visiting. Then again, I go away to my world to create more of the me that is not her.

After twenty-three years, and a whole life I've constructed outside of her, it is a controlled enrapturement I feel. I see who she is, a middle-aged woman beginning to loosen and sag in the normal places, weather-beaten, and I have to force myself to take this information in, since I had her surrounded by my love in an indestructible glow of the way she looked and acted then.

Now I watch who she is—controlling, tight, can't talk about her feelings, hardly refers to the past, not reflective.

I watch how I keep trying to resurrect her. She won't live and she won't die. I looked at her palm today, in the car. The lifeline clear and deep.

Jock on the floor

Jock had retired because of back trouble—he was in his sixties then. He would be in his shed as you came down the sandy track to the house. He was making string bags because after all it was making nets. It was something he could do in his retirement. I sat with him in the shed for half a day while he showed me how to make a string bag, and it was strange and comforting to be able to sit with him and make something. The string bag had essentially the same knots as he had used for making nets, before bought nets came in.

When I got back home, she rang to tell me Jock had died.

His lungs—he'd been smoking Log Cabin since he was nine. He had got out of bed one night and kneeled on the bedside mat and coughed up blood and then he died right there on the mat, heaving and grunting. Tommy had sprung up and tried to help him. Even then he was angry and pushed her away. Angry that he was dying, she said—she didn't take it personally.

Sorry to hear that, I said. There was a long silence.

I gave up smoking, I said. On the tenth of March.

That's strange, she said, her voice soft, So did I. On the tenth of March.

I think she stayed off tobacco for a few years.

She put his ashes on the mantelpiece next to a photo of her squatting near a rose garden in her nurse's uniform, before her marriage, when she worked up the Mental. Looking beautiful in her uniform.

It was at this time, during the veneration of the ashes, that she told me Jock could sing, one of the very few facts she mentioned about him—usually there was no small talk, just the practical detail of getting fish gutted or cooking a meal. She said that part of his courting was singing to her, down on the boat wharf at the ballast. She was seventeen and working shifts up the Mental and came down to Stockton with the other nurses to have a few drinks.

No one else I knew including the kids had ever heard him sing. We had heard him moan when he was drunk, and we had heard him grunt.

How complicated and quiet Jock was. The fact that he had a tender side, and had courted her.

A hundred sparrows

I can smell her fire from Violet's. I note the direction the smoke's coming from, and the fact that between here and her house, there aren't any people left on Stockton who have wood fires. She herself doesn't still have an open fire but a slow-burner fuel stove. There's a sump oil smell from the bottom of the palings someone gave her.

Violet holds my arm as we walk. In Tommy's back-yard the lobster pots of her dead husband are stacked four-high against a long section of the fence, and in the chicken-wire of the pots are knee-high weeds, and in the top layer of pots, which actually look like bird cages, are a hundred sparrows who flock upward as Violet and I go down the brick path. Tommy is already coming towards us, as if expecting us. She takes Violet's other arm and we lean back and look at each other behind Violet's shoulders, something we must always have done.

Any encounter was both fraught with possible social errors, and profoundly open to moments of heightened experience. Any slight opportunity would be taken, for these encounters. Usually everything happened with the eyes. There would sometimes be an accompanying movement. Violet couldn't see well but her hearing was acute. Everything had to be soft, silent, gestural. Whatever could be done in front of the blind.

Violet's birthday party

When Violet turned eighty-two we gave her a small party, Mum, Uncle Norm and me. We started drinking. Norm could still drink then, hadn't yet been forced onto cat's piss by his doctor. We were drinking in earnest, I forget why. Violet was on the muscatel. Without our really noticing, she got drunk, was obviously drunk, though her manner and personality didn't change. She admitted that this was the first time anyone had thought to give her a birthday party.

Including your childhood? Mum said.

Yes, Violet said. I better give this away. She pushed her glass to the centre of the table and got up, lurched to the outside toilet and was sick. Cleaned herself up, came back in and drank a glass of water, wiped her face on her apron and suggested a game of euchre.

Seriously? I said.

Documents

Mum had been collecting birth and death certificates for the ancestors. One day leafing through one of her folders I saw a document from the Mental Hospital on Stockton, from the 1930s, the patient Violet McLean, admitted because at home she had been 'sitting on her bed all day, not speaking or responding to anyone and not eating'. Someone had to mind her three sons who were toddlers. We wondered if she had been pregnant again and bashed by Pappy for it, and lost the baby. But who knows. The dates on the form showed she had been in the Mental for seven weeks and had been visited once by her husband Norman.

We put the form back in its plastic sheet and shut the folder and put it back on the shelf in the hall. I doubt we have looked at that document again.

Much later it occurs to me that Violet might have been grieving for Mum.

My father and mother and I visit Tommy

I don't know at what stage my father was able to visit Tommy again but somehow over time they had become friends and no one mentioned the past.

One weekend when I was in town visiting my parents we all went to see Tommy and then further north to the caravan park to see Norm. It was the thing they did every Sunday. At Tommy's, Dad went in and fixed something for her in the bathroom then we had tea. She was friendly but kept the radio on down low because she was listening for a race where there was a woman jockey and she had some money on her. She liked the horses' names and read out a few. This would once have been the cue for me to play word games and I watched to see would she look at me even briefly to acknowledge this: to my surprise she did, but not so my parents would notice. When we were leaving, Dad picked up his walking stick and we set off up the path, Mum poised to catch Dad if he fell. Tommy followed us, commenting on which of Jock's garden beds she was keeping up—broccoli, beans—and when we began to cross the road to the car she called to Dad, I see you've got a bent stick, Cliff! Ah yes! Dad said quickly in the same spirit, I fear it's always been like this! My mother let this go, looking sideways at me with some mirth and a deal of embarrassment. We crossed the road and Dad waved his stick around in the air.

Options

Years later, while I was in town, Dad was taken to hospital and they diagnosed a brain tumour, inoperable. Dad had been acting strange for some time and he and Mum were having family therapy.

The doctor said we should choose a hospice or a nursing home where Dad could go and have 24-hour care.

We were in the hall before going in to Dad's ward, and I said to Mum that I wanted to tell him he was dying so he could maybe come to terms with it. At least, I felt, he had the right to know. Mum said quietly, Susan, get realistic. He will only kick up a fuss. It won't be worth it. He'll get angry and die angry. This way we say nothing, he thinks it's an exacerbation of the ataxia thing, and he dies peacefully.

I took her point and we went in. I hope someone tells me when I am dying, if I don't already know.

After Dad died I learnt how to become friends with my mother, asking after her life, listening and not talking. She had upsized and now lived in a sunny house with three lounges arranged in a U. We lay on these lounges and talked. She remembered every house Dad had built—the addresses, whether brick or timber, recalled ordering in the materials, how much the build cost. I asked whether, after the family therapy, the counsellor had talked to her at all, on her own. Yes, she said, he did, and he had leaned forward and said, Well June, what are your options?

Oh? I sat up.

Well, what a revelation. I had *options*.

We lie on the lounges and talked to her about our childhoods. Mum had turned nineteen a few months after I was born. What was that like? 'I was ready.'

I started photographing my cousins and sisters. One day they were on the fence, 'riding' a mattress. Cousin David, Kathleen, cousin Phillip, Gwennie, Trisha, Barbie, cousin Janet, Linda.

Mum's PhD

My mother by now had twenty-eight A4 ring binders of papers making up her research into the family history on both sides. It's like she's done a doctorate, several times over. She knows the full story, as far back as she could go, sometime in the 1700s. But she can't watch 'Call the Midwife'. Too much poverty. I guess it makes the ring-binders vibrate.

In the Murphy book is a paper clipping from the *Newcastle Morning Herald*, 1906. It is about Violet's grandmother, who lived in Cook's Hill, once a poor suburb of small terrace houses, now a desired inner-city suburb with a good second-hand bookshop.

Titled 'Tired of Life—a woman's death', it says.

'Shortly after eight o'clock yesterday morning, Janet Grace Murphy, aged 52, was found by her son, Charles Murphy, hanging by the neck from a rafter in an outhouse at the rear of her residence, No. 11 Union-street, Newcastle.'

Charles had gone into the yard to feed his pigeons and noticed the door of the outhouse was closed, and called his mother. She didn't answer so he 'prized the door open with an axe and was horrified to find his mother hanging from the rafter by a rope'.

He went around the corner to get his friend James Woodbine, a wharfie, to help him cut his mother down.

When the doctor came he saw the body of Mrs Murphy lying in the yard, fully dressed, 'He found life to be extinct.'

Charles worked at Arnott's biscuit factory. He said his mother had called him at 7.30 that morning and didn't look well.

On the Death Certificate Janet's father and mother are listed as UNKNOWN, meaning that her six children, aged from 15 to 31, *did not know the names of their grandparents.* One of these children, Alfred Ernest Albert Murphy, was Violet's father.

Mum's years of fossicking had found these details though I was sure she had never told Violet about the grandmother who had hung herself in the outdoor dunny in Union-street. Mum found out what she could on her own, saturating herself in the family she hadn't lived with since age two, knitting herself into their history for as far back as she could go.

Violet walked on the beach

Especially when her kids had grown up and Pappy had died, Violet had the whole of her long widowhood to contemplate. I often think about the women I knew who had these long widowhoods, fifty years in some cases. Violet had 35 years; Grandma Mackie had 40 years. Before her eyes went, Violet walked for miles on the firm sand, halfway to Nelson Bay it seemed.

One day I came in from the dunes and noticed she was very flat in her mood. She was sitting in the breakfast room, her elbows on the table, her head in her hands.

Anything wrong Violet?

She lifted herself away from the table as if she ought to go and do some work, but then stopped and quietly said, Your Uncle Carl was just here, seeing I was all right, but—no one ever touches me. They don't hug me when they come in. I don't think I've been hugged since Pappy died.

Ah, Violet. I got up and went to hug her but she broke it after a short while and backed away and it was clear she wanted a hug from a man. And what she said was true, none of the three sons ever held her. My mother would have hugged her but Violet didn't encourage it—she had trained herself to let go of Mum and couldn't now attach herself, but just received Mum's homage, the food she brought over, company, grandchildren. There was no hugging. I don't recall either of my grandmothers hugging me. That was probably normal.

Violet was now ninety-two, and standing beside the radio on the fridge. I could see from behind she was crying. A singer was just reaching the high note of Danny Boy, which I somehow knew to be the F sharp above top C, if you played the song in the key of D. Another time I found her crying in the kitchen and realised it was the anniversary of Pappy's death. He must have been kind in private, she really missed him. Every anniversary she spent the day crying.

Later she was standing in the front door looking out at Stockton Bight, a darkening blur because she was almost blind. In fact she was smelling the sea. Hearing it thump. 'Ears still good,' as she said. You can't whisper, around her. Six of her faculties were kept going by different coloured tablets—blood pressure, constipation, sleeping—I forget the others. The doctor said her heart had swelled to twice its natural size, with the effort.

Carl her youngest son now began ringing her every day, so they would know when she went. One morning she didn't pick up. He rang Mum and said, She's gone, you better come over.

Violet's funeral

Violet died at home, laid back in her recliner, the remote in her hand. Barbie and I both spoke at the funeral and I found I had no tears. At the Beresfield RSL we ate tiger prawns and talked about spanner-crabs with my cousin Andrew, Clanka and Del's son, from Mooloolaba. His brother had a team of a hundred people selling bandwidth door to door. The brother leaned over and handed me his business card.

'Check our site,' he said.

People who fell in love forty years ago are being civil and sharing a beer but we don't talk about the dead at the wake. Another thing: there's no one from Stockton here. Violet outlived all her friends. Norm's wife Betty is leaning back against the wall near the husband who left her forty years ago and attempting to flirt with him. She's tall and thin and good-looking in an androgynous way. He is ignoring her, though if she asks a question he will answer her in a word or two.

She was getting drunker, and not getting the message. He was already very drunk, immobilised in an upright position on the wall, but knew to be polite at funerals. He was waiting for it to be over, and was perhaps beyond having an interest in his nephews' spanner-crab business or what was selling into China.

While Violet burns, I drive to her old haunts: the top beach, the riverbank, her back yard.

Tommy handed me a beer and muttered something about Violet. I took it to be sympathetic; she said she'd been feeding her tripe and parsley and that she held up well till the end. We work out that Violet died while watching 'Who wants to be a Millionaire', and we start telling death jokes.

Tommy's son Peter came to the back step. He shook my hand about Violet, and looked at the ground, nodding. He shook my hand for a while longer.

Although Violet was gone, Mum continued to go to Stockton every Sunday—it was in her blood by then. First she called on Tommy, then further north to Fern Bay to see her brother Norm. This went on for years.

Best friends

One Sunday when we got to Tommy's and pulled over, my mother took a bag off the back seat and showed me two flannel shirts.

These are for Tommy, you can give them to her.

Thanks.

When we came in Tommy was on her knees in the lounge room, leaning forward and cleaning the TV screen with the sleeve of her skivvy. I had owned that skivvy for a few years, now she owned it again. When she finished she dusted herself off and caressed her sleeve, looking at me while Mum was dealing with the food she'd brought. These under-conversations buried in clothing and gesture intermittently became Tommy's main vocabulary. She kept it up even though Violet was dead and she, Tommy, was now going blind.

She was going to be cremated like Jock, and have her ashes *mixed through his* and then thrown off the boat together into Stockton bight. Her son Peter was lined up for this job. But she had lived on and on, into her eighties, when, bent and thin, her wrists bird bones, she drank from a seven glass that she kept in the fridge between sips, and smoked Horizons, just an occasional one, and no bad word to say against Jock. In their heyday she had locked him out one night and the police had to come. But that was all gone.

Now she was listening to her transistor radio which lived on the small kitchen table with some tools. She listened to a commercial station where shock-jocks told people what to think. Sometimes she repeated things they'd said, maybe about migrants, maybe about people on the dole, and I just shook my head.
There would be no point arguing.

On the table was the note from her Meals on Wheels, Laurel Gordon,

No pork, Allergies—fish.

She had become allergic to fish.

The second dog, also called Blossom, had long since died, and Peter had brought Tommy a cat from the slipway, Vinnie, now a few years old and skittish with visitors. Mum was surprised the cat had wrapped itself around her legs. Tommy said, My animals always like her.

I realised Mum had become Tommy's best friend, an irony I thought worth celebrating somehow, whether an irony of tact, or of the principle of the eternal return, I don't know. They got on very well, both ignoring the frilly side of womanhood but women's women all the same, who stand by their man. Both now lived alone. Both owned no dresses or skirts by that stage of life. Tommy had owned no makeup for forty years; my mother still had a few tubes of lipstick and a compact. They didn't talk about anything too personal. They didn't like anything that was a lot of phooey. Politicians were a lot of phooey. They could sit in companionable silence for minutes at a time.

Mum never left Tommy's place on a Sunday without saying, If you need anything, *ring me.*

If Mum let herself think about it, she must have been disturbed or annoyed at my long and pointless crush on Tommy. Mum treated me more affectionately when I married and had my son; was obviously glad I had reformed in some way. She no longer had to make excuses for me for not having a boyfriend. 'Studying too hard.'

As I sat there watching them, I worked out that Tommy was only a year younger than Mum. They had been brought up on the principles of no skiting and no gossiping; it was thought bad manners to talk about yourself, and bad manners to talk about other people. This left the weather, food, animals, shopping lists, including ideas for things to look for in the op shop, and the garden, such as it was.

Tommy asked me about family but showed no other interest in my life. I realised that although she may have loved me, she didn't actually *like* me.

She thanked me for the birthday card I'd sent. She tried to read with a magnifying glass, and my mother had read it out to her.

I asked Tommy and my mother to sit beside each other so I could take a photo. Mum put her arm around Tommy's shoulder and I took three shots, Tommy rather stiff in the first one, melting towards Mum's shoulder in the second, almost snuggled in for the third, with a slightly naughty look on her face. I had read enough Freud to look at this image with some care.

Down the bottom end

Everyone knew Tommy, and came up to her on the street, and knew she was mostly blind so would identify themselves if she didn't recognise their voice.

In the good light in front of the bank she recognised a man called Harry and held his arm while they joked about his new mobility scooter. Most of the suburb by now were old people. He told her he loved the scooter, it had changed his life. She touched the scooter and he said, It happens so fast, old age—looking at her intently.

Every sign of age you could think of showed in her face and hands, shrinking, swelling, mild bruising, boniness. She smiled, enjoying Harry's company. She had known him most of his life.

And yet, he said, look, it took eighty years to get here! She laughed with him in the sun and we went into the paper shop to check her lotto.

On the way back to her place in the car, she said that Harry told funny stories about the time when he went to sea. How once someone had died on the boat and they had thrown the body overboard in its coffin and they had forgotten to weight it, and instead of sinking, *it raced along ahead of them, bouncing up and down with the waves*. They had to put on speed to catch the coffin and let down a lifeboat to get the dead man and weight him and rebury him. Harry said that all through this happening, the men could not stop laughing, they would heave something, and laugh, or start to say something, and laugh.

When we got back to her place, Peter was sitting on the back step waiting for her.

They got down to business and started talking fishing quotas. He'd had to sack his deckhand Whacka, who had learned to drive a front-end loader and gone to Western Australia for the mining boom.

Mothers

I continued to visit Tommy up till the time of her death, when she was eighty-six. When I was in town, I always went with Mum for the visits. I sat in a chair between them at one side of the small table and didn't say much, they did the talking. It was during those visits, which went on for nearly twenty years, that I realised that Tommy had no real interest in my life. I had never given her any of my books, she would only have been embarrassed, I was sure, about any personal stuff. But for some years I did talk about being a writer, and she never had anything to say to that, even when I received grants or prizes, she just nodded. Mum reacted in much the same way.

None of the three of us had much interest in femininity, we had that in common. But when I talked about going to demonstrations or about Women's Liberation or later feminism, or the book I'd co-edited, *The Penguin Book of Australian Women Poets,* and why we thought it was necessary, Tommy just looked at the table, the salt and pepper, her little radio, the form guide, and said nothing. It wasn't a world she could relate to, any more than she could respond when I said I now had a girlfriend, and we had been camping. The word girlfriend was anathema, obviously something not said, or not said with the meaning I gave it. Even less popular was the word lesbian, which I used a few times, in a normal voice, in a normal sentence—thunderous silence. Just shook her head.

Slowly I gave up talking about my life except for work—teaching in the writing program at uni—or a more popular topic, Ben, and how he had become a policeman. She was interested in that.

The other realisation I had, as I sat there listening to them talk, was that these two women, who had worked hard all their lives, been married to difficult men, kept their side of the bargain, who had both been dedicated to Violet, had both, in essence, been motherless. That was their bond. That and keeping silent about things that cannot be understood.

At her fire

More and more photos of Jock appeared from dark recesses of the house and were put on display in the lounge room, Jock sitting on a log in the bush with his hand on Blossom's head, man and dog looking intently into the camera, Jock on the Lobster Queen, leaving the wharf. I went around the room looking at each photo. That was the time she told me he could sing. She was at her fire burning pages from a foolscap book with neat handwriting in ink. It was Jock's logbook, I now saw. She was pulling out the pages, tearing them into strips and feeding them to the fire.

What are you doing?

Might as well burn it. Peter doesn't want it. Her voice was muffled with anger.

I could see where she was about to pull out the next few pages that Jock's entries were in pen and ink, in good clear handwriting. And later, I saw, as she kept tearing and burning, some few strips escaped and lay on the carpet, —in these Peter, when apprenticed to Jock, had begun to keep the entries. His were in biro and not neat, done only because he had to, it seemed. Scrawled. Whereas Jock's were almost copperplate.

It's possible Peter didn't care enough about his father, or about his own history, to want the logbook.

It's a historical record, I said, the museum might want it.

Let them want, they're not getting it.

When she went out the back for kindling I quickly bent down and rescued quite a few torn strips from the hearth and backed away, shoving them under my jumper. I had brought her some shopping which we'd put away, and now we had a pot of tea and the usual tomatoes on toast. All the time I was trying to hide the strips of paper and prevent them falling out.

What did he sing?

Come away, you rolling river—and—I loves Irene God knows I do—bits of Danny Boy—There'll be blue skies over –

Did you know where Dover was?

Atlases were actually invented then. (She threw me a winning smile.)

I drove down to Nobby's breakwater and parked looking out at the bight. I could see the ocean where a big metal ship the Pasha Bulker had gone aground not long before. A storm was getting up and the sky had turned the sea a luminous green and down towards the Wreck and the breakwater, an almost bilious green. I took out one of the torn strips.

7th Sep
big roll on from bad weather

punching wind
1 x 42 green lobsters Sydney markets
11 lb dog shark

The scarecrow

We glided over the bridge, my mother driving, crooners on the cassette, *You and the Night and the Music, Midnight Waltz*. I told my mother I was planning an article for the Stockton Historical Society. This group met at the Prawners' Club once a month and put out a newsletter. I told her I had an agenda with Tommy, to find out more about her past, or that era of Stockton when fishing and the steelworks were the main employers.

Be ready, my mother said, she looks like a scarecrow. Skin and bone.

The BHP had closed down years before. On Kooragang we drove under the long arms of the coal-loaders. Giant tankers were taking on coal for China. Also there were FRANZEN HEUFF SKANDIA. Across the river the Stockton fishing fleet was moored on the wharf opposite the Boatrowers, and was now smaller. I never thought Tommy would live on this long. She was in the same house, and usually wore a fishing jacket over a flanny, jeans and sneakers.

She met us at the door, more hawklike and bent, her scarecrow having turned to a wraith. I hugged her gingerly, engaging with her vertebrae that protruded from a back hunched over an almost concave stomach. Yet there was food in the fridge and she was dressed in good pants and a shirt and cardigan for town. We drank tea first. She was holding her shopping list which I saw had on it SAXBY X4 and a word that looked like chineok. The kitchen no longer smelled of cigarettes and beer.

Nice outside, I said.

Sun. Sit in that chair. She was holding my arm, feeling it through to the bone. Finally she let me go and I sat. My mother sat in her usual chair.

Anything happening on Stockton? Any news?

I wouldn't know. It's pretty quiet.

Yes.

My mother then said, Sad to see Julia go (meaning the Prime Minister).

Tommy looked at her from her bent crow position and started into a right-wing rant such as she heard on her kitchen radio.

Be that as it may, I said pre-emptively, How is Peter? Catching any fish?

He doesn't tell me.

Well, he's still eating, I said.

Still comes in here every day for his ginger beer, if I'm in my bedroom he doesn't come to check on me, I could be dead on the floor, drinks his ginger beer and goes. And the only way I know he's been, is the empty bottle on the sink.

There was nothing to say to this so my mother and I were silent.

The skin of Tommy's right hand had turned purple and the bones were covered with the thinnest draping of skin.

I need to go to the hardware when we go down town, she said. Get a new toaster. Then suddenly she said, This man came along, by the fence, onto this property up in the valley somewhere, and said he wanted to inspect the property for cut-down trees. And the owner said, I haven't cut down any trees, anyway, who are you? And the man took out a card and showed him he was from the government and had the right to come onto the property and inspect the trees.

I haven't cut down any trees, said the man, but all right, you can come and look, with your card. But I wouldn't advise you to go to the north paddocks. And so the government man thought right, that's just where he doesn't want me to go, I'll go there and went off to the north paddocks and soon his voice was calling Maaate! Call your bull off! And the farmer said, Show him your card!

We laughed and picked up the lists and the string bags for town.

Back at the house it was thrilling to see her eat a whole pie. She did it slowly like a cat, first sucking the juice out from the meat. Her hands seemed to be the same colour now but were quivering, and little tremors crossed her cheek in waves. Still, she was bearing up.

I went into the lounge room to the fireplace. She had been cleaning up and more photos had appeared on the mantelpiece. Jock at Mungo Brush in front of the tent. Jock at the slipway.

Looking down at the hearth I saw the poker Pappy had made for Tommy for her fire. It had some sort of heraldic head on it. I thought about how Tommy fished on the beach at night with Pappy, fishing and drinking and rolling cigarettes. Then how when he died I started fishing with her, down at the Wreck and in the river. Then how my mother had become Tommy's best friend, strange when you consider how hard it must have been for Mum to get through the time when I was 'too close' to Tommy, and how I had to be restrained from going there all the time, and needed to be pointed in the direction of men.

Last visit with Mum

I rang Tommy to see if we could visit—her voice seemed faint.

Up and about? I said.

I wouldn't say *about.* She took a breath. Anyway I'm home. I'm always home. Come over when you want.

This time the caverns in her neck were more pronounced and her hands were claws—she really was skin and bone. I judged she weighed about thirty kilos. Maybe thirty-five. She had lost her good mood and when I asked after her neighbour Betty Skews who I knew had moved into the old people's home on Fullerton Road, she was flinty and mean.

Why do you want to gossip like this? she burst out, I don't sit here talking about other people.

I leaned forward. Everything about Tommy had terrified me

for years. Her moods. The smell of her flannelette shirts. Suddenly all my old passivity with her crankiness surged into anger and for the first time in perhaps fifty years I spoke back.

What? This isn't gossip! I'm asking how a mutual friend is, can't I ask after someone's health? This is crazy!

Oh, what—she fumbled. Err—

I watched her closely now. She shrank back into herself and plucked at the table-cloth and readjusted where her little radio stood, shaking her head.

Well, she said eventually, Betty's OK. Still walks like a sailor, rolling along the corridors—

Now I saw how she operated. Sullen and cranky and remote till you called her on something, then she would crack and start being friendly. All I had had to do, all those years, was to *speak back* to her in a confident voice. Then she would crumble.

As if what she wanted was discipline.

That night I called her daughter Shelley.

I just had a breakthrough with your mother.

Oh yes?

I told Shelley about the Betty Skews conversation and how Tommy had *backed down*.

Yes, Shelley said. It took me till I was forty.

We were silent for a while.

Did she ever talk to you about her childhood? I said.

Not really, not in detail.

About the orphanage in Singleton? About seeing her father at the railway station one day? Realizing who he was?

No. Nothing like that. You probably know more about her than I do.

Tommy's shirts

A few weeks later Shelley rang—she'd had a call from Kay the neighbour who had been cooking for Tommy for months now.

Kay told me I'd better get down there. I'm leaving in the

morning.

I'll come and visit while you're there. Has she begun to die?

It sounds that way.

I drove down Mitchell Street staring out to sea, and stopped opposite Violet's house, that was. The beach was bare, and small—mere meters to the water, and superimposed on it was my childhood beach of sand hills and saltbush to the horizon, beyond which was the actual sea. The once hidden sea.

At intervals as I walked there were signs saying Save Stockton Beach. But that would mean taking down the breakwater which had caused the problem.

I drove to the bottom end and bought three excellent pies. The other customers in the arcade were extensively tattooed and large, and calling their children, Come *on* Kristy, Jayden, get here. *Here!* And once, to a two-year-old, *Fuck you Crystal!*

At Cardigan Street, Shelley greeted me with a whisper at the door. Tommy was asleep in Peter's old room—she now slept in his single bed.

How is she?

Sleeps a lot. Not really eating. I put some Sustagen in her coffee this morning and she had that. Then went straight back to sleep. I pulled the bedding up and tried to tuck her in and she got cranky and accused me of trying to euthanase her.

I went into the room and Tommy opened one eye and acknowledged me. I sat there, not saying anything. We had known each other for fifty-three years.

Finally a muffled voice from the blanket, How're you going?

I'm all right. Bit worried about you, I said.

Hanging in here.

I reached out and held her bony arm through the blanket. She fell asleep and I sat there watching her for twenty minutes. I knew it would be the last time I would see her. At the moment I got up to leave, she snorted and woke. I turned to her and said, without thinking, See you next time.

On my way to the kitchen, which seemed to take ages but was only the room next door, I lived though many scenes of our time together, which sprang to my mind's eye in quick succession—and while this was happening another stream of my mind was debating and chastising myself about saying 'See you next time,'—certainly not a recommended goodbye if you have no wish to encounter the person reconfigured as a father or a sister in some future life, if future lives exist. The spirit that carries over, if it does.

The funeral was to be for family only, but I said oughtn't they invite Kay the neighbour? And Mum and I were practically family, three generations of us had been Tommy's friend. We talked our way in, and met them at the funeral home over town. Tommy's tall grandchildren sat with their parents near the front. We were at the back of the small chapel, on the other side, from where I could see Shelley and her husband and grown children, seemingly unmoved, and past them, Peter, his face awash with tears.

No matter that they'd had a few running battles, or that at the end he visited and sat in the kitchen drinking the ginger beer she bought for him, but didn't look in on her. His eyes streamed.

He made no sound but cried throughout the short tribute read out by the funeral parlour man in his suit. Shelley must have given him notes. The funeral man mentioned that Tommy had a great sense of humour and was a keen fisherwoman. She had not wanted a big funeral. Peter kept crying soundlessly. At one point Kay got up and went forward to touch the coffin and said, Oh, Tommy—then went and sat down again. Neither Mum nor I seemed to have any tears. In fact I was numb. I felt nothing, and have felt nothing since.

After the funeral Shelley sent her son out to her car to get me two of Tommy's shirts she had saved for me. Pretty well everything else went to the tip.

Jock's logbook

Back home I put the shirts right at the bottom of the wardrobe and covered them up with other stuff.

I worked on the statue book for a few months and still couldn't get it to work. I put it back in its box, then started to clean out the cupboards. In time I got to the bottom of the wardrobe.

The smell of her shirts no longer terrified me.

At the bottom of the sewing box, the torn strips of paper.

7 Feb
Southerly gale
could not pull–
made lobster pots
sea rising

stopped this morning Big Ben
–down in river try Bream
tomorrow night weather permitting

25th Mar
1x60 Green prawns sold at ¼–
1x48 and 6 lb squid
had twelve shots from forts

7 March
BB no lobster

8 March
pull all pots
nothing 2pm

20 March
Full Moon
9 crabs 8am

24 March
– going down still blowing
from south east sewing bag
in net putting leads on
fixing ropes

blowing hard from South east
too much roll for prawning
all day
crab traps
buoys

9th May
made new net

4th May
Strained back on Tuesday
not go out

Painting boat bottom and
topside planks. Going off
slip Thursday

20th May
Had bad leg too sore to
work as could not straight leg

26th April
1x94 = 104 Bream at–
–mullet caught dead end
7 lb flathead " " "
3 lb jewfish " " "
for four shots. Sold Newcastle Fishermens co
11 lb bream Sold local

south east breeze blowing
waiting for sea to flatten

9th March
15 lb bream caught corner Walsh
sold local did three hauls

21st April
Raining and blowing
south sea starting
to rise and roll

15th April
Pulled boat up
scrubbed bottom

23rd April
southerly breeze
and roll rising

26th October
1x55 Green lobster
wind fair

3rd June
Raining very hard

east gale coming

10th June
33 lb Green Prawns
caught in mud
Sold Sydney

11th June
stayed home fixed –
put more leads and
towing too fast

21st June
river still in flood too bad
to go out fishing with net

29th July
4 lb dog shark
2 lb flathead
5 lb Perch
7 lb Mullet
4 lb Jewfish
41 lb Bream

10th September
Towed William J
Terrace in 2½ hours
2 hours to come back
punching breeze

the Mavis
shaft

Wash William J
washing soda

28th May
Wind blowing from south
and big roll running

6th Jan
77 lb Prawns
30 lb Grey Nurse

9 Davo

Solitude

Alone I walk and look. The shaggy verges of the estuary, met down any dead-end street, the spiky junkus plants, hummocky because whipper-snipped. I nibble on glasswort and samphire, salty, rubbery. Upturned dinghies lie on grass near the water or are chained to trees. On the small illegally-built jetty, hidden behind mangroves, I sit and watch swallows swooping low after insects.

Charlotte was in France for six weeks seeing family. I avoided working on the novel—I'd always written poems or short stories before and really had no idea what I was doing. I had gone to extreme lengths to find that out, including researching for the History of Narrative at UC, all in order to crack the nut of the novel. I could talk about the frame tale, the picaresque, I could give examples of parallel plots, or diverging plots, or nested stories, but none of this knowledge helped. I'd never been able to get the voice right. The statue—almost by definition—*had no voice*, in fact only recently her whole body had been concrete and marble dust. Come to think of it, that statue I had made and given to the gardener—it had big eyes but *no mouth.*

Other problems remained, and though in various drafts I'd tried to solve them, on rereading perhaps months later I found I wasn't believing them: how does she get rid of her wings? How does she know anything? I would have to fudge, page by page, her responses to everything. Rather, *she* would have to fudge. I considered moving the story forward in time so she could have a mobile phone and look things up, but then, how did she know how to read?

Obviously the task required great confidence and a sleight of hand. Also it needed some sort of intervention in the clichéd idea of a statue coming alive. I had read *A Winter's Tale* to see how

Shakespeare brought Hermione back to life. But Hermione had a life *before* she became a statue—whereas my person had been—who? No prior life. She had no childhood, which was another problem.

Then one morning I opened all the boxes in the garage and put the versions of earlier events on the big table in the main room, on the floor, on the lounge. Went around the room reading parts at random. Winter sun filtered in and it should have been a perfect work day. I felt overwhelmed and frightened. Put it back in the boxes. My character had undergone so many changes. There was no stability to the point-of-view.

Blackwattle Studios, Glebe

Lazing about in the house where the sun came in, one morning I found a piece of paper that had floated to the top several times, the original description of the statue coming to life.

I remembered the buzz of writing it, when I was living on the harbour in part of a big warehouse. You were not supposed to live there, and the front gates were locked at seven pm, but you could climb the gate, or get in by boat. Two men were also secretly living there, and naturally the caretaker knew we were there and treated us as unofficial night security. My studio was on the ground floor and had a concrete floor which I carpeted, from rolls of carpet I saw on the verge. Corrugated iron walls reaching to a double-height ceiling. The back door opened onto a small wooden porch suspended over the water.

I had come south from the residency in Armidale, cashed up, and bought some Bose speakers. One evening after the building emptied out, I was playing Joan Sutherland and Marilyn Horne singing the duet in Bellini's *Norma.* I went to sit on the porch. Behind me their rising voices interwound and leapt up to the ceiling and resounded along the metal walls. An eerie wind crept through the whole building which suddenly seemed loose. It made watery and wood-creaking noises in the night.

Inception of the character

The piece of paper recalled a day years before, when wandering the inner west I had climbed the fence near a no trespassing sign into an urban paddock somewhere in Leichhardt. Everything was quiet. It was a Sunday in the early eighties.

The paddock was full of statues, many life-size: Cleopatra, Tutankhamen, Diana, a group of Roman soldiers. A winged woman, her wings seeming to float in the sun. I looked at their faces as I walked among them, at their expressions. On a wrought-iron garden table was a top-half only Zeus. In the distance through a gate, was a house and a big back shed, no doubt where the statues were made. No one appeared. I stood still hardly breathing, when to one side over my right shoulder I *thought* I saw the movement of a wing. I turned, but the winged woman was completely still. Now I really examined her. Her skin was weathered and pocked from being outside—must have been in the yard for a while.

Her expression was one of indifference, although it might have been serenity. It's hard to tell with statues.

What if she *had* come alive—flown across the city, made a landing somewhere. Found clothes, and food, got a job. She would have to *lose her wings*. How would she do that—while I was inventing, a man appeared at my elbow, We are close, he said, is Sunday.

I know. Sorry ... Do you make the statues?

Is me and my wife and my wife sister.

Where do the statues go when they leave here?

Go on truck to our shop, he waved an arm to the west.

Do other people work here? I was fishing for time, hoping he'd offer me a look in the shed.

We have one man.

Now he turned to the shed and gestured to me to follow. A big open space with benches everywhere, plaster casts, statues waiting to go out into the yard, big hardback artbooks on high benches, Ancient Greece, Ancient Rome, the pages clay-smeared, a film of dust on everything. We walked the length of the shed, and came to a group of Roman soldiers, waiting in rows, all slightly different.

Quietly he said, Once we were work at night on big order when our man got frighten by these soldiers, he could hear them talking, not in the day, but in the night. So he had to leave.

And you replaced him?

Yeah. Next man is not so scare.

What is the name of the shop?

Garden Art, Haberfield.

At this stage when I was still in a sort of a fright of ecstasy, the statue had no name. A month later in a fiction workshop at Addison Road I said I had invented a character and needed a name. Finola asked me to describe her again. A winged woman, I said.

Is she Winged Victory of Samothrace?

I had to admit I didn't know.

The Winged Victory, Finola said, isn't she an emanation of Athena? Her name is Nike.

The shoe? I said.

The shoe company needed a logo Finola said,—pretending patience—and Nike is a fast runner. The tick on the shoe is her vestigial wing, I think.

She kept talking but I blurred her out. I had the image of Nike dressing herself from stuff dumped at the base of a full charity bin at the side of the Shell station in Annandale. Taking things out of boxes and holding them up. I felt I was watching a movie, and it was happening without my intervention. I watched as she dressed in a T-shirt and jeans and runners and went down Johnston Street, crossed the road near the junkyard and went into the park. Walking towards a bubbler, she is bailed up by a guy from the junkyard, out walking his dogs. He wants to know if she's new to the area. Her voice doesn't work at first. He thinks she's shy and encourages her, asks her name. Embarrassed, she looks down at her shoe.

Nike.

Well Miss Nike, anytime you want material for a retaining wall, bricks, timber, call by the yard.

Don't you think? Finola said. She had been talking the whole time.

What?

For thirty years people have been giving me postcards, or actual statues, or painted pictures of my character, and collaged her wings. In one case a good friend gave me part of her inheritance, bought me a year to write. I kept producing other, shorter books, unrelated, or not wholly, to the statue, books of poems, some of which won awards, but my big project was obstinate and I did not have the magic that animates long prose and makes you believe in it. I felt responsible to the people who had sent me a page from an old encyclopedia showing the Nike of Panaois, or had rung me with a reference to Nike *apteros* (wingless)—people talked about Nike as if she existed—still now people send things—an attachment in an email from a friend, Johannes, showing a crouched winged creature high on a cathedral.

The sheriff

My studio had other inhabitants. There was a water rat, sleek and personable, who came in and investigated the food. It ate the end off an avocado. Later I would find an esky to store the food. I could also smell a possum who ran about on the girders and sometimes at night I heard it on the walkways of the first floor.

My son came to visit and I saw from his expression that it confirmed a few of his views on me perhaps, that I *would* be living in a shed, and, better still, that it would be illegal. We hugged, sat on the porch overlooking the water and talked about nothing for a while. His car. The view.

He was by now a sheriff of the court at Parramatta and would soon become a serving police officer. When I asked him what court he was a sheriff of, he said the Family Court.

You mean divorce settlements and custody and people fighting?

Yes, the family court.

Hell, darling.

I know, I know. I had to remove a gun from a husband a while ago, a loaded gun.

Go on.

I just went really calm, spoke in a quiet voice while approaching him with my hand held out for his gun. He could have shot me but he handed it over. I surprised him by my manner, maybe.

As your mother, that scares me.

It's part of the job of the sheriff. Anyway, they're giving me a citation for it next week, an award, quite prestigious.

Very brave, very good.

Thanks mother.

In the skip

Inside the big gates at Blackwattle was a skip where broken statues were thrown. There were arms and legs, or headless women. There were not many men statues: women prevailed. Their broken arms and faces lay silent in the skip. Behind it was the open door of the statue-makers, their long thin workshop, the benches and moulds, the big artbooks they copied from. A man called Mario showed me around. They were hoping I'd buy something. There were terra cotta Chinese temples to put near the water feature in your garden. I felt at home there. I pretended to be interested in a birdbath.

Even though, for quite a while, there were many statues in my life, I still couldn't make the manuscript work. I would get a buzz on and think I had cracked it at last then days later reread it and think, No. Every morning I wake up to the red spines of the twenty-five or so notebooks I have kept in relation to this project and imagine them under the yellow plastic lid of the recycle bin. Then I open one from the year I lived at Blackwattle and I'm on a bus in Glebe sitting behind two St Scholastica's girls and one says, 'I page-turned for a woman the other day, a very hard Shostakovich thing. I've never page-turned before.' In a way it seems so *right* I don't want to throw it in the bin.

Taking the long view

Charlotte was writing a series of novels about life in Mesolithic Scotland. Clans, survival, living off the land, dealing with weather, hand-fasting, animals, healers, clan gatherings. Her mind could roam so far back in time, and I wondered how far forward it went. She came in early from looking through the telescope at the planets. I knew she'd been reading about the sky.

I said, Do you know what happens in the far distant future?

The sun expands, she said, till the periphery reaches earth. We are long gone, the seas have boiled away. Mercury and Venus have vaporised. The sun becomes a white dwarf still giving some light, then a black dwarf, denser, giving no light. Other planets, beginning with Mars, are still in orbit around it. Mars has two moons.

How many moons do the other existing planets have?

Venus has none.

Venus the planet of love, no moons?

None. Jupiter has I think 53 confirmed moons and 26 provisional. Saturn has 53, and 29 provisional.

At that stage, with the sun a black dwarf giving no light, are those moons still orbiting?

Still orbiting.

At my mother's

At my mother's birthday party we congregated at her place in Newcastle. Four of my sisters were there and my son and his wife and my two granddaughters came in, taking a drawing to their great grandma. They raced through the garden and up to the potting shed and wanted to make something. They hammered and sanded; they wrapped string around things and glued things to other things.

When their mother took them in to eat cake, I pulled up a chair near my son in the garden.

Gesturing at my mother he said, Aren't you proud of your mother?

Yes, she's in better nick than me.

Hard physical work.

Guess so.

I've been thinking, he said quietly, about your writing. No offence, but poetry, who reads it?

No one, no one.

Who buys it? You've done that, you've won awards, move on.

Oh yes? What do you recommend?

Why not try writing a best-seller? There must be a formula.

I may have looked blank.

Mum, let's say your heroine is a heterosexual CEO in—say, finance, deals with financial instruments—who, ahhh,—goes on a dating website.

I'll think on it. I see it has possibilities, son. How are the Eels doing?

There'll be bad publicity about them soon. Club's trying to hold onto the good men and keeps giving them presents, holidays, cars, a tab at Star Casino.

They live like celebrities.

That's what they are.

We should go in to lunch.

Cousin Janet had come down from Gympie with her husband Norm who, over lunch and under questioning, told us what it was like driving a tractor on a pineapple farm, spraying the pines for fifteen dollars an hour and no overtime.

To draw the conversation onto Mum, since it was her party and she is too well-mannered or too self-effacing to draw attention to herself, I pointed to a bookshelf with the many ring-binders of the family history she has compiled over twenty years of research. I looked at Janet and Norm and my sisters and said, Even though I'm a writer, Mum has written a lot more in volume than I have.

Yes Mum said, and mine is the authentic version.

Stations of the cross

Mallard drakes have bright green necks. I realise I have stopped inventing scenes for Nike, stopped dreaming about places she might go.

The estuary glitters in wind on a high tide fast running out. Across from us on the peninsula you can walk the stations of the cross, wooden crosses set in the bush and along the waterfront, with sayings from Mary McKillop. Things about compassion and the heart, I can't remember them. I can see a few of the crosses from here.

I have almost given up on the manuscript and I can feel the elephant leaving the room. Thirty years of creating scenes for a novel that might be a non-novel, a series of binnable pages. A level of farce in some areas of my life at the same time as an enormous sense of responsibility to the project, to *make* something of the idea, despite the fact it was a cliché, or even because of this.

I went to Melbourne for a week and stayed with Sal. Part of the time she was working hard at the Convent, doing animations. One day Ruth came around and told me that Greta was with some old men, the guys in the Vintage Vanguard club, they had her in their yard in some outer suburb. They had plans to fix her blinkers and replace the wooden tray in the back. We looked at each other without saying that we didn't expect this would ever happen.

Later Ruth wondered if the following day I might like to go to Majorca to look at the farm, she would drive, she had a silver '86 manual Mercedes and she liked driving out of Melbourne into the hills. We'd be going though small towns like Clunes, where they now had a Writer's Festival at a certain time of year.

We had a bit of trouble finding the way—which towns to go through—but when we turned off the bitumen onto the dirt road we were right. We rolled down the windows and sniffed the eucalyptus. It was a fine day with a light breeze, perfect for travelling.

The new owners weren't home. Dogs barked for a while but they were chained. I waited till they calmed, and said to Ruth I was going in over the gate. She didn't want to come. Fair enough. I went in anyway and knocked and tried the doors, locked. It occurred to me that we had never had a key, had never been offered one by the agent, had not thought to ask for one. Strange. I walked around the rectangle of the house, its walls emanating tobacco and cannabis, an old car seat on the pavers near the front door and a full ash-tray beside it. Everything stank. I stepped up a level to the dry claypan in front of the house. They had taken out the pepper tree

I planted to reduce the bareness, and for eventual shade. They had taken way the river stones I brought from the ballast on Stockton, which I had laid out around the pepper tree as a labyrinth. They had moved the vegetable bed further up the yard, for no apparent reason. We had been erased. There was a big tin shed which might or might not have been for growing cannabis, outside which the dogs were chained. When I climbed the gate, they gave some final barks. I asked Ruth if she would drive on to Bird's gate and we did that. Again, she wouldn't come in, and I thought, to be polite, I shouldn't go in either. We sat in the car and watched the place for a while. Nothing moved. It wasn't clear if it was inhabited. A light wind blew the dust of the claypan around her house into eddies that swirled and died.

Meanwhile there was news from Slovenia: Karmen, Joe's niece, texted to say he was not well, and in hospital. She was keeping an eye on him.

I went out to the veranda and thought of the time when I was eighteen and meeting Joe in Granville. How he had looked at me. I stared across the water.

The nuns have their own wharf, and a shed rented out to a surf club, where bikinied girls from Avoca take out their surfboats and train in the early mornings, rowing hard, the trainer on the rudder as cox, getting them to row in time with each other. There must be boys who do this too but this week there are only girls. 'Shell, you're going in a touch too soon! Shell!'

Joe dies

The new Amy St wharf ... the floating dock in Newcastle Harbour ... everything made me think of Joe that week, it was the week he was dying. At the age of 81 and after three heart attacks, the part of his heart that still worked was wearing out. Karmen, who was his doctor, rang to tell me, and to say Sonja was bringing him good food every day. I asked if next time Karmen was at the hospital she could ring me from there, so I could talk to Joe.

Late one night our time I heard his voice.

Susan? How are you.

I'm fine. How are you doing, Joe?

Ah, not so good, not really too good.

We talked for a while about old times, the café, the motor-bike, the house in Blacktown, the time we changed our name. Then we talked about Ben, and his voice softened.

Well I can see the doctor is coming. I will say ciao, Susan.

Ciao, Joe.

I knew it would be the last time I spoke to him.

In a few days came the latest news on his heart—he was having trouble breathing, he had stopped eating, he wanted to see Srecko and Branko, his brothers. Karmen was trying to arrange it. I rang Ben and we talked for a long time.

That night Karmen sent a photo in an email—Joe smiling from his bed, and looking already otherworldly, almost saintly, the light in his face, the strangely blissful look, and inside that, the vulnerability and innocence in him, which I could no longer ignore, and I stared at him until my eyes began to hurt.

It was mid-August. No news so I rang Ben's house. Karmen had rung there, she was in China. Joe had had to be resuscitated and was still alive.

Then a text from Karmen. She was back in Slovenia with Joe, and Branko and Sylvia had arrived, "yet we couldn't make any contact with him as Joe is now unresponsive, he can't talk or even open his eyes anymore. It makes it all so much harder as Joe had waited for this visit for so long and with so much Hope."

Ten hours later the last text. "Dear Susan I've just received a call from the hospital. Joe died this morning at 6.30. Karmen."

For a while, quite a while, I was numb, going about my daily business, taking calls from Ben, doing a certain amount of Slovenian cooking. I bought pork and veal mince and made the finger-sized sausages called cevapcici and when the best men arrived I barbequed the sausages for them. They weren't as tender as I had hoped but I kept making them when people visited and slowly improved. At some point I got out the cake-tin with the raised middle and made the traditional cake with the hole in the middle. Chocolate and plain, marbled, five eggs. I could do that. But still no tears. It wasn't till I took down from the shelf a Time-Life book called *The Balkans* and looked through it at black-and-white photos of the peasants in their scarves and their home-made clothes at the harvest or pitch-forking straw onto trucks or sleeping under a big tree in the middle of the day before going on with their labours, that I could cry, something about the pictures where the people looked so real, to me.

Early next day at low tide we took the tandem kayak out towards the oyster leases where birds would be foraging on the mudflats. At a certain point we stopped and it was my job to keep the boat steady while Charlotte looked through her binoculars at the birds who from this distance mostly looked brown and medium-sized. I couldn't concentrate much because of Joe, when I heard Charlotte mutter to herself, 'That third godwit is a whimbrel.' I nodded, as if I had a clue, and watched the water. The tide was turning. Within the tide, I could see a current, and within the current, an eddy. I couldn't read the birds yet but was starting to be able to read the water. Soon enough it had all moved on.

On the veranda a stream of cool air comes in just as magic hour happens on the water and in the trees on the peninsula. A golden light that lasts, today, for twenty-six minutes. Long enough that I can call Charlotte and we can watch it together.

Burramattagal

At Ben's house I find the remote and click on Channel 2, where the Eels are in trouble for breaking the salary cap. The club has been fined a million dollars and lost points in the competition. Still they play on. I watch a clip of a try in their last game. The close-ups, the mouth-guards, the tattoos, the embraces, the hard-nosed looks, the hugs, the jubilation.

I asked him how work was going. He was doing security at a mega-church. He talked about how his jobs had always involved him being hyper-vigilant, and how he almost felt he should now be working in a flower shop—anyway, he was looking for something new. He was learning ropes and knots, and would soon be interviewed for a deckhand job on the Sydney ferries. He could not imagine anything better than being on the harbour all day. I puffed out my breath in agreement.

Next day I was leafing through the Saturday paper while his girls were drawing pictures of aliens.

See this son?

What's that.

Tomorrow at Elizabeth Farm, an Eel festival, in Rose Hill. It's free.

Read it out.

"Attendees can learn more about the creature that helped give Parramatta its name and its importance to the Burramattagal people. Visitors can touch live eels, discover traditional weaving techniques and taste bush tucker."

What's an eel? Lily said.

It's like a snake, baby, it lives in the river.

I don't want to touch it!

Her sister Jade turned to her and said, Lily, remember the kids' farm we went to, remember that lady with the snake wrapped around her, and she let us pat it, remember?

Oh. Yes, but it was wrapped around her. If I put my hand in the river the eels will wrap themselves around me.

Maybe, I said, they'll have them in a big aquarium and lift them out to show you safely.

She doesn't want to go, Jade said.

Instead the girls came north with me on the train and had a few days holiday at Davo. On the second day they were on the waterfront collecting sticks and branches and began to make a cubby under the paperbark tree. They tried grinding the branches into the soil to make them stand up while Charlotte went to the shed and collected garden stakes and other poles and rope and string, and put these on the ground for them. Then Charlotte quietly took two of the stakes and leaned them toward each other and, leaving some overlap, tied them together.

The girls got the idea and did this again a metre or two behind Charlotte's stakes.

We sat out of sight on the veranda and watched them lay a long roof pole across the top V shapes in the tied stakes, then tie stakes along the sides for wall support.

Jade now began peeling the paperbark in big strips for the roof and walls and they laid these on—there was no wind. The front door of the cubby looked at the house, the back door at the water. Once it was finished they invented a password so only they could go in. Inside they sat cross-legged, inventing conversations between their toys while we made a picnic lunch for them, which they ate inside the cubby.

The next day the parents arrived to take them home and we were bereft. The cubby was on public land and couldn't be left there too long, but I wasn't ready to take it down. I made lunch and sat alone on a low stool inside it and watched the shore-birds feeding. I would have liked to be able to leave the cubby there and have lunch in it every day. Eating in the house, or even on the veranda, was no comparison to the experience of the cubby, the low stool and being near the ground, and having nothing to read while I ate, no print.

Indoors, I rang Ruth. We talked about Greta and how we missed her. I asked if there was any update on her repair. Ruth said last she heard, the men were sending her to Ireland for restoration.

At the big window looking onto the estuary. The hours in their stately stillness. The red tinge of samphire in the swamp plants.

For a while the only sound is birdcalls echoing across the water and the peaceful huff of the air-conditioner responding to the thermostat and turning on. And the different huff, more stagey and dramatic, of the fridge.

Go with the mad

I bit the bullet and emailed Nike to an editor/agent who it turned out did not have much to say. Her email said she thought it started well but did not sustain itself; it bogged down in reality—she didn't want to take it on. I rang her and said that it was hard to sustain—Maybe it was a mad idea, I said.

No, your idea is good. Just—Go with the mad.

I saw I would have to unhook the whole thing from incidents in my life, stop importing myself into Nike, be her and only her, do the whole thing afresh. I let that sit. There may not be time, but if there is, I'll give it a go. I simply have to stop being myself. Yes. The art of the novel.

Meanwhile

It was an oily day. The heat sat on the water and the saltmarsh, and the water surface had gunky swirls among the outflowing tide, plastic containers, among areas of clean and glitter, a different current. Still flowing out, faster than the rest of the tide, that seemed to sit by the banks, sullen in the mangroves.

Ben was by now working on the ferries and sending me short videos of the harbour from the Manly ferry, film of a huge cruise ship coming in, the bridge, the mesmeric surface of the water. He turned the phone to himself to record a message. Or once, when I mentioned a cracking thunderstorm going through the central coast, shaking the house, he messaged me:

'Big swells near the heads'.

Magic hour

When the lockdown lifted, Charlotte went to visit her grandchildren in Katoomba and I was alone for five days. On the second day Ben rang to ask, Are you home?

He was in Terrigal and could be here in fifteen minutes. I sprang up from my embrace with Melancholia on the lounge and tidied the house, putting unwashed frypans in the oven, emptying the benches.

We sat on the back veranda and he stared at the water while we talked for two hours—it was the first time we'd had together alone and in person for many years.

Ben had his French bull-terrier there, a black dog called Betty. Betty checked the place out then napped on a rug Ben had brought. Our safe topic was the Annandale house, where we were both happy. We talked about Beni Bizarre and the kids' parties and the twin dwarves who had come to his show in the park so long ago. Then our topic roamed to Glebe and how at sixteen he liked to go on Friday night to the trots at Harold Park. He had friends at school who were running a book, or learning how, when he was in Year 10. He said one boy always had the form guide and a little transistor to his ear at recess and lunch, when he studied the guide while listening to races.

Some kids' fathers owned greyhounds and exercised them round the streets of Glebe in the early mornings. There was a row of small terrace houses that looked down into the bowl of the racetrack, where the trots jockeys lived. Information filtered through to the kids, who gave each other tips.

Ben would meet his friends at the gate of Harold Park, and looking their most adult they'd get in by saying 'My father is in there'. Then one kid would give him a tip and he'd go and lay a bet and sometimes he came away with a night's betting earnings of eight dollars which was a lot to him then.

I stared at the water and thought it was no wonder he liked Charles Bukowski who in his stories was always going to the track.

I didn't mention it but thought of how different my perception was of Harold Park—to me the words called up the small stage in the back bar of the hotel across the side street of the racetrack, where the performance poets were doing their thing.

Later we walked Betty to the wharf and I asked how the girls, now nine and eleven, were going, with him or Louise home-schooling them for fifteen weeks so far during the lockdown. Well, he said—Lily was self-motivated and able to work, Jade missed her friends and did the least possible, he had to encourage her.

Still, she's a child, I thought, and probably wants her childhood. She prefers dancing to studying. We stared out at magic hour raking the island with golden light that would last maybe ten minutes longer. Anything can happen.

Acknowledgements

First, I want to thank my son Ben whose presence has greatly enriched my life, and his wife Louise and daughters Lily and Jade.

Next, close family, my mother June Mackie, and the Mackie sisters: Linda Russell, Gwennie Smith, Mark Smith, Kathleen Mackie, Trisha Butchart, Barbara Mackie.

The Clutterbuck sisters, Charlotte, Victoria, Harriet and Lucinda. John Moen, Joce Moen.

I want to thank the people who have helped me with editing, or sometimes with money, food, or a place to work: or with encouragement: please accept my gratitude.

Charlotte Clutterbuck, Gail Bell, Victoria Ramsay, Barbara Holloway, Paul Gillen, Sal Cooper, Kate Grenville, Kim Mahood, Karmen Fuerst, Harriet Clutterbuck, John Moen, Linda Russell, Kathleen Mackie, Jed Buffier, Conrad Buffier, Rose Mackie, Barbara Mackie. Saysana Sirimanotham, Matthew Fraser, Ken Neven, Bernadette Brennan, Paul Cliff, Skye Blomfield, Ruth Cunningham, Trudy Clutterbok, Halinka Rubin, Christina Slon, Bar Finch, Patsy Asche, Alex Kaufman, Victoria Dawson, Fabian Loschiavo (Mother Abyss), John O'Connell (Mr Cha Cha), Trisha Moylan, Noel Lee. Marti Marosszeky, Susan McMichael, Sarah Rice, Jo Rendell-Short, the Canberra Library Book Club people. Joci Stenson, Colette Olivia, Maureen Bettle, Colin Beaton, Pat Beaton, Pam Blakeley, Peter Matthews, Sandra Marsh, Rhiannon Bowman, Gina Baker, Fiona Britton, Julie Chevalier, Gail Nason, Peter Lach-Newinsky, Mike Ladd, and The Metropole Poets.

David Musgrave my publisher

Gleebooks, and the Darlinghurst Bookshop

Ethan Cochrane for the music

The generations of my family

In particular I thank Charlotte for her love and for her understanding of narrative and tone: our many conversations over the years.

A Note about the Author

Susan Hampton grew up in Inverell and Newcastle, NSW, and lived in the inner west in Sydney for many years, before buying a farm in Victoria. She now lives on the Central Coast of NSW with her wife Charlotte. She studied at Newcastle, Macquarie and Sydney Universities, and has taught writing at many Australian universities. She has five sisters, and a son and two grand-daughters.

Susan has won many grants and awards for her work. *The Penguin Book of Australian Women Poets*, which she co-edited, became a set text on many writing courses. *Surly Girls*, performance pieces and short stories, won the Steele Rudd Award in 1990. *The Kindly Ones*, a long narrative poem, has been described as '... a weird satirical travelogue written by one of the Furies ... It is an extraordinary poem: bold, bitter, intelligent and fantastical.' It was shortlisted for the NSW and Victorian Premiers' Awards for poetry, *The Age* Book of the Year Award, and the ACT Book of the Year Award. It won the 2006 Judith Wright Award.

Printed in Australia
Ingram Content Group Australia Pty Ltd
AUHW021107150224
390461AU00005B/11

'Joy McKean to me has been an inspiration in our industry. In a workplace mostly dominated by males she stood her ground and earned the respect she so rightly deserves. As a songwriter, well, I haven't enough room here to speak of her inventive melodies and beautiful turns of phrase like 'a lot more dinnertimes than there were dinners', magical stuff from her song 'The Biggest Disappointment'. Joy helped lay the foundations of the house we all share and love called 'Country Music'. She and Slim opened the door to that house to many of us and gave us encouragement right when we needed it, and for that I'm truly grateful. Joy is a national treasure.' **Troy Cassar-Daley**

'Joy McKean has been the backbone of so much of the Australian Country Music industry and a lot of us would not be where we are without her.' **Kasey Chambers**

'At a time when women were yet to consider a career in music, Joy was making her mark. Her strength and determination became the leading light that many of us have followed. I am extremely grateful for not only the example that Joy set as an accomplished lyricist, but for the generosity and significant contribution she has made to the Australian Country Music family. I also believe that Australia had a great mate in Slim, because he had such a great mate in Joy.' **Beccy Cole**

'Quite simply, one of our greatest songwriters. A pretty good yodeller too!' **Paul Kelly**

'Joy McKean is a trailblazer – an inspiration to us all in the way she has lived her life – meeting challenges head-on, pioneering the early days of the travelling shows and through it all, documenting and speaking for all Australians through the legendary songs that have come from her pen.' **Lee Kernaghan OAM**

'They say behind every great man is a great woman...but I say in Slim's case, she was right beside him. Joy McKean is embedded deep in the foundation of Australian country music. She's a pioneer, but not the kind sitting in the wagon. She's the one out front with axe in hand making a road where there is none. She's an extraordinarily talented and formidable woman who I'm honoured to say has been not only a true believer in me, but a very loyal friend. Slim and I had one strong thing in common. We married up. WAY up!!!' **Keith Urban**

'Singer, songwriter, travelling performer before all that was invented, wife of a remarkable man and matriarch of a remarkable family, Joy has lived a life so far unlike any other.' **Don Walker**

Also by Joy McKean

Another Day, Another Town
I've Been There … And Back Again